Walt Disney and the Promise of Progress City

Praise for Walt Disney and the Promise of Progress City

"[Sam has] captured much of the attitude and events of the times, and hit on much of Walt's drive and inspiration. [His] research into materials and people who were important in one way or another is exemplary. The notes from Buzz Price, John Hench, and Marvin Davis, for example…the apparent influence of Victor Gruen's theories…a relationship that developed with James Rouse—all insightful. It is clear, well-researched, and useful and thoughtful to anyone studying urban planning."

Marty Sklar
Disney Legend and Vice Chairman (Retired)
Walt DIsney Imagineering

"I thought I knew a lot about Walt Disney World and especially EPCOT until I read *Walt Disney and the Promise of Progress City*. This book really details how Walt Disney thought, which I found fascinating. I will now view Walt Disney World in a whole new way."

Lee Cockerell
Executive Vice President (Retired)
Walt Disney World

"One of the more interesting aspects of *Walt Disney and the Promise of Progress City* is how Sam connects the dots. So to Gennawey's way of thinking, it's a fairly logical series of events that leads from Disney driving the design of his new animation studio in Burbank to him then coming up with a site plan for Disneyland. Then—using the urban sprawl that happened in and around Anaheim in the late 1950s / early 1960s as his inciting event—Walt begins exploring the idea of building a city of the future in central Florida."

Jim Hill
Jim Hill Media

"Sam's writing is terrific; he truly enriches the discussion. Not only may you learn something new about the chosen subject, he'll likely open up another perspective on it for you, too."

Al Lutz
Founder, MiceAge.com

Walt Disney and the Promise of Progress City

Sam Gennawey

Foreword by Werner Weiss

Theme Park Press
www.ThemeParkPress.com

Theme Park Press publishes its books in a variety of print and electronic formats. Some content that appears in one format may not appear in another.

Editor: Bob McLain
Layout: Artisanal Text

ISBN 979-8-89609-166-0
Printed in the United States of America

Theme Park Press | www.ThemeParkPress.com
Address queries to ben@themeparkpress.com

Contents

EPILOGUE

Foreword

It was November 1965. As a pre-teen fan of Disneyland, I was excited by the news that Walt Disney Productions had secretly acquired 27,443 acres 12 miles south of a town I had never heard of—Orlando, Florida. It was an enormous amount of land. I knew that Disneyland had around 60 acres within its railroad loop and probably twice that much acreage for parking and other uses. It seemed that Mr. Disney had enough land in Florida for hundreds of Disneylands—or for an entire city.

According to the initial news, there would be a City of Tomorrow, a City of Yesterday, and a number of major industrial plants. There were no details about what Walt Disney had in mind for these cities. The news quoted Walt Disney explaining that it would be three years until opening—a year and a half of planning followed by a year and a half of construction. I could hardly wait until 1968. But how would a California teenager be able to visit Florida?

In that pre-internet era, it was hard to follow newspapers in other cities. I was lucky to have an older brother in college on the East Coast who knew that I was a Disneyland fan. When *The New York Times* published a longer article in February 1967 about Disney's plans for Florida, he mailed it to me. The article quoted Walt Disney, who had died two months earlier, describing his plans for something that he called EPCOT—the Experimental Prototype Community of Tomorrow. Walt Disney's vision was of a real city that would "never cease to be a blueprint of the future, where people actually live a life they can't find anywhere else today." So this was the City of Tomorrow! The article said nothing about the City of Yesterday.

I was much more excited about EPCOT than any East Coast follow-up to Disneyland. Living in California's Orange County at the time, I was watching the birth of the city of Irvine. My father had even taken me to the offices of William Pereira to see the architect's master plan for transforming the Irvine Ranch from orange groves and cattle grazing lands into a planned city. Although the Irvine Master Plan seemed to be an improvement over the haphazard growth elsewhere in Orange County, it still seemed so conventional, relying on automobiles and housing tracts, with no public transportation, no revolutionary ideas, and no cutting-edge technology.

But EPCOT would be another story! *The New York Times* article described a city unlike any other. No vehicles would be allowed at ground level. Instead, there would be two underground road levels, one for passenger cars and one for trucks. Elevated PeopleMovers—just like the PeopleMovers that would be coming to Disneyland later in 1967—would provide public transportation. An illustration showed a 30-story mega-structure with residential neighborhoods radiating from it in all directions. A cutaway illustration showed an indoor transportation lobby with PeopleMovers, a monorail, and the road levels below them.

It was October 1, 1971, before Walt Disney World actually opened. EPCOT was nowhere to be found. It was explained that EPCOT would be part of "Phase Two", and that what had opened was only the first part of "Phase One". Visitors had no reason to complain. They were treated to a $400-million extravaganza. The biggest attraction was, and still is, the Magic Kingdom theme park, similar to the original Disneyland, but with many elements larger and more elaborate. The Florida theme park was on the shore of a beautiful blue, man-made lagoon connected to a natural lake. A championship golf course, two resort hotels, a campground, and recreational facilities also clung to the bodies of water. A twin-loop monorail system provided transportation between the distant parking lot, the theme park, and the hotels.

By the time Walt Disney World opened, I was a student at the University of California at Irvine, where I took every class in urban studies and urban planning available to undergraduates. As someone fascinated by cities and by Disney parks, I was still waiting for EPCOT to get the green light—but each year, that seemed less likely. Walt Disney's successors continued to quote him about EPCOT, but conveniently omitted any references to people living there. During the 1970s, the annual reports to the shareholders of Walt Disney Productions included beautiful Imagineering art showcasing concepts for EPCOT, but it evolved into a theme park, not a real city.

Epcot Center opened October 1, 1982. My first visit to Walt Disney World was just a few months later. I thoroughly enjoyed Epcot Center—but I couldn't help but wonder what EPCOT would have been like if Walt Disney had not died the year after he bought those 27,443 acres. Would EPCOT have delighted enough residents and visitors to make it successful—as a business venture and as a living laboratory for innovative urban solutions? Would EPCOT have been able to renew itself continually over time, rather than becoming a stagnant relic from the era when it opened?

In 2009, I began reading a Disney fan blog called SamLand, written by a professional urban planner named Sam Gennawey. In this blog, I found someone who shared my interest in cities and Disney. I was hooked. Sam applied his insight and experience in urban planning to explain why guests had such positive experiences at Disney parks. We traded email. It turned out we would both be at the Epcot International Food and Wine Festival that year, so we met each other there.

I learned that Sam had always been interested in cities. As a child, he would destroy his mother's flowerbeds developing and rebuilding little cities in them. Instead of taking a direct path toward urban planning, Sam's career included selling stereos, opening his own record store, running a record company, moving to Chicago to run another record company, joining Mercury/Polygram, serving as the marketing director at a radio station, and inventing a lucrative way to promote records. After all that, Sam went back to college to prepare for a career change to urban planner. Why planning? Sam explained to me that he couldn't figure out how to make money as a historian, so he combined that passion with his love for the game SimCity. "Voilà! Planner," as he put it.

I was thrilled when Sam told me he was writing a book about EPCOT. I was honored when Sam invited me to write the foreword. And I was fascinated when I read Sam's manuscript.

Sam presents EPCOT not as a brief vision in the final years of Walt Disney's life, but as a decades-long journey that leads up to EPCOT. Sam provides a detailed look at what Walt Disney's EPCOT would have been like. And, best of all, Sam addresses the question of whether EPCOT would have worked.

I've been to Epcot many times, but thanks to this book, I've now also been to EPCOT.

Werner Weiss
Yesterland.com
September 2011

Preface

Walt Disney was not content to be the most influential entertainment figure of the 20th century; he also wanted to become the most influential urban planner of the 21st century. What was his motivation and how did he intend to implement his vision?

My obsession with these questions started long ago—but it was not until I was reading *In Service to the Mouse* that I fully understood why. The book is the autobiography of Jack Lindquist, Disneyland's first president. He was fortunate to learn his craft directly from Walt Disney. One of those lessons was that the best solutions usually came after a great deal of observation. Lindquist began to notice a certain type of guest that came to Disneyland. He said: "In the early days of the park, there were a lot of people, particularly women with small children from six to ten years of age who drove up in the morning during the summertime and bought general admission tickets for about $2.50 a day. We started seeing the same people doing this day after day: Buying tickets and dropping off their children." I realized I was one of those kids.

From 1967 through 1973, my mother would take my brothers and me to Disneyland quite often. This was during the period when you paid for general admission, and tickets for attractions were a separate charge. We did not go on many attractions because that would cost a lot of money. However, we did enjoy Walt Disney's beautiful park. Even better, there were a few attractions that were free, including Adventure Thru Inner Space, the Golden Horseshoe Saloon, and Great Moments with Mr. Lincoln. My favorite was the Carousel of Progress.

The Carousel of Progress is a time travel story—a giant turntable takes the audience from the 1890s to the "near future" and beyond. The show did not end when the turntable made its final stop. Guests were invited to jump on to the stage and ride the Speedramp to the upper level to view the incredible 6,900-square foot model of Progress City. Every childhood trip to Disneyland meant another spin inside of the Carousel of Progress. I knew the script by heart and would quietly sing along with the chorus. By the time we got to the final act, the one with the super-rich family celebrating Christmas, I would start to move to the edge of my seat. It would not be long before I could weave through the crowd and be one of the first to make my way to the Speedramp that would take me to the model of Progress City. That way, I could linger just a little bit longer than the rest of the crowd and just soak it all in.

The Progress City model was one of the most amazing things I had ever seen, and it made a big impression on my young mind. Every chance I got, I would stop and stare at the 115-foot diorama for as long as I could. I would listen to the narration as it promised that living in Progress City would mean a great, big, beautiful tomorrow where we would all lead rich and rewarding lives. It sounded wonderful, and I wanted to know more. What would life be like in Progress City? Was the project even possible? When can I visit?

Let's journey together as we attempt to answer the questions I have asked myself since I was a little boy.

A Word about Words

Before we begin our journey, it may be helpful to define some of the terms used throughout this book.

When I talk about **EPCOT**, I refer to the vision originally outlined by Walt Disney in the mid-1960s. EPCOT was an acronym for Experimental Prototype Community of Tomorrow. The evidence for this vision can be found in drawings, documents, a propaganda film, and the Progress City scale model at Disneyland.

The new town of EPCOT would morph into a theme park called **Epcot Center**, which was later shortened to **Epcot** in 1995. Epcot Center is the 260-acre permanent World's Fair that opened on October 1, 1982, and attracts millions of visitors today.

Disney World is the name of the Florida Project as Walt had envisioned it. In his vision, Disney World would include the city of Bay Lake; Reedy Creek,[1] the non-incorporated demonstration community of EPCOT; an East Coast Disneyland; an airport; an industrial park; and other amenities. **Walt Disney World** refers to the tourist resort we see today that consists of four theme parks, two water parks, two entertainment districts, seventeen resorts with a total of approximately 22,000 rooms, and 468,000 square feet of conference meeting space.

Disneyland refers to the theme park that opened to the press on July 17, 1955, and to the public on July 18, 1955. **The Disneyland Resort** refers to the 461 acres that Disney owns in Anaheim as well as the 49 acres under long-term lease agreements. The resort contains two theme parks, three hotels with approximately 2,400 rooms, 180,000 square feet of meeting space, and a retail/entertainment district.

---

1   Later renamed Lake Buena Vista by separate legislation.

Early on Walt Disney instituted a protocol for his artists and his employees where everybody went by their first names. That is why I will refer to Mr. Disney as **Walt**. This is not meant to indicate intimacy or informality. I will not be extending the same convention to the other personalities who are part of this story. When I refer to **Disney**, I am speaking of either Walt Disney Productions or what is known today as The Walt Disney Company.

The principal designers for Disneyland, Walt Disney World, and the other projects were **Imagineers**—a portmanteau of "imagination" and "engineering". The term was used by the people who worked at WED (Walter Elias Disney) Enterprises, later to be known as Walt Disney Imagineering (WDI).

Moviemakers designed Disneyland and many theatrical terms have crossed over and have become part of the vocabulary. The employees are called **Cast Members** and the visitors are called **guests**. There are no rides at the theme parks, only **attractions** and **adventures**. At the theme parks, those areas that are accessible to guests are called **onstage**; those areas off-limits to guests are called **backstage**.

As we make our way I will refer to, and define at that time, urban planning concepts and terminology.

Chapter One

Magic Highways USA

Speculating about the future is always fun when viewed through a rear-view mirror. Like many baby boomers, I was riveted to the television when "Uncle Walt's" program was about to come on. As much as I enjoyed all of the shows, one Disneyland episode really stuck with me: "Magic Highways USA", the story of the past, present, and future of the American highway system.

"Magic Highways USA"—which first appeared on ABC on May 14, 1958—is an example of the Disney "educational" film, a genre born out of necessity in World War II. To keep the studio open during the war, Walt and his team of artists made training films for the United States government. Through this experience, they expanded the vocabulary on how films can both educate and entertain. After the war, Walt continued to experiment and began to produce the *True-Life Adventures* nature film series. These films were critical and box-office successes. Walt said, "We have long held that the normal gap between what is generally regarded as 'entertainment' and what is defined as 'educational' represents an old and untenable viewpoint." He added, "I would rather entertain and hope that people learned something than educate people and hope they were entertained." "Magic Highways USA" ends with a speculative look at the future of automobile transportation.

When Walt wanted to produce a film that had a strong educational responsibility, he often turned to Ward Kimball. So it was that Walt chose Kimball to produce and direct "Magic Highways USA" with a script written by Larry Clemons. Kimball was the perfect man for the job. He had directed the landmark three-part "Man in Space" series first broadcast on March 9, 1955. The series was a big influence on the way the public looked at the opportunities that came with space exploration. President Dwight Eisenhower was so impressed that he had the films shown in the White House to drum up support for the space program. Eisenhower said, "I want to show some of our stuffed-shirt generals that don't believe in this stuff how it's going to be."

The Kimball signature style was called "science factual". He would take the audience step-by-step through a complex subject. At each step, Kimball would provide additional information and context, to create a strong foundation for the next step. Visually, Kimball was gifted at using limited animation that could be read in a glance, and his incredible wit resulted in clever word play. For the climax of "Magic Highways USA" and his other films, he worked very closely with content experts to come up with carefully considered projections of a realistic future.

There is a familiar pattern in the Disney educational programs. Walt's team had a knack for making the most boring subject something of interest. They start out with a long shot that provides a panoramic overview of the topic and then narrow the focus to a specific problem or opportunity that becomes the subject of the film. With the stage set and the topic clearly defined, a history lesson unfolds that tells us where we have been and gives us hints as to where we are going. Finally, by blending facts with pure speculation, the film gives us a peek into a future where everything seems plausible. The next objective is to make sure the audience has the same understanding of the primary topic, no matter how much they knew before the program started.

"Magic Highways USA" begins with Walt looking over a scale model of a then (1958) modern-day freeway overpass. He reminds us that, due to the vast size of the United States, "distance was a challenge"; and American progress can be measured by our ability to overcome that limitation. People respond best when they are motivated. The best motivation is clarity of mission. The television program reassures us that we have met this challenge before and have conquered it.

To demonstrate dramatically how quickly transportation technologies have evolved, Walt begins his opening monologue by standing behind a model of a Conestoga wagon. While he explains what the program is about and how we have been able to overcome our limitations, he moves behind a model of a space-age, hyper-modern car with huge fins, a glass canopy, and lines that resemble a fighter jet. Disney educational programs are not subtle. The first objective is to capture audience attention.

Our trip through time is a montage, taking us through America on foot, horseback, train, trolley, and finally, the automobile. In the show, the history of our nation's highways begins with the Pilgrims.[2] From footpaths to trails to roads, we follow the progress and development of our transportation network all the way up to the modern highway of the 1950s. These images are accompanied by the delightful instrumental "Nation on Wheels" by famed film and television music composer and Disney Legend George Bruns. The highlight is the engineering miracle of the day and the height of civilization—the four-level interchange in Downtown Los Angeles. However, we end up in a world where we may have overcome the

---

2   Unfortunately, because of the biases and prejudices of the day, any contributions from Native Americans will have to wait for the updated version.

challenge of distance but have created new challenges. The automobile has taken over and created an imbalance in our quality of life. But not to worry!

When "Magic Highways USA" first aired, the Interstate Highway System was still a new thing for many Americans, and the segment underscored that our national highway system not only would be important to progress but would also define what it means to be an American. The pursuit of happiness is dependent on individual mobility. Movement equals freedom. Buses filled with children going to school, trucks loaded with food and livestock, a jet fighter body on the back of a flatbed truck—each image reinforces the point that every aspect of our lives, even our defense, is dependent on our highways. The highways are the lifeblood of everything great in America.

We learn that every problem has a technological fix. When that fix creates new, unexpected problems, we will simply find another technological fix. That solution then leads to other problems, and the cycle continues. For better or for worse, this is the definition of American progress.

Walt said, "The automobile has created a highly industrialized America of abundance and made us the most mobile people in the world. But with all the pleasure the automobile has given us, it has overloaded our highways." This observation is the setup for a look into the future and how technology, creative thinking, and hard work will help us solve the problems we have created for ourselves.

The next segment outlines the process of planning and building an interstate highway in the 1950s. From an urban planner's perspective, it is remarkable how the fundamental development process has remained the same. It is a lot of fun, however, to watch how much the technology has changed over the years. Plus, modern audiences would be horrified at the destruction of forests and historic structures. We have come a long way with regard to environmental and preservation issues.

After all this destruction and building in the name of progress, we begin to realize that our quality of life is being negatively impacted by the growth in the use of the automobile. The segment ends in a crescendo of car horns, trucks, whistles, and construction noises. We are looking at a future where traffic congestion becomes the new normal. Life is out of balance. What are we to do?

Ultimately, "Magic Highways USA" was a loving plug for the new federal interstate system. The Federal Highway Act of 1956 provided for 41,000 miles of roadway, with the federal government paying 90 percent of the bill and local communities picking up the remaining 10 percent. This level of federal involvement was unprecedented even by the standards of the Depression-era New Deal, when the federal government typically picked up 30 percent of the costs for projects and relied upon local communities to fund the rest. The initial cost of the interstate system was $26 billion. It came to be the largest public works project in United States history. Once the freeway system was completed, American drivers could drive border to border without ever seeing a stoplight. I believe it is safe to say that Walt Disney World would never have happened without the interstate highway system.

A Rear-View Mirror

To lighten the mood, Kimball begins with a rapid-fire montage of comical solutions to our transportation problems. While this animated sequence makes us laugh, it also sets us up for the final segment. Kimball takes us from the absurd to the sublime.

Walt describes this final segment as a "realistic look at the road ahead and what tomorrow's motorists can expect in the years to come". The presentation is a projection from leading transportation experts; it represents the best thinking at the time and a sincere look at what the future of our highways could look like. After polling the experts, Kimball concludes that what we want is more speed, safety, and comfort.

For me, the fun comes from looking back more than fifty years to see how many of these predictions came true and which missed the mark. This show is a wonderful record of yesterday's tomorrow. Yogi Berra was right when he said, "The future ain't what it used to be."

Most of the misses were based on the false assumption that the United States would have an endless energy supply. Imagine highways where the roadbed would become illuminated at night and radiant heat would keep the pavement dry in rainstorms and melt away the snow. Instead of enclosing highways in air-conditioned tubes as the show predicts, it turned out to be more practical to install air-conditioning in each vehicle. We did not get fog-dispelling devices or the combination flying ambulances with fire suppression and tow truck capabilities.

The show proposes a whole array of new construction technologies, including a nuclear reactor that would melt mountains and build tunnels. Imagine something that resembles a giant iron melting away the stone and making a perfectly sized tunnel. The program also projected far into the future and advocated highway escalators as a way of getting up steep slopes, or highways that go under the ocean so we can drive to destinations on different continents and leave our planes and ships behind.

The list of hits is impressive. For example, the program predicted that cars would become more powerful and highway signage would need to change to accommodate the faster speeds. Digital displays, rear-view televisions, and geographic mapping systems with traffic information have indeed become commonplace. The integration of telecommunications technology has become reality. The use of technology to monitor roadway congestion and to track vehicles has also been widely implemented.

The program also explores how our cities would be organized. The show commented on the decentralization of our urban areas and the growth of the suburbs, which would become the trend for decades.

Of course, some ideas were implemented differently than proposed. These include radar screens for our windshields, which would enhance vision the same way that many infrared systems do today. The show proposed cantilevered highways along giant cliffs. Although there is not a highway running down the center of the Grand Canyon or next to the Acropolis, there are some stretches of Interstate 70 through Glenwood Canyon in Colorado and parts of the Blue Ridge Highway in North Carolina that reflect the vision in the film. On a more practical level, home refueling stations have been implemented for some electric and natural gas vehicle owners. The show also predicted that we would only need to push a few buttons and our automobiles would determine the best route and drive us there. Today, we have the satellite navigation piece, but nobody is brave enough to let their GPS drive them to their destination. Yet.

The final segment continues to look even farther over the horizon. Will we become a society where we will park our sun-powered electro-suspension car right in our own office, or program our recreational vehicle and let it drive us to our location while we read the paper or watch television in the back? Will we begin to use rockets to transport goods? Those questions have yet to be answered.

The show does remind us that the one thing we do know for certain is that happiness would only come when we have a complete network of interstate super-speed highways. "Magic Highways USA" is the story of how Walt Disney believed that we could solve any problem with the right technology, creative thinking, and good old-fashioned hard work.

Could Walt predict the future? Maybe…maybe not. We do know that he had a forward-leaning vision unlike any other. One example is how Walt insisted that "Magic Highways USA" be produced entirely in color. At the time of the debut broadcast, the penetration for color televisions in the United States was less than 1% of households. He knew that change was coming.

Chapter Two

A Clean Sheet of Paper

Once Walt found the location for Disneyland, he tried to buy as much land as he could afford, but even that would not be enough. He had to make a lot of compromises to get Disneyland built. Once inside Disneyland's front gate, Walt could control what his guests saw as they strolled through his park. But outside the front gate, he was powerless to control the tacky urban blight that was growing up around the perimeter. By the early 1960s, Disneyland was surrounded by low-quality tourist-oriented motels, restaurants, and services. Thomas Edison said, "Discontent is the first necessity of progress." Walt, a big fan of Edison, was indeed discontented about the way Anaheim had developed around his park; he called the area "a second-rate Las Vegas".

As with every opportunity that faced Walt, he was not satisfied with the status quo and knew he could do it better if given the chance. In the world of animation, the typical way to start is to pull out a blank sheet of paper. Walt knew the next time he decided to build a theme park that he would reach for the largest canvas he could find and buy enough land so that he could control what was in the frame. Just like the movies.

In 1959, Walt was given a chance to do it the right way. A billionaire offered him a chance to build another Disneyland in Palm Beach, Florida—only this time, Walt would get to design the city that surrounded the park. Walt knew that there was a huge untapped market for another theme park on the East Coast. According to Harrison "Buzz" Price, a land use economist who advised Walt, although the Palm Beach project ultimately did not move forward, it became a defining moment for Walt: this is when he became obsessed with building a city.

One thing Walt knew for certain: an East Coast version of Disneyland would make his brother, Roy Disney, happy. Roy was the business genius who supported Walt's efforts. For Roy, the theme park would greatly reduce the risk of any project and become the money machine that would allow his brother to do whatever he wanted. What could go wrong?

You Can't Top Pigs with Pigs

After a tough opening day and some negative reviews, Disneyland turned out to be a smash hit when it opened to the public in 1955. The park turned sleepy Anaheim into one of the fastest-growing cities in the United States. The economic windfall to Orange County was unimaginable. It seemed that every city in America wanted a Disneyland.

There was only one problem. Over the years, it became a well-known fact that Walt Disney did not like to do the same thing twice. He said, "I've never believed in doing sequels. I didn't want to waste the time I have doing a sequel. I'd rather be using that time doing something new and different." He liked new challenges and he already had a Disneyland. What was the point of building another theme park?

Walt said, "It goes back when they wanted me to do more pigs." The *Silly Symphony* cartoon *Three Little Pigs* became a huge success in 1933 due in part to "Who's Afraid of the Big Bad Wolf", a hit song that resonated with Great Depression audiences. Theater owners were clamoring for a follow-up. Walt hesitated. He proclaimed, "You can't top pigs with pigs."

Nevertheless, Walt could be practical when necessary, and he had ambitious plans for the animation studio. Those ambitions cost a lot of money. Therefore, he relented and produced two follow-up cartoon shorts. Unfortunately, Walt was right—the follow-up films did not have nearly the impact or commercial success as the original.

In 1959, twenty-six years later, Walt found himself in a similar dilemma. With an opportunity in Palm Beach before him, he saw that it would be possible to design a new town where people could live, work, and play. His city would function as well as Disneyland and his Burbank studio. It would be a suitable neighbor for his theme park. More importantly, this would not be a sequel.

Of course, the development would feature a bigger and better Disneyland-type theme park. Walt knew the park would help fund the rest of the project, but he was not sure if Disneyland-style entertainment would work on the East Coast. You would think another Disney park anywhere would be a no-lose proposition, but the reality was that Disney films had not done as well in the Northeast as they had in the rest of the United States. Plus, the failure of Freedomland—a Disneyland-inspired theme park built in the Bronx by an estranged Disney associate—made Walt pause. He wanted to be sure.

So he worked his way into four pavilions at the 1964–1965 New York World's Fair, using the opportunity to test the market. The Disney pavilions were a smash hit, and Walt realized that his style of entertainment would work with the "sophisticated" Northeast crowd. Walt also benefited from his sponsors' huge investments in facilities management, ride systems, Audio-Animatronics, and other technologies. Walt's curiosity about the feasibility of an East Coast Disneyland was satisfied. Now he was ready to pursue his dream city.

Changing Expectations

For Walt, EPCOT would be a way for American corporations to show how technology, creative thinking, and hard work could change the world. He saw this project as a way to influence the public's expectations about city life, in the same way his earlier work had redefined what it meant to watch an animated film or visit an amusement park.

Walt's EPCOT—the Experimental Prototype City of Tomorrow—is not the permanent World's Fair that is at Walt Disney World today. Rather, it is the city that Walt described to us just before he died—his vision of a city of 20,000 residents that would be built from the ground up on virgin land and packed with new ideas in planning, design, construction, and governance. If the project were built as Walt had envisioned it, most residents and visitors would know that the name is an acronym.

Building EPCOT would be Walt's most ambitious project. It seems he was following Albert Einstein's advice: "If at first, the idea is not absurd, then there is no hope for it." Walt was always curious about how to do things better through technology, creativity, and hard work, and that curiosity was the primary inspiration for EPCOT. Plus, he hoped people who visited EPCOT would learn lessons that they could take back home with them. Disney Legend Joe Potter, who helped to build Walt Disney World, said Walt was interested "in what attracted people, held their attention, and moved them in and out."[3] Architect Royston Landau called Walt, a "technological-gimmick-obsessive". Author Richard Schickel said in *The Disney Version*, "Disney's gift, from the beginning, was not as is commonly supposed, a 'genius' for artistic expression...it was for the exploitation of technological innovation."

An inspiration just as important as his curiosity was Walt's sense of romance. Imagineer Bob Gurr, the man responsible for many of the vehicles at Disneyland and Walt Disney World (e.g., the Monorail, the PeopleMover, and the Omnimover), described a moment he shared with Walt on the company's prized Grumman G-159 Gulfstream airplane. While looking at a drawing of EPCOT, Walt pointed toward the center of the map and

---

3 U.S. Army Maj. Gen. (Ret.) William Everett "Joe" Potter—graduate of the Massachusetts Institute of Technology (MIT), an engineer who helped plan for the invasion of Normandy during World War II, and governor of the Panama Canal Zone from 1956 until his retirement in 1960—worked for two giants: Walt Disney and Robert Moses. Potter said, "If you said to either of them, 'That's impossible, that will cost a lot of money, or people will be against it,' you didn't last long." Potter did last—ultimately becoming a Disney Legend—and played an important role in the Florida leg of our journey to Progress City.

said, "Here is where the park bench will be where [my wife] Lilly and I will sit on Saturday nights, and watch people walk by..."

Walt said, "Somehow I can't believe there are many heights that can't be scaled by a man who knows the secret of making dreams come true." He was fond of saying that this secret could be summarized in four Cs: Curiosity, Confidence, Courage, and Constancy. He added, "The greatest of these is Confidence. When you believe a thing, believe it all over, implicitly, and unquestioningly." Philosopher-psychologist Erich Fromm agreed and suggested that, "Creativity requires the courage to let go of certainties." Walt must have always been confident that the EPCOT project would work—and it probably would have worked had he lived long enough to infect enough people with his dream, like he had done so many times before. According to Roy Disney, this project was Walt's obsession right up until his death. Roy said, "On the day before he died, Walt lay on the hospital bed staring at the ceiling. It was squares of perforated acoustic tile, and Walt pictured them as a grid map for Disney World... Every four tiles represented a square mile and he said, 'Now there is where the highway will run... There is the route for the monorails.'"

Author Ray Bradbury, a good friend of Walt's, was asked if Walt was an optimist. Bradbury responded that Walt was not an optimist but an optimal behaviorist, a person who believes that "I behave at the top of my powers. Whatever gifts God gave me, I've tried to find out what they are, and make the best use of all my talents." Bradbury added that Walt "knew that he could function in architecture, and later he used that power and raised it to its highest degree." He summed up his view of Walt's optimism by stating, "Optimism cannot come first; behavior comes first, and out of behavior comes happiness." Walt wanted to build an entire planned community based on this belief. He wanted to change the public's expectations of what a city—and happiness—could be.

Unfortunately, Walt died before his most ambitious dream could be realized. Roy Disney was nearing retirement when his brother died in 1966, but he decided to stay on and make sense of Walt's ideas for the Florida Project. Roy and his "boys" wanted to create something that would make his brother proud. They started with the best of intentions. The State of Florida's legislators apparently agreed—they granted Disney unprecedented land use and development rights. Roy and his team knew that the first phase would include the obvious elements like an updated Disneyland, resort hotels, campgrounds, and the infrastructure necessary for long-term development.

But without Walt, the dream could not be realized. Over time, the idea of building a city was scrapped in favor of a theme park. A mountain retreat also came very close to being built but was scuttled soon after Walt passed away. Only an arts college made it off the drawing board close to the way he had envisioned.

Historian Joseph Corn said of projects like EPCOT, "Technological utopianism, a creed once widely held by historians and the general public alike, has been dealt a number of serious blows. It has become at once compelling as a topic of historical inquiry and problematic as a guide to public policy." Walt's EPCOT dream had become a historic case study. What lessons could we learn?

Chapter Three

A Timeless Way of Building

Fascination with the Progress City model on the upper level of the Carousel of Progress show building fostered my interest in learning about urbanism and what it takes to create livable, sustainable cities; and it compelled me to absorb as much as I could about the process that leads to beautiful, functional, and meaningful places. Walt seemed to know how to do that instinctively. He was never formally trained in urban planning, but he has made a significant impact on the way we perceive, design, and build cities. He was the right guy at the right place at the right time—because he understood "the timeless way of building."

The timeless way of building is a concept first conceived by Austrian architect Christopher Alexander, the first recipient of the medal for research ever awarded by the American Institute of Architects. He taught at the Department of Architecture at the University of California, Berkeley for thirty-eight years. His ideas influenced architecture, planning, object-oriented computer programming, and the Traditional Neighborhood Design and Sustainable Environmental Design movements. He was also a major influence on The New Urbanism community of city building professionals. Alexander was able to combine a scientific perspective with a view based on "beauty and grace," and the results have been profound.

One of the most fundamental and relevant discoveries from Alexander's research has been the realization that "human feeling is mostly the same, mostly the same from person to person, mostly the same in every person". Some would argue that this could not be true as we are all individuals and we have different experiences, backgrounds, cultures, and education. Alexander acknowledged that "there is a part of human feeling where we are all different" and "each of us has our idiosyncrasies, our unique individual human character" and "we often concentrate on…talking about feelings, and comparing feelings". Nonetheless, Alexander's forty-year research has shown that those individual qualities account for only 10 percent of human feelings. The other 90 percent are the "stuff in which we are all the same and we feel the same things".

One of Walt Disney's greatest gifts was his ability to understand and tap into those universal feelings. As one of the most influential artists of the 20th century, his creations have crossed the boundaries of time and culture, and his work is still relevant today. Walt knew how to create and tell timeless stories. As many of his filmmaking peers would say, he was the best story man in the business. But timeless stories were not enough for Walt; he also wanted to create timeless places.

The Quality Without a Name

The only way to build beautiful and functional public spaces is to learn the code that unlocks the riddle: how do such places happen? We have all experienced environments that exhibit the timeless way of building. Alexander said these places reveal "the quality without a name". Think back to a place where everything seems just right. You cannot quite put your finger on it, it is hard to explain to somebody else, and your words will always seem inadequate—but there is something there that transcends other places you have experienced. Alexander suggested, "There is a central quality, which is the root criterion of life and spirit in a man, a town, a building or a wilderness. This quality is objective and precise, but it cannot be named."

Why does this matter? When you consider that there are billions of people in the world, the challenge that the Imagineers had to create spaces that appeal to such a broad range of opinions and cultures would seem insurmountable. However, Walt and his design team understood what Alexander meant, and they achieved this "quality without a name"—the quality that appeals universally to all people—in many parts of Disneyland. Surely, this is one of the reasons for the park's tremendous success and why guests keep coming back. Had he lived to build his other environmental design projects, Walt would have infused them with the same quality. "Success is doing ordinary things extraordinarily well," according to business philosopher Jim Rohn; this was one of Walt's greatest strengths.

Walt was not the first person to produce animated films, but he elevated the art form to a level that has yet to be topped. In *Designing Disney's Theme Parks*, cultural historian Karal Ann Marling wrote, "The painstaking art of animation was, after all, the art of perfecting the world. It was a world over which Walt Disney exercised total, beneficent control." Walt wanted to have the same impact on the art of three-dimensional spatial design with the opening of Disneyland. Millions of visitors come to the Disney theme parks to experience the Disney "magic". So what exactly are they looking for? In *DisneyWar*, James B. Stewart defined the Disney magic as that moment when "people's apprehension turns into awe and delight". When Disney guests step into the environment based on a timeless way of building—an environment that has the quality without a name—they realize that they are in a place where their dreams can come true.

Perhaps you have witnessed how a carefully designed, immersive environment can make a significant impression on the individual and can quickly change one's mood and behavior. Walt had the vision and desire to create such a place. As a result, he changed the way we look at the public realm. How did he do this? Why are some places filled with life while other places seem so lifeless?

Christopher Alexander suggested, "What we call 'life' is a general condition, which exists, to some degree or other, in every part of space: brick, stone, grass, river, painting, building, daffodil, human being, forest, city." Alexander added, "The key to this idea is that every part of space—every connected region of space, small or large—has some degree of life." Most importantly, "This degree of life is well defined, objectively existing, and measurable." A space that demonstrates a high-quality, positive experience for the majority of people is one that has a "higher degree of life". Understanding what these measurable qualities are can help to unlock the riddle of how to create wonderful places.

Many urban planners and architects find it important to be able to measure how successful a space or structure is. Alexander tried to be more precise by saying, "We are going to pay attention to what we can see and what we can identify and what we can know." That is the start. It is also important that the knowledge be shared, that it be "put in some kind of experimental form, that another person can then be convinced of." Architect Matthew Frederick provided one definition for sharable knowledge. He suggested, "If you can't explain your ideas to your grandmother in terms that she understands, you don't know your subject well enough."

If you are a city planner and see your role as a resource management expert, then the solution is to demand that everything be measurable. So how do you measure something as seemingly intangible as a "higher degree of life"? How do you describe that quality in a way everybody can understand?

The Higher Degree of Life

When I refer to a place that has a "higher degree of life", what do I mean? The formal definition of a "higher degree of life" is a space that is filled with the "quality without a name". Let's start with this simple test. When you enter a space that feels right, you know it possesses that "quality without a name" immediately, even if you are not able to articulate why you have these feelings.

If you are asked to list why you have such positive feelings, you soon discover that your words are inadequate. It is almost impossible to truly capture the experience in such a way that it can be shared; however, you know the quality does exist, because you have just experienced it.

A couple of examples at Disneyland illustrate how various elements come together to create spaces with a higher degree of life. The first example comes just as you enter Disneyland. The second example is more subtle yet just as powerful.

In an informal poll at a Disney D23 convention, Disney's official fan club, I asked participants to describe that moment when they first felt the "magic" of Disneyland. For many, it was the emotional transformation you experience when you walk from the front courtyard where the large Mickey floral display is located through the tunnels under the railroad tracks to Town Square.

In *101 Things I Learned in Architectural School*, Matthew Frederick teaches us that "our experience of an architectural space is strongly influenced by how we arrive in it". The space is a stage and "we mentally connect visual cues from our surroundings to our needs and expectations. The satisfaction and richness of our experiences are largely the result of the ways in which these connections are made."

Walt used a well-known architectural trick called "denial and reward". This is achieved by deflecting the first view of Town Square by the use of tunnels that pass under the railroad tracks. Walking through the tunnels provides a moment of disorientation that aids in making the effect work.

The first courtyard is symbolically the same as a lobby in a theater. It is a gathering place. From this point, you have to make your first decision. Do you walk through the left or right tunnel? The tunnel you enter through is a highly personal choice, and for many guests, picking one side over the other becomes a tradition. Personally, I always enter from the left-hand tunnel, the one near City Hall.

Employing a movie metaphor, the tunnels create the physical equivalent of a "cross-dissolve". In a movie, a "cross-dissolve" superimposes the tail end of the first clip on the beginning of the second clip, and fades the clips in and out. When done correctly, the effect moves the story along while the audience barely notices the transition. When done poorly, it jars the viewer. The transition through the tunnels provides the same impact, but as a spatial experience. The tunnels are a cross-dissolve from one reality to another. The Disney parks are filled with such treasures.

As you enter the tunnel, the view is limited until you have passed all the way through. Frederick said, "Frame a view, don't merely exhibit it." The best way to create a richer, more dramatic view is to discreetly frame it, screen it, or deny it altogether and reveal it after you have passed through the portal. It has been suggested that by walking through the Disney portal, you are leaving the world of today and assuming your role on the stage that is on the other side. The reward will be a land that has a higher degree of life and possesses the quality without a name. For many, this transition is successfully implemented and profound.

Doing the Right Thing

Creating great places may seem like an impossible task and one left to chance. It is not. We operate with three levels of knowing. The first is simplicity, which is the worldview of a child or uninformed adult. These people are fully engaged in their own experience and are happily unaware of what lies beneath the surface of immediate reality.

The second level is complexity. This is generally how most adults view the world. These people are aware of the complex systems in nature and society, but cannot identify clarifying patterns and connections.

The third and highest level of knowing is informed simplicity. This is an enlightened view of reality and is founded upon an ability to discern or create clarifying patterns and connections. According to Christopher Alexander, places that demonstrate a higher degree of life can be achieved by the proper application of shareable positive design patterns; the ability to do so is a strength of informed simplicity.

When we have experienced a space that has a higher degree of life, how can we explain why we feel that way to others? How do we express the positive qualities such that they can easily be shared? In *A Pattern Language: Towns, Buildings, Construction*, published in 1977, Alexander (with co-authors Sara Ishikawa and Murray Silverstein) suggested a system of fundamental building blocks that can be combined to create wonderful spaces that "make people feel alive and human". This system consists of 253 patterns that lead to rooms, streets, and districts that work. Each pattern consists of a specific problem that recurs in our environment. The pattern provides "the core of the solution" and is described so that "you can use this solution a million times over, without ever doing it the same way twice". The patterns are numbered and arranged within a hierarchy that stretches from a macro look at large regions down to a micro look at the proper placement for climbing plants.

Each pattern is scored by importance with up to two asterisks. Approximately one-third of the patterns are marked with two asterisks, which suggest the connection between place and experience is an "invariant". Those patterns are a "deep and inescapable property of a well-formed environment". Patterns marked with one asterisk are valid, but subject to more research. Patterns that are unmarked are based on empirical data.

When used properly, the patterns can be used like an alphabet; various combinations provide the ability to tell an infinite variety of stories. As outlined in *A Pattern Language*, the combination of patterns can provide an infinite array of solutions for environmental design.

What do I mean by combining patterns? Let me use this example. When preparing a gourmet meal, you must combine the ingredients just right. Adding too much of the wrong thing or mixing the ingredients improperly will spoil the result. When you get it right, the result is something that is greater than the sum of its parts. That is when you have achieved a higher degree of life. The urban planner and architect want to achieve the same result with the built environment that a great chef achieves with the meal.

Alexander's book teaches us how to discern or create clarifying patterns within complex mixtures. Pattern recognition is a crucial skill for an architect or urban planner who must create a highly ordered environment amid many competing and frequently nebulous design considerations.

The Wizard of Bras Porch

Here is another example of a place that demonstrates a higher degree of life inside of Disneyland. To illustrate how properly applied positive design patterns can create spaces that have a higher degree of life and that possess the quality without a name, I will use one of my favorite spots in Disneyland. Those of you who have visited the park have certainly walked by it. Those who have discovered this spot will know exactly what I am talking about. Let's grab a seat on the Wizard of Bras porch.

As you enter Disneyland and stroll down Main Street, U.S.A. on your way toward Sleeping Beauty Castle, you will pass the Silhouette Studio on the right-hand side. Next door to the studio is a frilly Victorian façade with a small front porch. A few steps lead to a bench and two chairs that are bolted to the floor. This is the spot.

Depending on your point of view, you can analyze the porch in a number of ways. The city planner would notice that this is the only building along the west side of Main Street that is set back from the build-to line. A build-to line is a way to regulate where a building's façade must be placed. Urban life is predicated on proximity, walkability, and immediacy. Within a commercial business district, setting buildings back from the sidewalk makes them less accessible to people passing by, reduces the economic viability of first-floor businesses, and weakens the spatial definition of the street. The façades along Main Street are right up to the build-to line forming a street wall that helps to create an outdoor room. This porch is the one exception. Or as city planners like to say, it is "non-conforming".

From the perspective of a planning historian, the porch represents the passage of time. You could assume that this may have been the last house on the block that was not torn down during the growth of the central business district. Typically, over time, as the community would become more prosperous, the land uses along a major transportation corridor would change from primarily residential to primarily commercial. It is not hard to imagine that, at some point, this home may have been converted from a house into a commercial building. As the city gained more wealth, converted residential structures and storefronts with wood façades would give way to taller masonry commercial buildings. Nevertheless, in relationship to the adjacent buildings, this porch still clings to its residential-like quality and heritage.

The theme park historian knows that the real history of the porch is very different. For many, this is known as the "Wizard of Bras" porch. When the park opened in 1955, many of the shops along Main Street were licensees. Walt didn't have enough money for everything and leased bits just to get things done and to raise some extra cash. One of the first vendors was Hollywood-Maxwell's Intimate Apparel Shop. If you needed undergarments while visiting Disneyland, this would be the place to go. Here you could buy lingerie, brassieres, and torsolettes at the only store in the park to sell such goods. Plus, you got a history lesson about the world of underwear in the museum located inside the store. The shop lasted less than one year and closed in January 1956. The reason this porch even still exists is up for speculation. Some experts have said it was built so that guests would have to be adult size in order to see the showroom window. Others have said it was meant as a resting place for men while their lady companions shopped inside. It could also just be an aesthetic decision and a way to create a greater variety of storefronts along Main Street.

From the Imagineers' point of view, the door may not open any more, but the façade has been cast in a new role. If you could open the door, the porch would lead to Fargo's Palm Parlor offering "Predictions that will haunt you" and are "Bazaar, Whimsical & Wizard". In the tradition of honoring important people in the history of Disneyland, the window on the second floor is a tribute to Imagineer Roland "Rolly" F. Crump who specializes in "designs to die for"; the examples featured in the window design are his sketches for the Museum of the Weird, a project that would later become the Haunted Mansion.

If we use Christopher Alexander's pattern system, we are able to describe precisely why the Wizard of Bras porch is so special. Main Street demonstrates a very high degree of life. It feels alive and has what Alexander calls the "Magic of the City". Functionally, the Main Street corridor is between two "Activity Nodes" and becomes a "Promenade". The corridor is designed to be a "Shopping Street" with a "Market of Many Shops". The atmosphere is almost a "Carnival" and it is not uncommon to see "Dancing in the Street". Main Street becomes "Common Land" and a "Public Outdoor Room".

The façades were designed in a way that creates the appearance of "Individually Owned Shops", even though we know that is not a reflection of the reality inside. There are "Street Cafés", "Food Stands", and occasionally people "Sleeping in Public" in Town Square and in the Plaza Hub.

Although the façades imply that there are many structures along Main Street, the reality is that there are only four very large buildings. However, the clever design of the "Building Complex" breaks down the large structures through the use of small storefronts, which creates an experience that becomes a "Pedestrian Street" lined with a "Family of Entrances". The street becomes "Positive Outdoor Space" lined with "Connected Buildings". As Alexander says, "The simple social intercourse created when people rub shoulders in public is one of the most essential kinds of social 'glue' in society."

The "Paths and Goals" are designed to help propel you forward. The edges of the street are defined by the "Building Fronts", which play a similar role to the build-to line mentioned earlier. All of these patterns have combined to create the "Pedestrian Density". From Town Square to the Plaza Hub, this area is filled with "Common Areas at the Heart", a place for social groups to informally gather. For every social group, there is a space to call its own while still being connected to the whole.

The Wizard of Bras porch is an example of a "Half-Hidden Garden" or, more specifically, a "Private Terrace on the Street". Sitting on a protected, elevated space allows the people on the porch to look down at the passing traffic and feel secure from the people below.

When guests are enjoying the porch, it becomes an "Activity Pocket". When people sit on the steps—as they frequently do—the steps become "Stair Seats". Places like this porch help enliven the street and offer "eyes on the street", providing a greater sense of security for everyone. The porch is part of an "Intimacy Gradient" of public spaces and becomes a semi-public space.

Without such a space, the transition between the public and private realm can sometimes seem harsh and abrupt, and an opportunity is lost. A porch can also function as an "Entrance Room". Building these types of spaces within our environment is an opportunity to create places that bridge the transition between the private and the public realm. In the United States, a house with a front porch has traditionally served this function. The end result is a tranquil space, just out of reach yet still connected to the hustle and bustle below.

The Wizard of Bras porch is a wonderful spot to sit and watch the passing parade of guests. The view is hypnotizing in the same way as looking out at a river or a lake. Alexander describes what you are experiencing as a "Zen View" made up of a "Tapestry of Light and Dark". For many, the porch serves as an effective "Place to Wait" and a "Sunny Place".

Because of the well thought-out combination of positive design patterns, the porch has become an "Outdoor Room", which is an open-air space that provides relief and reflection. While sitting on the porch, the space is activated by the "Opening to the Street". The porch is too narrow, however, to satisfy the "Six-Foot Balcony" pattern, which would have made the space more functional. To overcome that limitation, there is a "Half-Open Wall" that protects the guests from the surrounding traffic. Placing a low wall or some other element defines the space.

Overall, the porch is made up of "Good Materials", and the "Perimeter Beam" creates a strong frame for the opening. Alexander would suggest that the pitched roof is a good example of a "Roof Vault" and that the low railing acts as a "Low Sill" that expands the seating capacity on the porch. The thick columns create a "Column Place". The extra bit of detail at the capital (top) generates a "Column Connection", and when you stand across the street, you notice the "Roof Caps", those extra little details at the peak of the roof that do not have to be there, but would be missed if they were gone. The wooden floor provides a contrast to the asphalt and bricks on the street below, and the "Floor Surface" is warm and inviting. Even the front door strengthens the space with "Solid Doors with Glass".

How a structure is built can also contribute to a higher degree of life. The "Half-Inch Trim" is the suggested application of decoration. Most importantly, the porch functions as a wonderful "Seat Spot" and a proper "Front Door Bench". In addition, the "Ornament" is appropriate for the style of the architecture.

What may matter most is that the Imagineers were thoughtful enough to include a place to pause and reflect, relax and unwind, yet still be a part of the action. As the other Disneyland-type parks have grown much larger and grander, they have eliminated this type of space. That is one reason why the park in Anaheim feels more intimate than the others. This is a perfect example of a space that has that quality without a name and achieves a higher degree of life. The Wizard of Bras porch example only scratches at the surface of how to use *A Pattern Language* to describe the experience of a space so that it can be shared and possibly duplicated elsewhere.

Wholeness

Another way to understand if a space achieves a higher degree of life is to determine if it demonstrates a quality that Alexander called "Wholeness"—the quality a space has when the "local parts exist chiefly in relation to the whole, and their behavior and character and structure are determined by the larger whole in which they exist and which they create". Wholeness is achieved when positive design patterns are combined to create centers. When multiple centers coalesce, they become those spaces that have that quality without a name. The Wizard of Bras porch is a space that possesses wholeness.

To achieve wholeness, you need to unlock the power of centers. Centers represent the combination of elements, objects, and patterns that can be measured and appreciated. It is important to remember that a center is not just one grand object like a solitary mountain on an empty plain. A strong center could be thought of as more like a mountain range. A center is something greater than its parts, even if there is one element among the parts that is the "first among equals". Alexander called that spot the "Resting Place".

An isolated center has no life. It gains strength when combined with other centers. As the centers converge, they transform the environment, which increasingly "comes to life". Alexander said this starts to happen when the centers "are packed and overlapped to fill the space...each one helping and intensifying the others".

Walt would strengthen, or in his words, "plus" his landscapes by combining positive design patterns and creating multiple centers. In the early days of Disneyland, many of the attractions shared the same physical space. The Frontierland area could be explored in a variety of ways, including pack mules, trains, stagecoaches, and Conestoga wagons. Tomorrowland could be experienced from above in the Astro-Jets, below in a submarine, or in a futuristic vehicle such as a monorail or WEDway PeopleMover.

There is much to say about centers and how to identify which ones are in play within any given space. When centers are combined correctly, the results are exceptional places instead of merely acceptable, or worse yet, regrettable, places.

Alexander stated there are four key ideas about the structure of centers. First, centers themselves have life; and second, centers help one another. Alexander said, "The existence and life of one center can intensify the life of another." Centers are made of other centers. He stated, "This is the only way of describing their composition." Finally, "A structure gets its life according to the density and intensity of centers, which have been formed in it." The process is very organic. This is not like a machine. The boundaries can be blurred. The elements will be subtle in their distinctions. Each center supports and strengthens the others. This is why it is so hard to create such places consistently. Alexander does offer some help, however.

Centers Are Measurable

Centers allow us to measure which spaces are more "alive" than others and to share that information objectively. Alexander made five assertions about centers. To illustrate these assertions, let's apply them to a public place that may be very familiar.

Imagine you are at Disneyland or the Magic Kingdom, and you are standing in the Plaza Hub just in front of the Partners statue. Walt Disney and Mickey Mouse face south, welcoming the guests as they enter the park. Disney Legend and long-time Imagineer Blaine Gibson created the sculpture.

Alexander's first assertion is that "centers arise in space". Centers have to start in a specific place. Walt wanted a specific, identifiable space at the center of his park that would clearly orientate guests to the various "lands", or what planners would call "adjacent activity nodes". The Partners statue is at the center of such a place, and it is called the Plaza Hub. This hub serves as a distribution point. Its function is at the heart of its design. This circulation pattern is known as the radial plan or—in "Disneyspeak"—the hub-and-spoke. We will revisit this topic in more detail later, because the creation of a strong center would be at the heart of the EPCOT project as well. The Partners statue is a strong center element; Alexander would call this "Something Roughly in the Middle".

The next assertion is that "each center is created by a configuration of other centers". The Plaza Hub is a distinct place with clear boundaries. This boundary is further defined by a curb that surrounds the park. The textures are distinctly different and obvious to the eyes and feet. Each boundary enhances and embellishes the other. Each center strengthens every other center.

The Plaza Hub is framed by gateways to the various lands. Beyond the gateways are activity nodes that further enhance the Plaza Hub center. The result is the Hub has the feel of an outdoor room. The feeling is more pronounced at Disneyland than at the Magic Kingdom due to Disneyland's smaller scale.

An open plaza would be boring and lifeless. Even a plaza that features minimal amenities or a solitary piece of public art would not be saved. You see traditional traffic circles everywhere, and they do not possess that quality without a name. The Plaza Hub is different because of the way positive design patterns are combined to create new centers. For example, planters are used as a median that separates the Hub into two distinct spaces. Along the outer ring are benches where people can rest and watch passers-by. The presence of these guests helps to animate the area. The inner ring within the planters and facing the statue is a much more intimate space.

There is a special relationship between the Plaza Hub and the castles that dominate the northern edge. First, there is the contrast between the immersive environment of a main street in small-town America at the turn of the 20th century and a medieval castle as the "terminating vista" that encloses the space. Imagineer John Hench acknowledged, "There are a couple of contradictions that occur on a rational level. Like having a castle at the end of Main Street. It doesn't belong on Main Street, but it does belong at the end of a vista like this." This contrast should feel odd, but it does not. In fact, the contrast of the two cultures feels reassuring. Hench called it "a strong point". That was just the quality that Walt wanted, and something best accomplished by somebody with a background in film. As we will see, Walt's vision for EPCOT would be a collection of such spaces, with each space strengthening the others.

The Plaza Hub is a perfect spot to reflect on how positive design patterns can combine to create a powerful center that is both meaningful and functional. Quite simply, the Plaza Hub works because everything you see supports everything else you see. The dominant elements work because of the supporting details. The supporting details are enhanced because of the discipline provided by the dominant elements. The Plaza Hub orients and reassures the guests with minimal signage and direction. This space bridges every culture and speaks a universal language.

The Fifteen Fundamental Properties of Beauty

In Alexander's opinion, beauty is not subjective but objective. Through his research, as documented in *The Nature of Order* series of books, he has determined that all centers begin with at least one of fifteen fundamental properties and that at least one of these properties is at the core of any space. When that property is combined with others, the whole is greater than the sum of the parts.

A space can have different Levels of Scale, which is a balanced range of sizes that is pleasing and beautiful. A Strong Center enhances good design by offering areas of focus or weight. Like the earthen berm that surrounds Disneyland, Boundaries provide an outline that focuses attention on the center. Alternating Repetition repeats various elements, which creates a sense of order and harmony. Positive Space is when the background reinforces rather than detracts from the center. Good Shape uses simple forms that create an intense, powerful center.

Local Symmetries refers to organic, small-scale symmetry that works better than precise, overall symmetry. Looping and connecting elements promote unity and grace, a property called Deep Interlock and Ambiguity. Contrast means the unity is achieved with visible opposites. Gradients are the proportional use of space and are another pattern that creates harmony. Texture and imperfections suggest uniqueness and life; Alexander calls this Roughness. Similarities should repeat throughout a design to create

Echoes. The Void is created by empty spaces that offer calm and contrast. Only what is essential should be used, while avoiding extraneous elements; this is called Simplicity and Inner Calm. Finally, the design of a space should be connected and complementary, not egocentric and isolated. This creates the quality of Not-Separateness.

Good design comes from combining positive design patterns and creating centers. Combining centers creates wholeness. Each piece works together to create places based on a timeless way of building that captures a higher degree of life. The results are places that you want to return to frequently.

Walt somehow knew right from the start that building in a timeless way was best. He would apply these positive design patterns not only at his movie studio but also at his home and at his theme park. Walt's ambitions as a city builder were to apply those qualities to something much bigger than Disneyland. He wanted to build a new town that possessed the quality of wholeness; he wanted to bring back the qualities of life that would rescue our humanity. If he were to succeed, he might just change the world. Again.

Chapter Four

The Burbank Studio

Walt Disney and his brother Roy founded the Disney Brothers Cartoon Studio on October 16, 1923. Their first studio was in the garage behind their Uncle Robert Disney's place at 4406 Kingswell Avenue in Los Angeles. They soon moved out of the garage and down the street into a small office at 4651 Kingswell Avenue. It was not long before their thriving animation studio expanded into the office suite next door.

The studio continued to grow, and soon the brothers outgrew the Kingswell facility. They purchased a lot at 2719 Hyperion Avenue in the Silver Lake area of Los Angeles in 1925 and began building. Their new studio opened in 1926. The Hyperion studio quickly became a creative beehive.

In 1929, Roy insisted that they rename the company Walt Disney Productions as a very real reminder as to who was the creative force behind the animation studio. Roy told Disney archivist Dave Smith, "It was my idea. Walt was the creative member of the team. His name deserved to be on the pictures."

Physically, the studio grew in an unorganized fashion; by 1931, the 1,600 square foot facility had expanded to over 20,000 square feet. A two-story Spanish Revival building and soundstage joined the original one-story stucco building. Over the years, additional buildings were added as needed, and the studio grew to more than 73,000 square feet by the time the Disney brothers moved to Burbank.

With the 1937 success of *Snow White and the Seven Dwarfs*, the Disney brothers thought it was time to build a proper animation studio from the ground up. In 1938, they bought 51 acres in Burbank and selected Frank Crowhurst as chief contractor and Bill Garity as project supervisor.

Walt tapped Karl Emanuel Martin "Kem" Weber to be the architect.[4] His

---

4 Born in Germany in 1889, Weber graduated from the School of Decorative Arts in Potsdam in 1912 and began to work for architect Bruno Paul. Weber worked on the German pavilions for the 1910 Exposition Universelle, a World's Fair held in Brussels, and for the 1915 Panama-Pacific International Exposition in San Francisco. Unable to return home due to Germany's involvement in World War I, Weber remained in the United States and explored opportunities in California. His early work was mostly for residential structures in various historic revival styles such as Mayan, Egyptian, and Minoan. He was also the Art Director for

design reputation was solidified by his work in the Streamline Moderne style. Walt chose Weber for the studio project not only because of Weber's solid reputation as an architect and industrial designer but also because of his experience with film set design. Still, even with an accomplished architect handling the project, Walt was involved in every aspect of the project, though his priority was on function and not design. He wanted to enhance the movie-making process, and he would do that through a thoughtful efficient structure. Christopher Alexander said, "Process plays a more fundamental role in determining the life and death of the building than does the design." The design of the Burbank studio was all about the process.

Weber and Disney quickly completed the design, and by 1939 they were ready to begin construction. The first of the Disney staff moved in on Christmas Eve, and the rest moved in by the spring of 1940.

One Man's Vision

Walt and Roy's facility in Burbank was the first movie studio solely dedicated to the manufacture of animated films. All design decisions were based not on architectural interest or beauty but on how the solution could enhance the filmmaking process. In a 1940 interview, Chief Contractor Frank Crowhurst said, "Walt wasn't particularly interested in any architectural effects. We have a functional group of buildings... They allow their masses of construction to express style rather than surface ornamentation. It's no good for me or Weber...or anyone else to try to tell him how a building should look. He isn't interested."

Walt wanted to do everything he could to encourage the maximum creativity and efficiency of his artists. For example, to create the perfect animation desk, Walt asked Frank Thomas, one of his most trusted animators, to design one based on his experience. Then Walt had Weber refine the design and fabricate the desks. Weber was also responsible for the design of the other pieces of furniture and the unified studio signage. In *Building a Company*, author Bob Thomas claimed that "[Walt] planned the Burbank studio down to the contour of the chairs".

In press releases, the studio was described as "a self-sufficient, state-of-the-art production factory that provided all the essential facilities for the entire production process". In *Walt Disney: The Triumph of the American*

Barker Brothers, a large, influential furniture store in the Los Angeles area. Weber also worked as an industrial designer, with some of his work shown at the 1928 International Exposition of Art in Industry in New York.

Imagination, Neal Gabler, the well-known movie critic, wrote, "Walt saw the Studio in psychological terms. From the moment he started talking about the planning of the Studio, he always had in mind the psychological effect of the physical space, because Walt didn't believe good work came out of tyranny. Studio heads at that time believed...anxiety was the source of productivity. Walt didn't operate that way. He felt that if people were happy, they would create well."

The Burbank studio was designed to provide the artists all the comforts of home. There was a snack stand, barber, cleaners, a buffet-style restaurant, and health club. Every part of the facility was air-conditioned by a custom-made General Electric system. This was very rare at the time; it not only ensured the artists' comfort, but it kept dust off the painted celluloid sheets as well.

This attention to detail was not just Walt being a benevolent boss; it meant that his artists really had no reason to leave work. The Disney Studio work environment was unique at the time, but it would become the prototype for modern-day high-tech companies and other high-performance organizations after World War II.

A Machine for Making Movies

At the time the Disney brothers built their Burbank studio, most Hollywood movie studios were a jumble of hastily built soundstages and administrative buildings that doubled as stage sets—movie studios were not called "film factories" for nothing. Walt wanted something very different for his creative, talented staff. From the outset, he intended that his studio be based on an easy-to-navigate site plan and timeless architecture. A little tour reveals that he succeeded.

We enter the Disney Studio through one of three gates. The internal circulation system is a grid of streets, typical of the Midwestern cities where Walt grew up; the logical grid roadway pattern makes it easy to find our destination.

The two main streets on the Disney lot street grid are Mickey Avenue, which runs north–south, and Dopey Drive, which travels east–west. At the intersection of these two streets is a very famous street sign. The sign was originally meant to be a temporary prop for the 1941 movie *The Reluctant Dragon*. At some point, it was given permanent status, and it has become one of the most identifiable and photographed spots in the studio. Upon close inspection, you can see that the figure of Mickey Mouse does not match the studio's standard of the day—it was not carefully made, as it was assumed that the sign would be removed right after filming.

The internal roadways are very narrow curb-to-curb. A narrow road naturally promotes traffic calming and encourages walking, bicycling, or small carts as the preferred method of travel. Walt intended that moving around his studio would be a pleasure, unlike the experience one found at other movie studios in the area. With that in mind, he pushed the parking areas to the edges of the property.

The buildings are set back from the interior streets and lined with grass lawns and oak trees. Even the utilities are placed underground and hidden from view. The overall effect is less a factory and more like a suburban office park. The entire studio feels very intimate and welcoming.

At the center of everything, both physically and psychologically, is the Animation Building. For the building's architectural language, Walt selected the popular Streamline Moderne style because it emulated the sensation of speed, efficiency, and modernity in a distinctly American way. Walt wanted to build an efficient and functional movie-making machine—what could be more functional than an architectural style that reminds people of an aerodynamic train or an airplane? The principles behind Streamline Moderne successfully express Walt's intentions for the facility.

The design of the Animation Building captures architect Louis Sullivan's advice that "[a] proper building grows naturally, logically, and poetically out of all its conditions". Overall, the massing of the buildings features horizontal elements and clean lines. The buildings repeat various elements throughout the studio campus, which creates a sense of order and harmony; this design pattern is called alternating repetition.

In keeping with Modernism, there is a lack of architectural detail. The Animation Building design relies upon the thoughtful use of exterior materials, such as the flat ground-floor bricks that are held together with recessed mortar and arranged in pairs, one on top of the other, with the result that the building seems to hug the ground.

The California desert inspires the color palette for the exterior of the Animation Building, with the terracotta, cream, and green building colors arranged in a gradient—a choice not only beautiful but also functional. Walt wanted the color of the exterior to calm the eyes for the artists, who look at saturated colors throughout the workday.

The street grid in this part of Burbank does not follow on a true north-south-east-west orientation. The Animation Building ignores the local street grid so that the building's orientation allows for the maximum number of windows that face true north. It has been known for centuries that north light is the best for artists because they get constant light with a silvery quality that brings out the cool, purplish, greenish atmospheric colors. When windows face north, the quality of the light tends to be shadowless, diffuse, and neutral or slightly grayish most of the day and throughout the year. The animators and color stylists could paint all day and the subject would not change. The windows were fitted with special metal awnings that could be adjusted by the occupants of each office. Even today, the north-facing windows of the Animation Building remain unobstructed to let in the natural light.

The view below the north-facing windows has changed considerably over the years. Originally, an earthen berm was built to hide the view of Alameda Avenue. When the Team Disney Building was erected, a reflecting pool was installed. Today, the reflecting pool has been paved over, and the plaza has been dedicated to tributes for Walt, Roy, and the other Disney Legends recipients.

Form Follows Function

Architect Louis Sullivan once proclaimed, "Form follows function." That is a good way to describe how Walt approached the design for the studio. As we continue our tour, we see that the layout for the buildings—and their relationship to one another— follows the production path for an animated film.

The filmmaking process starts on the third floor of the Animation Building, with Walt and the storymen. Walt's office suite is located in wing 3H on the third floor, in the prime northeast corner. The suite is made up of a formal office as well as a working office. There is also a small kitchen and an apartment where Walt would occasionally spend the night. (He enjoyed the apartment so much and found it so useful that he decided he would create the same type of living quarters on top of the fire station at Disneyland.)

As the film production progresses, the storymen hand off their work to the layout men and directors located on the second floor, where the work is divided up. The assignments are passed along to the first floor, and the hundreds of animators go to work. In the basement are test cameras where the dailies—the raw footage prepared each day—can be shot and sent back up to the animators for their review.

When the animation cells are ready, they are transported in underground tunnels to the Ink and Paint Building, across the street to the east just below Walt's view. The tunnels allow the delicate drawings to move from one phase of production to another without concern for the weather. Once the cells are painted, they move south, toward the Camera and Cutting Buildings.

Ultimately, all of this attention to detail became a double-edged sword. Some artists would say that the plush new facilities lacked the intimate nature of the Hyperion studio and made it difficult to interact with Walt and other team members. That interaction was central to the early success of the organization; unfortunately, the lack of contact was one factor that led to a labor strike that started on May 28, 1941. Disney historian Paul Anderson said, "When they moved to the Burbank studio, a lot of the artists complained that it seemed very compartmentalized and that there was a real class system among the various echelons and levels of the artists."

Walking Along the Grid

We continue our tour by walking north along Mickey Avenue. Across the street from the Animation Building we see the Hyperion Health Club, Commissary, and the Roy O. Disney building (1976). At the end of the street is the Michael D. Eisner Building. The 345,000 square foot Michael D. Eisner Building (formerly Team Disney) was designed by Michael Graves and opened in 1990. The building pays tribute to the film that made the Burbank studio possible: *Snow White and the Seven Dwarfs*. The building is an example of pure Post-Modernism, and the façade is an interpretation of the Parthenon with 20-foot dwarfs holding up the pediment.

Facing the Michael D. Eisner Building across the Legends Plaza is the five-story Frank Wells Building, built in 1997. Architect Robert Venturi had the challenge of being sympathetic with both the adjacent original, modest low-slung Kem Weber buildings and the Post-Modern, temple-like Eisner Building. The Wells building features loft-like office spaces surrounding a large, open interior courtyard. The façade is a porcelain enamel image of film reels on a filmstrip background. Public areas are done in black and white with a patterned terrazzo floor and brushed aluminum panels holding digitally pixilated marble that creates a black-and-white image. The Wells Building is also home to the Disney Archives.

The street that runs south of the Animation Building is Dopey Drive. Across the street is the Studio Theater—first used to mix the soundtrack for *Fantasia*—and Soundstages A, B, and C, specially built to mitigate the noise from the nearby Bob Hope (formerly Burbank/Glendale/Pasadena) Airport. The airport was originally a Lockheed production facility. Its strategic importance was one reason why the Disney Studio was taken over by the military during World War II.

Although Walt wanted to design a new studio from the ground up, not everything was original; in the end, he moved a number of buildings from the Hyperion lot, including the Employee Center and Studio Store plus the Hyperion Bungalow. The Shorts Building was made up from two different Hyperion structures, with one half built in 1934 and the other in 1938. This move was driven as much by emotion as it was by practicality. According to *Disney Twenty-Three* magazine, "The easternmost part of the building is where Walt and his team created *Snow White and the Seven Dwarfs*. How could he leave that behind?"

Soundstages and the Backlot

As live-action films became part of the production mix, Disney expanded the capabilities of the studio, by the construction of soundstages and a backlot. The live-action sequences in *Fantasia* with conductor Leopold Stokowski were filmed on Stage One, built as part of the original project. In 1949, Disney added Stage Two. Jack Webb paid for the project so that he could film the *Dragnet* television series. *The Mickey Mouse Club* was also filmed on Stage Two, one of the largest sound stages on the West Coast. Stage Three, featuring a huge water tank, was built in 1954 and was specifically designed for *20,000 Leagues Under the Sea*. The studio continued to expand in 1958 with the addition of Stage Four. In 1988, that building was divided and Stage Five was born.

A common feature at most movie studios is a backlot, which is an area with permanent exterior sets for outdoor scenes. Backlots are part of the magic necessary in filmmaking. Building façades that represent various time periods frame the backlot public areas. The façades are merely decorative fronts and not complete buildings. They can easily be "dressed" to represent any location or setting needed for the production. At Disney, there were four themed backlot areas: Western Street, Zorro Plaza and Zorro Street, Residential Street, and Town Square. Each area was added as production needs demanded. The three-dimensional sets found in the early Disney Studio backlots are the forerunners of the themed façades that are used today at Disneyland. Over time, the backlot was slowly removed and replaced with office buildings and production facilities such as Stages Six and Seven.

The backlot also housed shops that provided the crafts and services necessary for live production, including the Machine Shop, which was originally built to service the cameras and other technical equipment. The Machine Shop was also where Walt built many non-film–related projects, including his Carolwood Pacific home railroad and many of the vehicles, watercraft, and attractions we see today at Disneyland. While the Machine Shop no longer exists, the Electric/Plumbing Building still stands next to the Special Effects Shop, as do a Paint Shop, Sign Graphics, Craft Services, and the Mill.

Walt had five earthern berms built around the north and east edges of the property to shield the film productions from the surrounding community. There was also a small berm, used for films, that protected a lake on the south end. The use of this landscaping feature can still be found at Walt's home and at Disneyland.

Today, on-site shooting has taken the place of backlot façades for the most part. Universal Studios has maintained a large backlot, but the other famous major studio backlots have been torn down and repurposed.[5] This was the fate of the Disney Studio backlot as well.

Expansion

The Disney brothers also owned property south of Riverside Drive, where Walt originally wanted to build his Mickey Mouse Park. However, part of the Riverside Drive property was eventually sold and is currently under the Ventura Freeway. The remaining land became home to the Feature Animation and the ABC Buildings.

Robert A.M. Stern designed the Post-Modern 240,000 square-foot Feature Animation Building in 1994 at a cost of $54 million, with details and materials influenced by Kem Weber's original Animation Building. The four-story structure, currently headquarters for The Walt Disney Company Feature Animation department, was specifically designed to act as a buffer between the pedestrian-oriented studio lot and the bustling nearby freeway. Inside is a screening room with a lobby that can be used when the rest of the facility is closed.

When Disney purchased ABC Television in 1995, they decided to move the leadership from New York to Burbank. Disney engaged Aldo Rossi to design the ten-story ABC Building, which was completed in 1998 at a cost estimated to have been between $75 and $90 million. The building is approximately 300,000 square feet and divided into three areas. A serpentine pedestrian bridge over Riverside Drive connects the facility to the rest of the studio, and a parking garage goes six levels below grade.

The water tower is an iconic visual element of the studio and is no longer in use. The 135½ foot tower cost $300,000 and held 150,000 gallons of water. It is also a rare example of Roy's influence on Disney design. While most water towers stand on four legs, the one at the Disney Studio has six. There is no functional reason, although Roy did claim it would be more stable in an earthquake; but, more importantly, he simply thought it would look better.

---

5   For example, MGM sold off Lot 2, which contained the large train station that was featured in the Andy Hardy movies, and Lot 3, which contained a lake and a jungle. Twentieth-Century Fox redeveloped its backlot, which became the Century City mixed-use development designed by Welton Becket.

Virtually No Limitations

The Disney Burbank studio is a rare example of a Hollywood movie production facility that is still relatively intact. Walt was able to design the facility with virtually no limitations. None of the other major Hollywood studios was built with such a singular vision. Although the backlot has given way to new office buildings, every new act of construction has enhanced or embellished what was there before. For Disney today, many of the backlot functions have been moved to the Golden Oak Ranch near Newhall, California; we'll talk more about Golden Oak Ranch later.

Walt continually received letters from fans asking if they could tour the studio. Walt knew that the animation process was not the most exciting thing for visitors, so he began to develop something grander. He started toying with the idea of an amusement park adjacent to the studio. He felt there was a need for a three-dimensional environment in which guests could interact with the characters.

The studio eventually produced more than just movies and television programs. Many of the attractions in the early days at Disneyland were designed, developed, and fabricated on the lot and trucked to Anaheim. For example, most of the park's vehicles were built at the studio, including the Main Street vehicles, the monorail trains, and much of the *Mark Twain* riverboat.

Walt Disney Productions may have started out in a simple garage, but they ended up at Walt Disney's state-of-the-art animation factory. This may be the only large-scale construction project overseen by Walt that did not compromise his vision. The Burbank studio is a pure expression of the way Walt viewed the built environment and how to control it for his own purposes.

Chapter Five

Carolwood Drive

You can learn a lot about a person by taking a look at his or her personal space. Once you enter the person's home, you might be able to get a peek into his mind. Walt Disney's Holmby Hills home was his sanctuary away from the studio and a place for him to dream about new projects, new ideas. Let's explore what Walt's home tells us about him.

When Walt and his family moved into their home at 355 Carolwood Drive, his mind exploded with new interests—interests so powerful that they led to the beginning of Imagineering, Disneyland, and the desire to build a city of his own. Behind the earthen berm that protected his home from his neighbors, Walt could be with his family, entertain his friends, immerse himself with his hobbies of miniatures and model railroading, and escape the pressures of his movie studio. This allowed him the space to explore other creative ideas.

Birth of a Railfan

Even as a little boy growing up in Marceline, Missouri, Walt was fascinated with trains. Marceline was a rail town created by the Santa Fe Railroad as a refueling station. In 1938, Walt confided, "To tell the truth, more things of importance happened to me in Marceline than have happened since—or are likely to in the future."

Before he was married, Walt's father, Elias, worked for a short time as a carpenter for the Union Pacific installing track from Ellis, Kansas, to Denver, Colorado—so perhaps that set the stage for Walt's fascination with trains. But, to young Walt, it was his Uncle Mike Martin who had the most glamorous job in the world. Uncle Mike was an engineer for the Santa Fe Railroad. He would come to the Disney home, sit with the family on the front porch, and fill the young boy's head with stories about life on the rails. These stories made a profound impression on Walt.

When Walt turned fifteen he decided he would go to work for the railroad himself. He signed up to become a "news butcher", just like his hero, Thomas Edison. A news butcher walks up and down the train aisle selling sodas, apples, newspapers, and other small items. This was also the first time that Walt rode in the cab of a steam locomotive. To get started, Walt borrowed $30 from his brother Roy so he could post a bond, a requirement for getting the job. This loan was the beginning of a long financial relationship between the brothers. By the end of the summer, Walt returned home, somehow having lost all of his profits and the bond money.

Many years later, Walt would learn that some of the Disney animators were also railfans. Ollie Johnson lived in La Cañada, California, and owned a one-inch–scale live steam locomotive. In 1936, Walt visited Johnson and realized for the first time that he could have his own personal railroad. In the late 1930s, Walt bought his nephew Roy E. Disney an HO-scale electric train set. HO is the most popular scale of model railroading in the world, with a scale ratio of 1:87.1, which is 3.5 mm to 1 foot. Walt assembled the train and would play with it when he visited his brother's family. This was Walt's first real experience in model railroading, and it most certainly was not to be his last.

Walt's passion for trains was so strong that he would occasionally take his wife, Lillian, to the rail yard just to watch the trains moving about. In Katherine and Richard Greene's outstanding book *Inside the Dream*, Lillian said, "We'd stand and watch the trains come in and after they'd go by, he'd watch the vibrations on the tracks." She noted, "I wondered why he did that. [To Walt,] [t]hat was recreation."

High Iron

On October 20, 1945, after Walt had attended a party at animator Ward Kimball's house, he was inspired to take his railfan hobby to the next level. Kimball was one of Walt's famous Nine Old Men of animation, a two-time Academy Award winner, who is most famous for animating such characters as Jiminy Cricket, the Mad Hatter, and the Cheshire Cat. He also produced, directed, and co-wrote "Magic Highways USA" and the "Man in Space" segments for the *Disneyland* television show. A renaissance man, Kimball was a founding member of the incredible Firehouse Five Plus Two, a Dixieland jazz band made up of studio animators that became world famous in its own right. In *The Story of Walt Disney*, Walt went so far as to say, "Ward Kimball is one person that I can truly call a genius."

Kimball owned a house in San Gabriel, a suburb near Los Angeles. When Walt arrived for the party, he learned that in 1938, Kimball had installed a narrow-gauge steam train in his backyard—a full-size 1881 Baldwin "Mogul" (2-6-0) coal-burning steam locomotive from the Southern Pacific's Owens Valley narrow-gauge line that Kimball had restored and decorated with his own artwork on the headlamp and cab. He called his locomotive the *Emma Nevada*, and it ran on Kimball's Grizzly Flats Railroad. He parked the train in an engine house and built 800 feet of track on his property. He was such an avid train buff and so enjoyed inspiring others that in 1990 Kimball donated his train to the Orange Empire Railway Museum in Perris, California, where it can be seen today.

On the weekends, Kimball would fire up the locomotive and ride back and forth. The October 20, 1945, party was one such occasion. Kimball invited Walt to join him in the cab and let him run the steam locomotive. This was Walt's first turn at pushing the Johnson bar, which is a lever that adjusts the steam engine valve timing and, therefore, the speed. He got a chance to ring the bell and pull on the steam whistle of a real, live steam train. It brought back childhood memories of his days as a news butcher. Once Walt started to play with Kimball's train, he was hooked. Kimball described what came over Walt as "a railroader's 'high iron' in his blood" that "he just hadn't discovered ... yet!"

This party reignited Walt's passion for trains; now he wanted a railroad at his own home! Plus, this dovetailed with Walt's doctors' suggestion that he find a hobby as a way to relax. Walt told his nurse, "Yeah, Kimball is always relaxed. Maybe it's because he's got such a wonderful hobby running that big steam train in his backyard." However, Walt's home at the time was not big enough. That would soon change.

The Chicago Railroad Fair

By Christmas 1947, Walt had set up an electric HO-scale model train outside his office. When Kimball learned of this, he ran into Disney Legend Ollie Johnston's office and said, "There's something up in Walt's office you've gotta see." This became an open invitation for all of the train fanatics at the studio to express their love for the hobby.

Walt had received the train set from Lionel Trains as a gift. In 1934, when Lionel had been on the edge of bankruptcy, Walt granted a license to Lionel to manufacture a small electric handcar powered by Mickey and Minnie. The toy was an immediate hit, sold more than one million units, and saved the day for the toy maker. Lionel continued to manufacture the toy until 1937. There was also a Donald Duck railcar toy that included Pluto. As a thank you, Lionel pledged to give Walt all the model railroad equipment he wanted.

Like many bosses at the time, Walt was very remote from his staff and did not fraternize much with the employees. As a result of his enthusiasm for trains, Walt's relationship with Ward Kimball was an exception. When Walt heard about the 1948 Chicago Railroad Fair, he realized it was an opportunity he could not pass up. Knowing of Ward Kimball's love of trains,

Walt called him up. As Kimball recalled, "Kimball, this is Walt. There's a swell train show they're opening in Chicago down by the lake. It's supposed to be the biggest event in railroad history and I want to go." Kimball said, "Wow, I want to see that." As a result of the trip, Walt and Kimball would forge a lasting friendship that went beyond the work at the studio.

The two men traveled cross-country to this massive event. The Chicago Railroad Fair was set up on the lakefront site of the 1933 Chicago Century of Progress World's Fair. More than one hundred thousand railfans were in attendance. The fairgrounds were divided up into themed "villages" representing different tourist destinations and hosted by different rail lines. The different venues included a replica of the French Quarter in New Orleans, a dude ranch, a slice of a national park, and Indian pueblos. Costumed attendants and appropriate food added to the illusion.

When Walt and Kimball arrived at the Chicago fair, they were treated like royalty. They were introduced to railroad executives and rode on vintage and modern locomotives. The men rode in the cab of Chicago's first locomotive, Pioneer, and they helped the crew fire-up the Baltimore & Ohio's replica of the *Tom Thumb*, America's first steam locomotive. When the men helped run the historic *DeWitt Clinton*, the first steam locomotive to operate in the State of New York, Kimball said it was "one of the greatest thrills of my life. It was like shaking hands with George Washington."

The trip continued after Walt and Kimball left Chicago and traveled to the Henry Ford Museum and Greenfield Village near Dearborn, Michigan. It seemed as if Henry Ford collected one of everything. On display were kitchen appliances, furniture, knives, and guns. It is likely that Walt and Kimball were especially intrigued by the museum's exhibit depicting the history of transportation with bicycles, tractors, planes, trains, and automobiles.

Greenfield Village is a park adjacent to the Ford museum featuring historic buildings that have been moved to this location, restored, and put on display, including Orville and Wilbur Wright's bicycle shop, the original Ford assembly shop, a 1913 Dentzel merry-go-round, and a sternwheeler riverboat. There is an operating steam train that ferries guests around the property. One of the highlights for Walt during his visit was Thomas Edison's Menlo Park Laboratory. As we shall see in due course, this trip would be a critical component to the development of Disneyland.

After spending so much time with Walt on the trip, Ward said, "Walt Disney was just a down-to-earth farmer's boy who happened to be a genius." Walt would discount this description. He said his success "was built by hard work and enthusiasm, integrity of purpose, a devotion to our medium, confidence in its future, and, above all, by steady day-by-day growth in which we all simply studied our trade and learned".

This was only the beginning; over time their mutual interest in trains deepened even further. In 1948, after Walt took another ride on Kimball's Grizzly Flats railroad, he noticed that there was no train depot. Walt offered Kimball a deal to dismantle the train station featured in the 1948 film *So Dear to My Heart* and rebuild it in his backyard. Kimball thought this was a good idea since he was the one who did the research for the art director of the film; a rare book in his collection called *Buildings and Structures of American Railroads* documented pictures of a Victorian "gingerbread" depot on the Pottsville branch of the Lehigh Valley railroad in eastern Pennsylvania that became the model for the 1948 film set. The men agreed to the deal, and Kimball dismantled the three-sided set piece and spent a lot of money making the temporary structure into a functioning building. Later on, after construction for Disneyland had begun, Walt asked Roger Broggie, the head of Disney's Machine Shop, to see if he could get the depot back from Kimball. Kimball said, "Hell no, that's not fair." So Walt used Kimball's blueprints to build a copy, which he installed in Frontierland.[6]

Walt's immersion into the hobby of model railroading was a real boost to his creative juices. After riding in the cab of Kimball's narrow-gauge train, taking the Chicago trip, and forming stronger bonds with the artists who shared this passion, Walt could not get enough of trains. Trains would become the catalyst that would propel him toward new ideas beyond making movies, such as transportation systems and the built environment, and the best way to integrate them. By the time Walt returned from Chicago, he knew he needed to take this reenergized interest in trains and do something with it. He would begin with his home.

---

6 When the New Orleans Square station platform in Disneyland was built in 1962, the original Frontierland depot was moved across the tracks and became the inspiration for the Toontown depot that was added in 1993. This time the Imagineers copied the design but added a cartoon twist called "Squash and Stretch". the effect that keeps the volume of an object constant while it is expanded and contracted in seemingly unnatural ways. Or as former Disney animator Preston Blair explained, "When a sandbag moves through the air, it will 'stretch' in the direction of the movement. Then, when its progress is arrested, it will 'squash' out." Blair added, "If it were alive (anything can happen in a cartoon!), it would also squash from anticipating the action in which it stretches. The proper use of Squash and Stretch will strengthen an action. It is essential in creating a feeling of weight in characters." Toontown depot was the first time someone at Disney designed a building that looked fat and inflated with air with no right angles.

Holmby Hills

Walt may have started out with an electric scale model train in his office suite, but now he wanted something more, something a bit larger. He wanted something with a boiler. He was learning about live steam scale locomotives and decided that he needed a proper layout in the backyard of his home. All he needed was property big enough to accomplish this goal. Lillian agreed that buying a new home was a good idea, although her reasons were quite different. Letting her husband set up a train layout would give him another reason to stay home more often, with fewer trips to the studio.

Walt and Lillian found the perfect location: a five-acre property at 355 Carolwood Drive in the Holmby Hills section of Los Angeles, not far from the studio. They purchased the property on June 1, 1949, and the family moved into the custom-built house in 1950. Walt was so excited that he wrote his younger sister, Ruth, "I am going to take time out to play with my train." Lillian's plan seemed to be working. What Walt would create at his new home was a very personal, carefully designed, intimate experience that reflected his interests and a place he could share with his friends and family.

Much of the train was laid out in a space Walt called "Yensid Valley". Yensid—Disney spelled backwards—is also the name given to the wizard in the "Sorcerer's Apprentice" sequence in *Fantasia*. Just like Walt, the wizard would raise one eyebrow to Mickey Mouse to show his displeasure. Walt decided to name the locomotive the *Lilly Belle*, in honor of his wife, and to call the system the Carolwood Pacific Railroad Company after the street where they lived. The train traveled the "Fair Weather Route"; other physical highlights along the track included the "Janss Pass" and the "Canyon Vista".

The prototype locomotive for the *Lilly Belle* was a Central Pacific American 4-4-0. Walt's train was built at one-eighth scale with a 7-inch track gauge. The layout consisted of 2,615 feet of track, with enough switching options so that he could travel almost a full mile without running on the same track in the same direction. At one point, the train crossed over a 46-foot-long wooden trestle bridge over a valley while another part of the track passed under the bridge.

Eleven switches controlled the network of tracks, and all of them could be operated electronically from a control board located in Walt's 834-square foot barn, which was also used to store his train. The barn is a scale model of one used in the film *So Dear to My Heart* and reminiscent of the barn from Walt's early days located on the Crane Farm, the 48-acre Disney property in Linn County near Marceline, Missouri. Walt hand-built most of the barn's workbenches.

According to Roger Broggie, the man who ran the Disney Studio Machine Shop, "The first time the locomotive ran was on December 24, 1950." They pulled the train out of the Machine Shop, laid down some track, and gave people rides around the soundstages. The first time the train would make the circuit around the Carolwood property was on May 7, 1951.

Lillian loved flowers and wanted her personality, as well as Walt's, to become part of the house. She worked with landscape designers Jack and Morgan "Bill" Evans to build a garden on the north side of the house. When Walt rolled out his plans for the track layout, Lillian immediately noticed how the train was due to run right through her new garden. Walt needed a way to get the track all the way around the house, so he figured out a compromise. He would just dig a tunnel and go underneath the flowerbed.

Walt called on Spencer Olin, one of the studio's attorneys, to draft an agreement between Walt, representing the Carolwood Pacific Railroad, and the rest of the family for the rights to tunnel beneath the flowerbeds. The attorney suggested that Walt did not need to do this since he already owned the property, but Walt said, "Lilly has made up her mind that I shouldn't run right through the middle of her garden. She wanted to have a large window put in so her friends can look out at her flowers while they're playing Canasta." He added, "I just want the right to run my railroad."

This would be no ordinary tunnel. Walt wanted to create a bit of drama. He proposed that the 90-foot tunnel be designed with a slight S-curve in the middle, such that a rider would not be able to see the exit when the train first enters the tunnel. For a brief moment, passengers were completely in the dark. In *Inside the Dream*, artist Herb Ryman recalls the foreman on the job suggested it was cheaper to build it straight. Walt's angry retort was, "It's cheaper not to do it at all." As you would expect, Walt got his tunnel the way that he wanted it. He named it the "Rorex Tunnel" after Jack Rorex, the construction supervisor who gave him the idea of the S-curve.

A Bigger Train

Walt's backyard miniature railroad provided him many hours of enjoyment. Walt enjoyed the physical work of building the rolling stock—the vehicles for his railway. He was especially proud of the yellow caboose, with its miniature pot-bellied stove. It took Walt almost one year to hand-build that one piece of rolling stock. The details are so precise that it contains a miniature calendar dedicated to Ward Kimball's Grizzly Flats Railroad.

The Carolwood Pacific became a way for Walt to relax and enjoy time with his friends and family. Frequently, people would be invited to the house and take a ride. However, the good times would not last forever;

an unfortunate accident put an end to the Carolwood Pacific and set in motion the need for Walt to find another place to play with his train. One Sunday, a guest engineer was running the *Lilly Belle* and went too fast around a curve. The *Lilly Belle* turned over on its side. The whistle broke off of the locomotive and a jet of high-pressure steam escaped. A five-year old girl was attracted to the mayhem and accidentally stepped into the jet's invisible steam. Although the resulting burns were minor, that was enough for Walt. Walt always said of his backyard railroad, "If it isn't fun, let's don't do it." He called Roger Broggie and told him to take the train back to the Machine Shop. Walt would have to play with his trains somewhere else.

According to Kimball, "The Carolwood Pacific Railroad project introduced Walt to the notion of outdoor entertainment. Disneyland made it possible for Walt to have a larger train than the miniature that ran at his estate." Kimball knew what Walt was thinking. He knew that Walt was going to build a park so that he could "have a full-size steam train...that he could have fun operating himself on the days when the park was closed". That somewhere else would become Disneyland.

From Yensid Valley to Disneyland

Walt had seen how well the berm worked at the Burbank studio, so he had Bill Evans build an earthen berm around the Carolwood property to shield the backyard from the neighbors. As Walt told his daughter Diane, "I built that bank up on the canyon so when I was down there playing with my trains, my neighbors wouldn't be annoyed." Walt was so pleased with the work of the Evans brothers that he asked them, "How about you fellows landscape Disneyland for me?" Although Jack passed on the offer, Bill accepted and became the landscape architect for both Disneyland and Walt Disney World. According to Imagineer and author Jeff Kurtti, "[Bill Evans'] forthright approach and innate understanding of how landscaping fit into the art of place-making was a talent that must have not only pleased Walt aesthetically, but was a godsend to his evolving design and construction of Disneyland."

Imagineer and Disney Legend Marty Sklar said, "Bill Evans defined Disney theme park landscaping, and trained just about everyone who has created theme park stories in living environments." In *The Making of Disney's Animal Kingdom Theme Park*, Melody Malmberg explains Evans' approach: "The first consideration was guest comfort—shade and shelter. The second was screening visual intrusions—creating a berm, a ring of earth and vegetation surrounding the park to hide the real world; or using strategic planting that camouflaged a building or electronics or lighting.

The third principle was telling a story through landscaping—creating the right look for the setting, from the mixed broadleaf forest of Tom Sawyer's Mississippi River banks to the serene gardens of Japan."

Imagineers Number One and Two

Walt's passion for trains led him toward a creative relationship with two giant talents that would have a profound effect of many of the things that were to come: Roger Broggie and Harper Goff. Broggie was the mechanical genius that took Walt under his wing and encouraged him to build things with his own hands. Goff was an intuitive designer and an artist with impeccable taste. Broggie became a critical player in the development of Disneyland and Disney World and is considered by many Disney historians as the original Imagineer. As Roy E. Disney said, "Any mechanical things you had to do, what you said was, 'Call Roger, he'll know how to fix it.' Without him, Disneyland would never have happened."

Broggie started at the studio in 1939. He helped devise the multiplane camera, which added depth and movement through space to animation. Broggie would rise to the position of vice-president and general manager of MAPO, Inc., the manufacturing and research arm of WED Enterprises. By the time he retired in 1973, he was vice president of research and development for WED Enterprises.

When Walt decided to start his backyard railroad and build a live steam locomotive, he turned to Broggie for help. Broggie taught Walt how to use the various shop tools. Walt took great pride in all of the miniatures that he had built. Imagine those conversations.

Another important figure in the development of Disneyland and other Disney theme parks was Harper Goff. His influence on the design of the theme parks cannot be overstated. Goff was born in Fort Collins, Colorado, in 1911 and moved to Santa Ana, California, with his family in 1920. He began taking classes at the Chouinard Art Institute, which later become part of CalArts, the art school founded by Walt. He went on to work at Warner Brothers as a set designer with credits ranging from *Casablanca* and *Sergeant York* to *The Adventures of Don Juan*.

It was only by chance that Goff came to work for Walt. Goff absolutely loved model steam trains and was part of a growing brotherhood that worshiped this hobby. In 1951, Goff was shopping at Basset-Lowke in London—the place to go if you wanted to buy a new scale-model live steam locomotive. He spotted a new engine that he really wanted, only to be told that it was on hold for another gentleman. The shopkeeper suggested that Goff return another day; if the other buyer did not want it, Goff could buy it. To Goff's surprise, the gentleman in question was Walt Disney, and a partnership was born. Walt got the locomotive, but Goff got a new job.[7]

Walt asked Goff to sketch out a *True-Life Adventure* short called *20,000 Leagues Under the Sea*. Goff had other ideas. He was a huge Jules Verne fan and ignored Walt's direction. He drafted sketches for a live-action film based on Verne's book. Instead of being mad at Goff, Walt was impressed with what he saw, changed direction, and produced the classic film we enjoy today. Not only did Goff sketch out the film and convince Walt to produce it, he also designed the film's signature *Nautilus* submarine.

Walt's next challenge for Goff was a project he was calling "Disneylandia", or "Walt Disney's America". This is the project that would ultimately evolve into Disneyland. Goff used his hometown of Fort Collins as the model for Disneyland's City Hall, and he was the principal designer for Adventureland. He used his experience as the art director for the movie *African Queen* to create the Jungle Cruise. When Walt decided he wanted the Golden Horseshoe Saloon in Frontierland to look like the one in *Calamity Jane*, he asked Goff to work on the project. What Walt did not know at the time was that Goff was the art director for *Calamity Jane*. Goff simply pulled out his blueprints of the movie set. Watch the film today, and the resemblance is clear.

Goff continued to work on films for other studios; his credits include *Willy Wonka and the Chocolate Factory* (1966) and *Fantastic Voyage* (1971). He later returned to Disney and was the person responsible for the basic design concept for the World Showcase at Epcot Center. It was Goff who first suggested that the pavilions be given equal space along the waterfront and be made up of scale models of iconic, historic structures. He also worked on the Japan, Germany, and United Kingdom Pavilions.

In addition to his visual talents, Goff played the banjo in Firehouse Five plus Two with fellow railroad fanatic Ward Kimball. He was working on Tokyo Disneyland when he passed away in 1993. As a result of Goff's involvement in designing Disneyland, author and Disney history expert Jeff Kurtti dubbed Goff the "Second Imagineer".

---

7   Today, that locomotive is on display at the Walt Disney barn in Griffith Park, Los Angeles.

Chapter Six

The Anaheim Project

Walt Disney seemed to be the embodiment of the old adage that if you follow your bliss, you will find the greatest happiness. When he became passionate about something, Walt would devote a great deal of attention and time to focus on that subject.

The stress of running the animation studio was taking its toll on Walt's health. His doctors advised him to find some hobbies that might distract him, and he ran with that advice to explore his fascination with railroading and what would be another prophetic hobby, that of collecting and building miniatures.

Who would have guessed that this love of miniatures and trains would lead to a utopian world that was shielded from the surrounding urban sprawl, where everything functioned as planned, everything was spotless, and people immediately felt at home? Walt's hobbies would translate into some of the most creative ideas of his long career.

First it was the miniatures. Walt's obsession with miniatures may have started after he visited the Thorne Collection at the 1939 San Francisco Golden Gate International Exposition. Mrs. James Ward Thorne had commissioned and put on display thirty-two elaborately detailed scale-model interiors that represented various architectural styles and time periods. Each model was done at a scale of one inch to one foot, with an average size of three feet wide, eighteen inches deep, and two feet high. The models combined painstakingly accurate details, materials, and theatrical lighting. The result seemed like a little movie set; the viewer fully expected somebody to walk into the room at any moment. Day-to-day objects were left about, books were open, and cabinets stood with the doors slightly ajar as if someone had just removed something. Each model contained all the signs of daily living.[8]

Walt started to amass what eventually became a huge collection of miniatures. Everywhere he traveled, he picked up more pieces for his collection. Then he took matters into his own hands, literally: he started to build his own miniatures.

8　The Thorne Collection now resides in a downstairs gallery of the Art Institute of Chicago.

He started to work with master model builder Ken Anderson to learn the craft. Starting at the Disney Studio in 1934, Anderson is considered to be one of the very first Imagineers. He went on to become an art director, color stylist, and layout artist. In 1951, Walt pulled Anderson out from the Animation Department because of his background in architecture. He was put on Walt's personal payroll and was given the assignment to develop a series of dimensional dioramas similar to the Thorne Collection. The two men worked together and hand-built many of the scenes; Walt's interest in miniatures grew stronger.

In *Designing Disney's Theme Parks*, Karal Ann Marling describes when *The New York Times* critic Bosley Crowther came to the Disney Studio to visit with Walt. Crowther noted that Walt was "almost weirdly concerned with the building of a miniature railroad engine and a string of cars". Marling said it was "Walt's growing determination to build something tangible and true, something perfect, a place where nothing could ever go wrong". She added, "Children love dollhouses and toy train sets because they give little fingers mastery over the dangerous, forbidden, frustrating world of grown-up things." While on a trip to Holland, Walt took his family to Madurodam, a new park featuring miniature replicas of famous European architectural landmarks. This trip further fueled Walt's interest in miniatures.

Disneylandia

Walt had figured out a way that he could combine his passion for railroads with his hobby building miniatures. The result would be a new form of entertainment: miniature dioramas with animated elements that represented different periods of American history would be installed in a train, and the exhibit would travel around the country. Walt would make money by charging admission to what he would call "Disneylandia".

Walt purchased three old rail cars with the intention of installing twenty-four displays. Each display would focus on a different theme from American history and culture. Harper Goff explained, "This traveling show would come to everyone's hometown. Walt's train would be there on the railroad tracks, and it would be a special event in Chicago or St. Louis or wherever."

Already thinking about the best guest experience, Walt proposed that people would enter from the rear, pop coins into the machine, a curtain would rise, the display would come alive, and guests would then walk to the next display and do the same thing all over again. Walter Knott, who had created Knott's Berry Farm in Orange County, California, had some old coin-operated machines that did something very similar, but without the Disney detail and storytelling.

The prototype for the displays was Walt's fully realized model of Granny Kincaid's cabin from the Disney film *So Dear to My Heart*. Walt hand-built a model of the film's cabin set. He rigged the display with a light that would turn on when a guest stood in front while a recording by actress Beulah Bondi, as Granny, would tell her story. He displayed the cabin at the 1952 Festival of California Living held at the Pan-Pacific Auditorium in Los Angeles. Walt used the opportunity to test the audience's reaction to the model. He told the press that it was a sample of Disneyland—A Miniature Historic America.

What Walt learned from his visitors was that the model as built was rather dull. To enhance the exhibit, he proposed having a miniature Granny sitting in the cabin and rocking by the fireplace. He called Roger Broggie and assigned him the task of figuring out how to make the miniature Granny rock in her chair.[9]

Because of this experience, Walt felt that static dioramas, like the Thorne Collection, would only attract modest interest. In his search to always find a way to do things better, he decided that each model should be inhabited by small animated people. This would be really something special, and he figured people would flock to the train station to see a show like that.

On a trip to New Orleans during the mid 1940s, Walt and Lillian had discovered a small clockwork bird in a gilded cage. It was a French antique around 100 years old. The Disneys loved the little mechanical bird and brought it home. The lifelike movements and the variety of actions the little figure would exhibit intrigued Walt.

When the time came to begin planning for the traveling dioramas, he showed the bird to his Imagineers and asked them to figure out how it worked. To his way of thinking, if artisans could build something like this one hundred years ago, his guys could use modern technology and do it one better.

This exercise in reverse engineering was the birth of Project Little Man. Walt wanted to create a miniature figure of a man dancing on a stage. He had actor Buddy Ebsen tap dance while being filmed against a wall marked with a grid. A 9-inch mechanical man was built and was animated to follow Ebsen's movements. The figure moved through the use of cams and cables. This device was manufactured and tested.

---

9 Today, the model is on display at the One Man's Dream exhibit at Disney's Hollywood Studios at Walt Disney World, and the furniture is on display at the Walt Disney Family Museum in San Francisco.

The next step in mechanical figures was even more ambitious. This time Walt wanted a miniature three-dimensional animation of a barbershop quartet singing "Down by the Old Mill Stream". Think of a mechanical version of the Dapper Dans who perform at Disneyland and the Magic Kingdom. However, the engineering team discovered that working at such a small scale made the project too difficult; the technology was just not there to do the job as Walt had envisioned it. Roger Broggie said, "We got as far as building the guy in the chair and the barber behind him. Then the whole job was stopped and they said, 'We're going to do this thing for real!'"

The next project featured a much larger figure. Walt wanted to build a Chinese restaurant at Disneyland. He told his Imagineers, "Out in the lobby will be an old Chinese fellow like Confucius—not an actor, but a figure made out of plastic. Now the customers will ask him questions, and he'll reply with words of wisdom." The trick would be "an operator in the back of the figure answering questions and making the lips move". The figure made it into production, but was never seen by the public. Once again, Walt's ambitions and vision were well ahead of the available technology.

By 1952, Walt was seriously looking into the feasibility of the traveling road show and authorized a study to be done. The study revealed that the project would never make money. Issues cited in the report included changes to the American railroad industry, with its lack of direct routes, and the high cost to maintain the highly fragile mechanical shows. Walt decided to change direction. Instead of a traveling train show, Walt drafted a plan to use the same type of animated dioramas and tour department stores. The department store idea was rooted in a prior success. In 1935, Macy's of New York had featured a display built by movie actress Colleen Moore of a miniature castle with tiny portraits of Mickey and Minnie over the fireplace. The display had been a hit, causing sidewalk traffic to back up. What Walt proposed was to build up to twenty displays that would come to life when guests deposited coins into the slot. This plan also had problems and it, too, was shelved. Jeff Kurtti said, "Plainly, the idea had simply outgrown its logistic constraints and its ability to pay for itself, let alone turn a profit." Walt pushed aside the traveling Disneylandia project, but in its stead, the place-based Disneyland was born.

The Origins of Disneyland

The story of Disneyland's origins has been told many times before in every way imaginable. The official line came from Walt himself in a 1963 interview when he recalled, "It came about when my daughters were very young and Saturday was always Daddy's day with the two daughters. So we'd start out and try to go someplace, you know, different things." Walt continued, "I'd take them to the merry-go-round. Sit on a bench, you know, eating peanuts. I felt there should be something built where the parents and the children could have fun together. So that's how Disneyland started." In another interview, he added, "While they were on the merry-go-round riding around 40 times or something, I'd be sitting there trying to figure out what you could do."

To honor those moments, Disneyland has a park bench and a horse from the Griffith Park merry-go-round on exhibit inside the Opera House on Disneyland's Main Street, U.S.A. Both items came from Imagineer Tony Baxter's collection.

It has been said that Walt may have been dreaming of owning an amusement park as far back as 1911, when nine-year-old Walt and his younger sister, Ruth, were regular visitors to Electric Park in Kansas City, fifteen blocks from their home. What they saw was a magical place where a train ran around the perimeter and landscaping was carefully designed. The park rides were integrated into the landscape and the grounds were well maintained. Every evening, there was a fireworks show at closing time.

The first time Walt seriously considered the idea of an amusement park to fulfill a real need came during the Hyperion studio days. He was inundated with requests from fans to meet Mickey and Minnie. People wanted to tour the animation studio. Guests touring movie studios was not a new concept. At Universal Studio just down the road, Carl Laemmle had been selling tours to his studio since 1915. People paid twenty-five cents for admission, which included a box lunch and a chance to climb up into grandstands and watch silent pictures being made.[10]

Walt was not so sure that tours at his studio would work. As a showman, he felt that watching the animation process was not all that exciting. However, if he could enhance the tour experience with, say, a park, maybe it could work. To make the idea even more appealing, Walt had surplus land by the time he moved to Burbank.

Mickey Mouse Park

By 1947, the talk of a place called Mickey Mouse Park was accelerating. In Burbank, Walt owned sixteen acres adjacent to the studio. The land was south of the main facilities between Riverside Drive and the Los Angeles

---

10 The practice stopped when talking pictures were introduced. Universal Studio resumed giving tours in 1964 with the famous Harper Goff–designed Glamor-Trams and a more highly programmed guest experience.

River. Walt said, "When I built the studio over there I thought, well gee, we ought to have really a three-dimensional thing that people could actually come and visit."

Walt was thinking of all kinds of ideas. In one very early concept, he had guests boarding a scale-model live steam train and touring the sound-stages. On August 31, 1948, Walt sent a memo to one of his production designers, Dick Kelsey, that outlined his early ideas for Mickey Mouse Park. The memo was sent days after Walt and Ward Kimball had returned from the trip to Chicago Railroad Fair and Henry Ford's Greenfield Village. Walt was motivated.

In the memo, Walt suggested that guests would enter a Main Village featuring an old-fashioned town square, a railroad station, a town hall, a fire station, a drug store, and other shops. The village also would have an opera house and a movie theater. The primary function for this space was to give guests an opportunity to meet some of the characters. Within the village, people could take rides on historic vehicles like a horse trolley and horse-drawn buckboards. Other areas would include a Western village and a carnival section.

Walt recruited a small group of artists from his animation studio and other movie studios, primarily Twentieth-Century Fox, to help him with this project.[11] The first announcement for a place called Disneyland was published in the *Burbank Daily Review* in 1952. The park was going to be located at the corner of Riverside Drive and Buena Vista Road.

When Walt applied for the necessary permits, the Burbank City Council turned him down. They did not want a permanent carnival in their city. One lawmaker proclaimed, "We don't want the carny atmosphere in Burbank! We don't want people falling in the river, or merry-go-rounds squawking all day long." Walt knew better. He assured them, "A word may be said in regard to the concept and conduct of Disneyland's operational tone. Although various sections will have the fun and flavor of carnival or amusement park, there will be none of the 'pitches', games, wheels, sharp practices, and devices designed to milk the visitor's pocketbook."

Still, he was unable to secure the permits and was forced to look else-where. As it turned out, there were other reasons that made the Burbank

---

11 Why so many people from Twentieth-Century Fox? According to artist Herb Ryman biographer John Stanley Donaldson, the studio had a backlot that was "five times the size of Disneyland. Having everything—from temple to tenement. A period riverfront had been constructed to thirty acres, replete with streets, buildings, and piers; a replica steamboat, the *Clermont*, side-paddled to a three-acre basin, excavated to depth of seven feet—filled with five million gallons of water." He added, "The place just needed a turnstile."

site unworkable. Two large infrastructure projects were being proposed adjacent to the site: the Los Angeles River flood control project proposed by the Army Corps of Engineers and the Ventura freeway expansion. More importantly, as Walt kept working on the problem, he realized that his dreams for his park were getting bigger and the property adjacent to the studio was just not going to be enough land.

A Graduate Course

Once Walt became focused on building an amusement park, he began to study everything he could about the subject. He visited dozens of parks to see what worked and what did not. On one trip with Art Linkletter, they visited Tivoli Gardens, built in 1843 in Copenhagen, Denmark. Linkletter said, "As we walked through it, I had my first experience of Walt Disney's childlike delight in the enjoyment of seeing families and in the cleanliness and the orderliness of everything. He was making notes all the time about the lights, the chairs, the seats, and the food." Linkletter asked Walt what he was doing and Walt replied, "I'm just making notes about something that I've always dreamed of, a great, great playground for the children and the families of America." Walt liked how Tivoli Gardens was kept clean, was decoratively lit with popcorn lights outlining the buildings, and had outdoor entertainment. It was a park for both adults and children.

In doing his research, Walt often visited the Bradley and Kay amusement center at La Cienega and Beverly Boulevards in Los Angeles. He observed how the children used the facility. He knew the owners, Dave and Bernice Bradley, and was constantly quizzing them about their operations. He wanted to know how the rides worked, what people ate, and how people lined up in the queues. Bernice Bradley remembers, "Our park was very tiny. There was a carousel, a little train ride, and another little boat ride for children...Walt was out there almost every day, sitting on the end of the bench, watching how children enjoyed the rides." She added, "He also talked to a lot of the children, which is what he enjoyed the most. He challenged them. 'How was that horse you were riding? What color was it painted? Did you like it?'" Another nearby park where he could often be found was Beverly Park in Beverly Hills, also owned by the Bradleys. Walt also visited Coney Island, Knott's Berry Farm, Travel Town in Griffith Park, the Los Angeles County Fair, and Oakland's Fairyland. His team studied fairs, zoos, and even Forest Lawn Memorial Park cemetery in Glendale—at the time the most popular tourist attraction in the Los Angeles region before Disneyland was opened.

Admiral Joseph Fowler, Disney's head of construction, said, "Every summer Walt would send me to Europe for ideas. Often he would come

along. We'd go to World's Fairs, Oktoberfests, gardens, amusement parks—
you name it. He wanted to learn about operations, attractions...well, about
everything! He would just soak it all in. It was typical of Walt Disney."

Birth of the Imagineers

As the Disneyland project started to gain traction, Walt realized that he
would need to step away from the studio grind, get a fresh start, and train
his own team—artists known as Imagineers.

When Walt decided to build Disneyland, he knew he would need professionals to carry out his project. He first went to see architects William
Pereira and Charles Luckman. Pereira is now best known for designing CBS
Television City (1952–1953) in Hollywood and Marineland of the Pacific
(1954–1955) on the Rancho Palos Verdes peninsula. Luckman had operated Lever Brothers and partnered with Pereira to remodel the Flamingo
Hotel in Las Vegas in 1953. Their preliminary study for Disneyland did
not capture what Walt had in mind.

Next, Walt went to his friend and neighbor, architect Welton Becket.
Becket lived across the street from Art Linkletter's family, and at the time
was best known for his design of the Bullock's department store (1947)
in Pasadena. He later designed the Capitol Records Building (1954–1955)
in Hollywood. His imprint is felt throughout the Los Angeles region. After
Walt tried to describe his concept, he asked Becket if he could help. Becket
told Walt, "Walt, no one can design Disneyland for you. You've got to use
your own people. We can't help you. We don't have that kind of a background for this." His advice was, "Just use your own guys." Becket knew
that there was no architect in the world who could do what Walt demanded.

Roy Disney was not at all thrilled with the idea of Walt's park at first.
Walt said, "I couldn't get anybody to go with me because we were going
through this financial depression, and whenever I'd talk to my brother
about it, why he always started to get busy with some figures, so I mean,
I couldn't...I didn't dare bring it up." It was Roy who suggested that Walt
start a separate design company apart from the studio to help with the
Disneyland project. To fund this new adventure, Walt said, "I spent over
$100,000 that I borrowed on the insurance that I'd been paying on for 30
years. Even had to sell my home in Palm Springs to use that money to get
this thing to a point where I could show people what it would be."

Walt decided to name his new firm The Walt Disney Company. However,
that was quickly scuttled because it was too similar to the name of the
studio. So the design company became WED Enterprises. "WED" stands
for Walter Elias Disney. The company was incorporated on December 16,

1952. In 1965, Walt Disney Productions acquired WED for $3 million. WED Enterprises was the architectural, engineering, and research and development arm of the company.

People who worked at WED Enterprises were called Imagineers, a term that is generally credited to Welton Becket. In Harrison "Buzz" Price's book, *Walt's Revolution by the Numbers*, he talks about receiving a letter from Walt crediting him with the name. However, Price does not recall doing such a thing. He was grateful for the letter and guessed it may have happened while dining with Walt at the Corral Room, the executive dining room at the Disney Studio. Walt said, "We're always exploring and experimenting...we call it Imagineering—the blending of creative imagination and technical know-how."

WED Enterprises became a hand-picked crew who worked directly for Walt, not the studio. In *Inside the Dream*, Imagineer Rolly Crump remembers the company being called "Cannibal Island" because it "was gobbling up all the people that were in animation". Walt created an environment where work and learning would be fused together to support their taking calculated risks. Over time, a social organization of masters and apprentices took shape, and that strengthened the organization.

WED Enterprises was financed by a license agreement with Walt Disney Productions in which the design firm received royalties from the use and sale of the Disney characters. The studio also got the rights to use the name Walt Disney. WED Enterprises was not run for profit, but needed funds to cover the expenses of inventing things for the theme park and other projects. Walt called the design firm his "sandbox". Walt instructed his Imagineers, "All I want you to think about is that when people walk through...anything that you design, I want them, when they leave, to have smiles on their faces."

Location, Location, Location

In the world of real estate, they say that location is everything. The time had come to build Disneyland, and Walt needed to figure out the perfect location. Like most movie moguls, Walt had a great deal of faith in market research and test screenings. He would always insist that the final product reflect his standards, but that a little feedback from the audience was always welcome. With this in mind, he decided to go shopping for someone who could find the best location for his park. In July 1953, Walt hosted a party at his home and discussed the Disneyland project with architects Charles Luckman, Welton Becket, and William Pereira. Luckman introduced Walt to Harrison "Buzz" Price, who worked for the Stanford Research

Institute (SRI) and had recently finished two site-suitability studies for major corporations. This was the type of expertise that Walt needed; the next morning, Walt had WED employee Nate Winecoff call Price and put SRI under contract.[12]

In order for Price to get an accurate read on the viability of the Disneyland project, Walt had to clearly describe his vision for the park. Price needed to understand how this project would be different and better than other amusement parks. As Price recounts in *Walt's Revolution! By the Numbers*, the project description would enable him to identify analogs that would allow him to develop more accurate data for his feasibility analysis.

Walt and Price started with a discussion of the circulation plan. Before Disneyland, most amusement parks were planned with pathways based on a grid. There were usually four entrances or more connected to parking lots that surrounded the facility. Disneyland would only have one entrance. As Walt described it, the entrance at Disneyland would lead guests through a corridor that would be a stylized, turn-of-the-century main street. At the end of the corridor would be a circular plaza. From the circular plaza, pathways would lead to four different thematic areas. To move about the park, the guest always had to return to the circular plaza.

Generally, amusement park operators wanted all the street visibility they could get. Walt wanted to hide his park from the outside world. To create that barrier, he wanted to build a landscaped berm as he had done at the Burbank studio backlot and at his Holmby Hills home. All of the rides would be customized; there would be none of the typical thrill rides such as a roller coaster. Walt wanted to place an old-fashioned steam train around the perimeter; this would replace the train that he had given up at home.

Walt wanted his park to be in southern California, and he thought

---

12   Over his long career, Buzz Price worked on an estimated 3,000 economic feasibility studies, most of which were in the leisure-recreation-attraction field, including more than 150 projects for Walt and Roy Disney. It was Walt who suggested Price change the name of his firm to Economic Research Associates (ERA). Price ran ERA until 1969, when he sold the firm. After the sale, Price continued to work for a diverse clientele. He was one of the few non-Disney employees to be honored as a Disney Legend in 2003. He was hand-picked by Walt to be the director and chairman of the board for CalArts. Not only did he work for Walt and Roy Disney, he also worked on projects for Universal Studios, Knott's Berry Farm, Sea World, and Six Flags, as well as studies for museums, zoos, educational institutions, and international clients, including eight World's Fairs. Price's influence on the theme park business was so profound that he became the first recipient of the Lifetime Achievement Award from the Themed Entertainment Association. After Price's death in 2010, the honor was renamed The Buzz Price Award.

he would need about a quarter section, which is 160 acres. This amount of land was much larger than the area available to him adjacent to the Burbank studio. Also, he wanted to open the park in two years. Walt told Price, "It will be a place for California to be home, to bring its guests, to demonstrate its faith in the future."

The Feasibility Study

Having described his vision, Walt contracted with Price to produce a feasibility study for the Disneyland project. The study started in April 1953 and was conducted in two phases: the first phase was a ten-week study to determine the park's location; the second phase was a four-month analysis of the amusement park business. Price's firm was paid $25,000 to conduct the study.

Price knew that many of his clients already have at least partial answers to their own questions. He asked Walt, "Do you have any bias, any opinion, on where it should go in southern California? The study you are talking about is big." He reminded Walt, "The greater Los Angeles five-county area [Los Angeles, Orange, San Bernardino, Riverside, and Ventura] is at least 4,000 square miles. The eight-county area is even larger." Walt said firmly, "No, you tell me where it should go." Price suggested, "You own the Golden Oak Ranch out in Saugus, is that a consideration?" Walt replied again, "No, you tell me where it should go." Walt wanted to give Price as much flexibility as he could to find the perfect location.

As Price described the process, "The source of my opinions would be determined by a long and thorough study of the census data...some 40 or 50 major census tracts. That would give us direction for what would be the best choice." This analysis was all done without the use of computers. Every tally was done by hand on spreadsheets in a notebook. Thousands of calculations were made. Everything was mapped on plastic overlays.

SRI studied a broad set of variables, including the differences in temperature and wind velocity, fog patterns, the shift in population growth, the timing of freeway construction, taxes, and building code requirements. Price said, "We even did a job of tracking smog, because this was going to be an outdoor park and we didn't want to choke everybody."

Some sites were rejected early in the process. The team looked at Descanso Gardens in La Cañada as well as Chavez Ravine where Dodger Stadium would be built a few years later. As the search continued, SRI narrowed down the choices to an "amoeba" that was five miles on either side of the Santa Ana Freeway, which runs south from the Los Angeles County line to the city of Santa Ana. This brought the study area down to 150 square miles. Then the team continued to narrow down the choice even further to all of the available 160-acre sites that they could find.

SRI identified ten sites with four preferred and the others described as "almost sites". The SRI team recommended the Harbor Boulevard property in Anaheim as its first choice; Buena Park, where Knott's Berry Farm is located, came in second; Los Alamitos was the third choice; and the Willowick Country Club in Santa Ana was fourth.

In 2005, Price said, "We looked at locations in Los Angeles, near the beach. And the more I looked at it, I could see that the population of southern California was going south. We could see that with the new freeway, and the way construction and the people who would go to a theme park were headed, that this location, off the freeway in Anaheim, was the way to go."

Price said, "You always have an alternative ready because no one assumes you're going to have a clear slide into home plate." He added, "It wasn't a bad solution. It was a first-class property. The land was clearly available. We had a good relationship with the city manager of Anaheim. And, we could afford it–well, not me."

Price and his boss at the time, C.V. Wood,[13] presented the findings to Walt and Roy. Walt immediately selected the Harbor Boulevard site, but moved it down a quarter of a section to get farther away from the freeway. The site was 160-acres held by seventeen different property owners. Today, the Disneyland Resort has expanded and covers 510 acres, of which 461 are Disney-owned and 49 are under long-term lease.

"No one had ever heard of Anaheim, except on the *Jack Benny* program," said Price. "He had a skit where the announcer would say, 'Now leaving for Anaheim, Azusa, and Cucamonga.' But I showed it to Walt, and he took one look at the plan and asked me if I was sure. I said, 'Yes, without a doubt.'" According to Price, Orange County was preferable to the other areas in southern California because "[i]t was cooler in the summer and warmer in the winter, with predictable and fairly light rainfall". The deal was concluded in August 1953, and the property was purchased at approximately

---

13   C.V. Wood is one of the most mysterious characters in the creation of Disneyland. "C.V." stood for Cornelius Vanderbilt. Wood rarely appears in official histories of the park. He was appointed the construction manager for the Disneyland project and was a critical player in getting the park built; it would not have happened without him. Price described Wood as, "One of the strangest, damnedess [sic], boldest, smartest, most shameless and colorful characters ever to career through this business. He walked in the worn footpath of P.T. Barnum. He was the quickest numbers man I ever had for a client." Wood had a tendency to tell off-color jokes and Walt was not amused. Because Wood was good at getting the job done, Walt waited until Disneyland was done before firing him.

$4,500 per acre. It was all the Disney brothers could afford at that time. Price proudly boasts that "[t]oday [2005], the center of southern California's population is exactly four miles from Sleeping Beauty Castle".

Price was an ethical man and never took advantage of the insider knowledge that he gained while working for his clients. After he completed the location study for the Disney brothers, he identified one triangular property that was not part of the initial purchase program. He checked with Roy to see if it was something they wanted to buy and Roy declined. He told Price that it would be all right for him to purchase the property if he wanted to. The price was right, about $17,000. However, Roy's advice to Price was that it would be a bad investment. Roy felt that once the park opened, the property values around Disneyland would plummet. After all, Roy figured who in his right mind would want property next door to an amusement park? Buzz never bought the property.

On April 2, 1954, plans for the construction of Disneyland were announced. Anaheim seemed far out in the country at the time of Disneyland's construction. The Santa Ana Freeway had not yet reached Harbor Boulevard when construction started, and the freeway would not be completed until about three months after the park had opened. From Burbank, the drive would generally take at least two hours. Forty miles of the trip would be on surface streets weaving through construction zones along the old Anaheim-Telegraph Road. Even after the park had opened, nobody knew about the Harbor Boulevard exit and it was easy to miss the turnoff. The directional sign was only about 100 yards before the exit.

In *Inside the Dream*, Art Linkletter described his first trip to the Disneyland construction site: "We were driving through little villages I'd never heard of. We were driving through orange groves and dirt roads, when Walt finally announced that we had arrived at the site." Linkletter added, "I didn't tell him what I really thought—that he was out of his mind." However, due to Disneyland's success, Anaheim would end up becoming one of the fastest-growing cities in the United States by 1960.

Yes, If...

Buzz Price would be called upon frequently to weigh in on the viability of a Disney project, and he developed a research methodology that suited Walt and Roy's needs. The process that he used when working with Walt was a "Yes, if..." line of attack. Price said, "'Yes, if...' is the approach of a deal maker. It points to what needs to be done to make the possible plausible. 'No, because...' is the language of a deal killer. Creative people thrive on 'Yes, if.'" He added, "Walt liked this language."

Price refined this innovative research process by hosting more than 150 design workshops called "charrettes", French for "little carts". The workshop name was derived from the Ècole des Beaux Arts period, when students in Paris would bring their paintings to be judged by their masters in the carts; and in many cases, the artists would still be working on their wet canvases while on the move.

In modern usage, a charrette is a process whereby all those affecting and affected by the outcome of a project come together to collaborate on finding solutions. After extensive consideration and discussion, the group can begin to develop a consensus and establish clearly articulated performance goals that are specific, measurable, achievable, realistic, and timely. With these goals set, the project's success can be judged by the ability to meet or exceed the planning criteria. By using performance goals, it is easier to manage and comprehend a complex project. What may have appealed to Walt in this approach was the layer of storytelling applied to the technical process of spatial planning.

The Focus Group

In November 1953, Walt had Price conduct a charrette with four of the leading figures in the amusement park business. Price gathered William Schmitt, owner of Riverview Park in Chicago; Harry Batt of Pontchartrain Park in New Orleans; Ed Schott of Cincinnati's Coney Island; and George Whitney of Playland at the Beach in San Francisco. Price rented a hotel suite at the Sherman Hotel in Chicago during the annual amusement park industry convention and trade show. Representing Disney along with Price were Richard Irvine, president of WED Enterprises; Bill Cottreal, vice president of WED Enterprises; and Nate Winecoff. The men worked the "crowd" for over two hours in the old-fashioned way, as Price said, with "Chivas Regal and caviar", then a presentation. The Disney team used the famous Herb Ryman "lost weekend" conceptual drawing that Roy had used when he met with banks to fund the project. Price called this "a dog and pony show". After the presentation, he recalls that the "reaction was unanimous. It would not work." Price documented the group's reaction to the Disneyland proposal; he noted that they all agreed that all of the "proven moneymakers are conspicuously missing, no roller coasters, no Ferris wheel, no shoot-the-chute, no tunnel of love, no hot dog carts, no beer, and worst of all, no carnie games like the baseball throw".

Walt's proposal to build his own attractions was met with skepticism. The naysayers said, "Custom rides will never work. They will cost too much to buy and they will be constantly breaking down, resulting in reduced ride capacity and angry customers." They suggested, "Only stock off-the-shelf rides are cheap enough and reliable enough to do the job. And besides, the public doesn't know the difference or care." They also determined that there was not enough ride capacity to make a profit. After reviewing Marvin Davis' design for the park, they were even more skeptical. In their experience, the fatal flaw was the single entrance into the park. This would mean a bottleneck at the front gate, and that was unacceptable. They suggested the need for entrances all around the park next to parking lots and transit if Walt wanted to be successful.

"Most of Mr. Disney's proposed park produces no revenue but it will be expensive to build and maintain," said the focus group. "Things like the castle and pirate ship are cute but they aren't rides so there is no economic reason to build them. There is too much wasteful landscaping." They also found other examples of waste. Spaces like Town Square with its little park, City Hall, and a fire station were not designed to make any money. Those structures were a poor use of real estate and did not add to the bottom line. Even the Main Street vehicles like the horse trolley, fire truck, and omnibus would be money-losers because they also suffered from a capacity issue.

After reviewing other concept drawings, the men suggested that Walt's commitment to the little design details was just not warranted. They felt that "[p]eople will vandalize the ride vehicles and destroy the grounds no matter what you do, so you may as well go cheap". Even the level of design for the building interiors became an issue. Walt wanted the interiors to be as highly detailed as the exteriors. The men told the Disney team, "The interior finishing concepts of the restaurants are too expensive, especially since a hot dog and a beer are about all anyone eats at an amusement park." They said, "He will lose his shirt by over spending on things the customers never really notice."

Then they began to really tear the project apart. During the presentation of the Jungle Cruise, the men said that the ride would not work because the animals would be sleeping or hidden. Walt's desire for year-round operation was a bad idea, when 120 days was "the only way to go". Most importantly, the lack of "carny" barkers was certainly a bad idea. One critic said, "Without barkers along the midway to sell the sideshows, the marks won't pay to go in. Customers are likely to leave with money left in their pockets." Price summed up the thoughts of the participants with this statement: "Mr. Disney's park idea is too expensive to build and too expensive to operate." The focus group's advice to Price was, "Tell your boss to save his money. Tell him to stick to what he knows and leave the amusement business to people who know it."

Walt appreciated the practical tips; but he was always ready to compete when he thought he had a better idea, and the results of this focus group was the affirmation he needed to hear. Rather than being dissuaded, he was even more certain that his idea would work. Instead of another amusement park, Walt knew he was creating the first theme park. The difference between the two, as explained by J.G. O'Boyle in *Persistence of Vision* magazine, is, "A theme park is not ride-dependent. A theme park without rides is still a theme park. An amusement park without rides is a parking lot with popcorn."

After Price had completed his research, he predicted that first-year attendance for Disneyland would be between 2.5 and 3 million guests. The actual attendance that first year neared 4 million guests.

Chapter Seven

Disneyland and the Urban Experience

Disneyland did not start out to become a showcase for innovative urban design and planning policies, but that is exactly what has happened. Not only did Disneyland change the public's perception of what an amusement park could be, Walt's innovations have forever changed the public's expectations for the public realm and how we design these spaces.

In developing Disneyland, Walt and his team took a very comprehensive look at the amusement park industry to learn about what worked and what did not work. They took these findings and blended science with art. Buzz Price had told Walt, "Guessing is dysfunctional. Ignoring prior experience is denial. Using valid numbers to project performance is rational." Walt heeded that advice, but also knew that you cannot focus only on the numbers. Walt reminded his team, "After you get the numbers, you still have to make up your mind." The result is, as John Findlay noted in *Magic Lands*, "...a special suburban environment for pedestrians. It gave the middle class an irresistible combination of entertainment, commerce, and culture; presented ideas in a carefully arranged sequence of attractions; maintained uniformly high standards of cleanliness, service, and attractiveness; regulated the movement of crowds through limited space; and exploited moviemakers' techniques of industrial design in order to present a world that improved on reality."

Disneyland's environmental design and public space innovations were so successful that Walt would try to incorporate them in other projects: The site plan has a strong boundary and is protected from the outside world by a landscape element. The circulation realm is based on a radial or hub-and-spoke pattern. In the center is a space where guests can settle and get oriented. At the end of the pathways would be iconic architectural elements that act like a beckoning, pulling the guests forward. Born of a movie mogul's vision, the design of Disneyland is a reflection of Walt's cinematic and storytelling background. At the time, Disneyland set a new standard for cleanliness of public spaces. It also helped to renew public interest in historic central business districts. Pesky but vital infrastructure was cleverly hidden from the guests' view. Most importantly, Walt created through the park a special kind of public space that has connected emotionally with millions of guests.

The success of Disneyland convinced Walt that he might be able to take what he had learned and apply it toward building a beautiful, functional city where people not only played and worked but also where they lived. Walt had confidence in his creativity. He had already changed the world of animation forever. His studio was light-years ahead of other movie studios in function and design. His theme park redefined the world of amusement parks. Maybe now he could turn his attention to transforming the urban experience.

Reassurance

With regard to the spatial design process, there is a difference in approach between theme parks and the world outside the front gate. Each type of environment is driven by its own distinctive organizing system, and we must define the differences so that we make the right choices to create places that are simultaneously serviceable and vibrant.

The "real" world feels alive when there is a certain disorderly vigor. A theme park succeeds when there is a lack of visual contradictions. It is virtually impossible to blend these qualities without creating a space that feels uncomfortable and undesirable.

Jane Jacobs—noted author of *The Death and Life of Great American Cities* and savior of large areas of historic Manhattan—described "the city as organized complexity". Among other factors, architect Robert Venturi came to the conclusion that successful and dynamic urban environments contain a "messy vitality over obvious unity". Both agree that it is this quality that is necessary if a place is to feel authentic and resonate with meaning to the users. Such places are embedded with quality, variety, and surprise. As a result, the environment puts you slightly on edge, and you feel more alert and alive in a delightful way. There is a delicate balance, however. Too much of this messy vitality and you will only encourage fear.

When asked about this difference, Imagineer John Hench[14] said, "Most

---

14 Hench grew up in southern California. He started at the DisneyStudios in 1939 as a sketch artist on *Fantasia*. In 1954, after Hench completed a career in animation, Walt Disney selected him to become one of the first Imagineers. Hench considered himself as the "color guru" for the Disney parks. Through his influence, Walt understood how color could be used as a storytelling element, how color welcomes guests and helps them make decisions, and how color establishes the mood. Hench is the one who figured out how color "encourages the suspension of disbelief" and creates the illusion of reality. John Hench was a master teacher and influenced a generation of Imagineers. This was especially true after Walt's death in 1966. In 1998, Hench was given a Lifetime Achievement Award by the Themed Entertainment Association. In 2003, he released *Designing Disney: Imagineering and the Art of the Show*—required reading for those interested in theme park design. In it, Hench defines, in terms understandable to the layperson, how

urban environments are basically chaotic places, as architectural and graphic information scream at the citizen for attention. This competition results in disharmonies and contradictions that...cancel each other [out]." He warns, "A journey down almost any urban street will quickly place the visitor into visual overload as all of the competing messages merge into a kind of information gridlock."

Hench suggested that the only way to design a successful themed environment is to eliminate any visual contradictions. He defined a visual contradiction as "the active clutter that you see in the real world, which creates mixed messages, sets up conflicts, creates tension, and may even feel threatening". Hench taught his team, "If visual details disagree, guests experience active clutter, which has the same effect on the eye as a cacophony of noises has on the ear." Hench elaborated, "Walt wanted all the details to be correct. What it amounted to was a kind of visual literacy." He suggested that each space is like a "bead or charm in a necklace. The same thing was applied as you walk around the park. Continuity was the same. Whether you're slow or fast, what you look at is the same." This never-ending aspiration to eliminate every visual contradiction was in complete harmony with Walt's vision. One day, early in the park's history, while Walt was making his usual rounds, he spotted an employee dressed in a spacesuit, walking from the backstage area near Frontierland on his way to Tomorrowland; he decided he needed to find a way to make sure this did not happen again. Walt did not want guests to see anything that was not specifically designed for each space. In Walt's mind, this was a disconnect that destroyed the carefully constructed theme, and that was unacceptable.

By eliminating the visual contradictions, Walt had created a world that existed within the earthen berm that surrounded his park that was safe and clean. What he created was not a place about fantasy but a place about a sense of reassurance. Michel Sorkin, author of *Variations on a Theme Park*, noted, "The highly regulated, completely synthetic vision provides a simplified, sanitized experience that stands in for the more undisciplined complexities of the city." Walt himself said, "Physically, Disneyland would be a small world in itself—it would encompass the essence of the things that were good and true in American life. It would reflect the faith and challenge of the future, the entertainment, the interest

---

visual storytelling, character, and color come together to create a sense of place and harmony. He has influenced every park and resort since Disneyland. Hench had very high standards. At the opening of Disney's California Adventure in 2001, he reportedly said, "I liked it better as a parking lot." He stayed at Disney until his death in 2004, at the age of ninety-five. Imagineer Tom Morris described Hench as "the Philosopher of Imagineering".

in intelligently presented facts, the stimulation of the imagination, the standards of health and achievement, and above all, a sense of strength, contentment, and well-being." John Hench said that Disneyland "tried to present an undilutedly rosy view of the world; contradiction or confusion were qualities the planners of Disneyland associated with the defective, poorly planned, conventional amusement park." He added, "Disneyland offered an enriched version of the real world, but not an escapist or an unreal version. We program out all the negative, unwanted elements and program in the positive elements. We've taken and purified the statement so it says what it was intended to."

Evangelist Billy Graham once told Walt that Disneyland was "a nice fantasy". This did not sit well with Walt. He replied, "You know the fantasy isn't here. This is very real...The Park is reality. The people are natural here; they're having a good time; they're communicating. This is what people really are. The fantasy is—out there, outside the gates of Disneyland, where people have hatreds and people have prejudices. It's not really real!"

The park is made up of a series of spaces that unfold before you. Hench said, "You begin with the first scene and move through. You don't throw people into the fifth scene, where they cannot make sense of what is happening." The payoff is a sense of welcoming, worth, value, and security.

When somebody suggested the only reason people go to Disneyland was escapism, John Hench took offense and disagreed. He said, "There was never a Main Street like this. But it reminds you of some things about yourself." He added, "What we are selling is not escapism, but reassurance." A visit to Disneyland reassures us that things will be okay. Here, everything works, places can be clean, people can be nice, and the pace of the world feels right. Marty Sklar and John Hench have described the urban design for Disneyland as the "architecture of reassurance".

This quality is achieved by removing visual cues with messages that do not embellish the pre-determined narrative. In a concept drawing of Main Street, U.S.A. from 1953, artist Dale Hennesy included a church. Such a Main Street building would have been common and historically correct in a "real" civic center. However, Walt was not designing a reflection of a real town. He was designing Disneyland; Walt decided the church did not support the story, so there is no church at the edge of the Disneyland commercial district. Every tiny detail came under similar scrutiny from Walt. For example, when Bill Martin showed Walt drawings of Main Street, "[Walt] went over my plans with a fine-tooth comb. I'd drawn sidewalks on the blueprints with square corners and Walt said: 'Bill, people aren't soldiers! They don't turn in at sharp angles! Curve the sidewalks! Make the corners round!'"

Walt's Toy

In *Designing Disney's Theme Parks*, Karal Ann Marling suggests, "One of the consistent hallmarks of Disney architecture is its refusal to be avant-garde: reassurance, on the contrary, means using the familiar conventions of real-world architecture—and then 'plussing' them until the audience has to smile." Although he was no fan, Robert Venturi does concede, "Disney is nearer to what people really want than anything architects have ever given them."

John Hench said the architecture, colors, background sounds, music, and smells create an environment where "the order here at Disneyland works on people, the sense of harmony. They feel more content here, in a way that they can't explain. You find strangers talking to each other without fear." He added, "You actually find people patting strange kids on the head, which of course they wouldn't do anywhere else. Disney historian Michael Broggie[15] said, "[Walt] also thought the Park's atmosphere could be sophisticated yet relaxed enough that adults would feel comfortable allowing their 'inner child' to play, without feeling embarrassed." In 1963, Walt said, "The American child is sensitive, humorous, open-minded, eager to learn, and has a strong sense of excitement, energy, and healthy curiosity about the world in which he lives. Lucky indeed is the grown-up who manages to carry these same characteristics into adult life. That's the real trouble with the world. Too many people grow up."

Jeff Kober of World Class Benchmarking teaches in his workshops that the physical experience of passing through the portal of Disneyland communicates a concept he calls "emotional separation" when guests are forced to separate the experience of paying and the experience of entering the park. The experience couldn't be more effective. After a visit to Disneyland, British writer Aubrey Menen said she "spent the morning riding through dreams that lay somewhere at the bottom of my mind". Writer Matthew Arnold said, "Every aspect of the Magic Kingdom, from trash collection to efficient transportation to the providing of near-constant stimuli, works to achieve this same end: freedom from worries, from toils, from the feelings of insecurity that define the average person's workaday life."

For many guests, there is a sense of timelessness inside Disneyland. In *Disneyland Through the Decades*, author Jeff Kurtti said that frequently visiting the park "is revelatory in the drastic change you will see—and the almost complete lack of change you will see". If you want to get a sense how Disneyland has both changed tremendously and remained the same

---

15   Roger Broggie's son.

over the years, you might want to visit the museum on Main Street, where a model of Disneyland on opening day in 1955 is tucked into a wall.

Imagineer Bruce Gordon may have provided the best description as to why Disneyland works. He said, "Walt was hands-on with everything at Disneyland. This was his park, his dream. I always believed the reason Walt built Disneyland was that he wanted one." Bruce adds, "He wanted the biggest train layout; he wanted a place for all his toys. In the park he had an apartment above the fire station. Walt would get up early in the morning, before the park opened, and he'd drive his fire truck around Disneyland. People would think he was crazy, but he was only playing with his toy."

Site Design

Make no mistake. The spaces within the park are not representative of reality but become a hyper reality—stylized and tightly edited versions of the real thing. The buildings are shrunk and edited to meet the needs of the story that binds everything together. However, Disneyland is a legible urban environment.

As a result of the innovative site design plan for Disneyland, guests are provided with a comprehensible orientation and an environment that induces a change of mood. Key to this was Walt's decision to set his park within a strong boundary, with only a single entrance, and with a radial, or hub-and-spoke, circulation system.

Walt picked Marvin Davis to be the master planner for Disneyland.[16] From the very beginning, Walt was clear about his intentions for Disneyland. He told Davis, "I just want it to look like nothing else in the world. And it should be surrounded by a train." He said he wanted the railroad tracks on the high ground so guests could preview all the wonderful things that would be inside the berm. Davis described the site design process for Disneyland: "I was working in what they call the Zorro building as the project designer for master planning of the Park at the time. This was before they even knew where the Park was going." ... "Before they bought the property—I guess I must have done, well I know I did 129 different schemes for the solution of the thing...different entryways...until finally it developed into the scheme that it is now with the single entrance and

---

16 Davis was born in Clovis, New Mexico, on December 21, 1910. He attended both UCLA and USC in Los Angeles, California, and graduated with an architectural degree in 1935. Davis received the American Institute of Architects medal as the top student of his class. He went on to become a very successful assistant art director at Twentieth-Century Fox and joined the Disney organization in 1953.

the walk for the avenue, which is Main Street, up to the center of the hub. Walt's idea was to have the whole thing as radials from that hub."

In August 1953, Walt walked into Marvin Davis' office with the map of the property he just purchased in Anaheim. Walt took out a pencil and drew the exact placement of where he wanted his train. The drawing showed the railroad tracks running around the perimeter forming a triangular boundary. That basic outline still represents the boundaries of the park. Understanding that constraint, Davis knew what to do next.

Walt looked at all sorts of public spaces and their circulation patterns. He said, "I've been studying the way people move at museums and other entertainment places. Everybody's got tired feet. I don't want that to happen in this place." He called this problem "museum feet". He described the feeling when "the ache of having walked too much just to get through the place" made the visit unpleasant. He figured that he could mitigate this issue through better planning. "I want a place for people to sit down and where older folks can say, 'you kids run on. I'll meet you there in a half hour,'" Walt said. "Disneyland is going to be a place where you can't get lost or tired unless you want to."

Walt and Davis decided that the best solution to avoid "museum feet" was to lay out the park's circulation plan like a bicycle wheel. This is known as the radial plan. It has also been called the hub-and-spoke pattern because the pathways radiate out in every direction like spokes connected to a hub on a bicycle tire. Davis noted, "The overall shape of the park, with its single entrance, was Walt's and that was the key to the whole thing. Walt was very circulation conscious, and he wanted a single entrance so that they could control the number of people that came in, and know the number that went out, and know what's in the park." The benefit of this layout is that no matter where you go, it is easy to find a way to come back to a familiar central area. "[Walt] wanted to solve everything with the radial idea," recalled Marvin Davis in a 1991 interview with authors and filmmakers Richard and Katherine Greene. It gave "people a sense of orientation—they know where they are at all times".

This radial plan concept was so successful that the design pattern has been embedded in virtually every Disney theme park. Walt remarked, "The more I go to other amusement parks in all parts of the world, the more I am convinced of the wisdom of the original concepts of Disneyland. I mean, have a single entrance through which all traffic would flow, then a hub off which the various areas were situated." He added, "That gives people a sense of orientation—they know where they are at all times. And it saves a lot of walking."

Main Street is more than just a narrow pathway to get you from one point to another. One Disney executive called it a "mindsetter". J.G. O'Boyle said, "Main Street, U.S.A. has a more significant function—it serves as a meticulously coded social instrument designed to communicate a complex set of instructions—a theme—to each of the guests—instantly, harmoniously, and wordlessly." O'Boyle concluded, "That message is a reminder of our shared cultural identity."

At the end of Main Street, just in front of the castle, is a circular park called the Plaza Hub. This is the central gathering spot within the park. "Walt observed how families made decisions about what to do next," John Hench said." He concluded that they needed a lot of space, as they would stop and gather around with one child or two hanging outside the group." The solution was the use of "hubs—open, essentially circular spaces that afford views in many directions—[and that] facilitate decision making. From a hub, guests can see and point to many of the choices they might make." Hench added, "Decision-making is very fatiguing. Relating things that are unrelated is fatiguing… If you start wandering from one thing to another, not quite knowing what you want to see, you will wear yourself out." He suggested, "You come to a point in the park that we know is a decision point, we put two choices. We try not to give them seven or eight so that they have to decide in a qualitative way which is the best way." Walt and his team gave this careful consideration in an attempt to manipulate crowd flow. In the book *Vinyl Leaves*, author Stephen Fjellman wrote, "The Disney strategy is to disperse people as widely as possible and to keep them moving." Even the stores along Main Street were planned with interior pathways to mitigate congestion on the street.

We can use Christopher Alexander's pattern language to discuss the effectiveness of the Disneyland site design. For example, Alexander's design pattern, "Mosaic of Subcultures", describes how we have made most modern environments overly complex, which is disorienting and stressful. This pattern suggests that the solution is to break the city down into a "vast mosaic of small and different subcultures, each with its own spatial territory, and each with the power to create its own distinct life style". The results are "Identifiable Neighborhoods". Walt designed Disneyland so that it is broken down into smaller "lands" that are reached from a central point. The Plaza Hub becomes "Common Land", which is shared by each of the lands of Disneyland.

Some of the destination decisions had been made early in the design process. Davis stated, "We knew we wanted the fantasy rides up at the end of Main Street, once you go through the castle. Then the other lands just logically took their place." To eliminate the confusion common to visiting an unfamiliar place, each land has a "Main Gateway"; these gateways are all similar in design, are laid out to form a group, and are all easily visible from the Hub. Alexander calls this a "Subculture Boundary".

Guests standing in the hub can tell from each gateway what they might expect once they have passed through that portal. The guest can decide to walk east into the future toward Tomorrowland, north toward the castle drawbridge and Fantasyland, west toward the stockade at the entrance of Frontierland, or veer off path just a bit and enter Adventureland. Each path radiates out from and returns to the Plaza Hub.

Since Disneyland opened, research has been done to determine how the park influences guests on a subconscious level and what this means to human behavior. The structures along Main Street are both functional and symbolic. They reinforce our self-image and form a collective memory. John Hench said, "Part of it, I suppose, was Walt's exploitation of very old survival patterns. He had an instinct for this. I think that if anyone really wanted to take the time to examine it, he would see that these survival patterns are the basis for our aesthetics, our sense of pleasure." Hench was talking about the timeless way of building, which Christopher Alexander was able to document. The result is an environment that demonstrates a higher degree of life. Main Street, U.S.A. creates an opportunity for the guest to decompress and to agree to accept a mutually understood pattern of expected behavior. The visit becomes more slowly paced, less stressful, and friendlier. This is not a competitive urban environment but one that projects the idealized image of a different time and place.

The Building Blocks of Disney Theme Park Design

The Berm

At Disneyland, Bill Evans built a twenty-foot mound of earth—or berm—that completely surrounds the park. A berm is a narrow ledge or shelf generally made of dirt with the top or bottom of a slope planted with trees and plants to control a view. Along the top edge is a dense layer of plant materials. At Disneyland, the berm is one of the defining physical features; it is what separates the theme park from the rest of the adjacent development and from the world. The use of the berm was adopted from both the Burbank studio and Walt's home in Holmby Hills. The berm allowed Walt to control the environment, create a more intimate setting, and prevent visual and sound intrusions. Bill Evans taught Walt that "[t]rees alone won't do that. It takes about a hundred feet of dense trees to block sound, but you can do that with about twenty feet of earth."

Referring to the berm at Disneyland, Norman Klein says in *The Vatican to Vegas*, "Technically a berm was the shoulder of earth that obscured

Anaheim from visitors. As a narrative, the berm was the proscenium arch, marking the reassuring boundaries of the scripted space." The berm created a horizon for many of the vistas within the park. In the 1990s, the Disney Imagineers expanded the definition of the berm so that they could apply it to the stores and other indoor environments. Today, they consider the berm to be "the threshold…isolating the visitor from the street, and inviting a theatrical suspension of disbelief".

The Wienie

At the end of each pathway that radiates out from the Plaza Hub is what Walt called a "wienie"—typically a strong vertical physical element that functions as a view terminus. Walt observed that people move toward things that are inviting, and, borrowing from silent-era comedy films, he coined the term "wienie" to refer to such things. Why wienie? In *The Vatican to Vegas*, Norman Klein quipped, "The movie dog jumps on cue because someone wiggles a frankfurter off screen. That is what Walt Disney meant by a wienie."[17] John Hench defined a wienie as "A beckoning hand [that] promises something worthwhile; its friendly beckoning fingers say, 'Come this way. You'll have a good time.'" Historian Steven Watts says wienies "were the large visual attractions in each 'land', which caught the eye and drew people along preordained routes so that the crowds flowed smoothly". Wienies build memories and make for repeat visits. They are the centerpieces of the scripted space.

Virtual Reality

Disneyland is a virtual reality experience of the first order. The Imagineers applied cinematic techniques to three-dimensional spaces. At the time of Disneyland's design and construction, the movie industry was going through major changes to compete with television. Cinemascope and 3D movies were all the rage.[18] Norman Klein said, "The screen that surrounded and invaded and was immersive in scale seemed particularly appealing. It seemed modern, panoramic, wall to wall." The early Imagineers based many of the Disneyland design considerations on a basic theatrical storytelling tool called the "Elements of Setting". In the theater and motion pictures, production designers rely on six elements to frame the experience: location, time, historical time, seasonal time, daily time, and weather. John Hench tailored this approach especially for theme parks, saying that designers must

---

17   It has also been noted that Walt had a lifelong love of hot dogs.

18   While 3D movies are ubiquitous now, the technology was not highly successful at the time, and the fad ended in 1956.

focus on form, space, and time—with form being the story you are trying to tell. Hench said, "Disneyland wasn't really a radical step for Walt because even in the two-dimensional world of motion pictures space is implied. In fact, we used many of the techniques we had learned from the films and applied them to the third dimension. And when we set up a kind of story in our own mind, we would establish an imaginary long shot as if we were taking it with motion pictures." Karal Ann Marling warned, "The cinematic approach to architecture succeeds or fails with the first establishing shot."

In Walt's 1953 proposal for the park, he said, "Like Alice stepping through the Looking Glass, to step through the portals of Disneyland will be like entering another world." According to Jeff Kurtti in *Walt Disney's Imagineering Legends*: "For Walt, Disneyland was a world seen through fantasy, a place of warmth and nostalgia, full of 'illusion and color and delight.'" Kurtti continues to describe that "quality without a name" by saying, "Walt sought to create a 'storybook realism', an essence of genuineness and authenticity that is more utopian, more romanticized than the actual environments could ever be."

So it is that each of the lands at Disneyland represents a major cinematic genre of the early 1950s. Main Street, U.S.A. is home. Adventureland is movie exotica. Frontierland brings to life all of the Westerns that were on television and in the movies. Fantasyland allows Walt's animated films to come to life. Tomorrowland is a science fiction portal. John Hench suggested, "To design an enhanced reality we must intensify above all the visual elements of storytelling, creating a vibrant, larger-than-life environment."

Spatial Manipulation

In many respects, Disneyland is the world's largest toy train set. Of the locomotives that circle the park to the buildings along Main Street, Walt said, "It's not apparent at a casual glance that this street is only a scale model." He added, "This cost more, but made the street a toy and the imagination can play more freely with a toy." To achieve this effect, the Imagineers adapted a film technique called forced perspective and applied it to three-dimensional design. John Hench defined forced perspective as "a form of one-point linear perspective in which receding space is compressed by exaggerating the proximity of the implied vanishing point to the viewer". In film, the process adds depth to the image. In three-dimensional design, the illusion adds height. The perspective is "forced" because the first floor of a building is full scale, the second floor is smaller in scale, and the third level is even smaller. As the structure continues to rise, the materials continue to get smaller in scale. Forced perspective is used to adjust the scale of the architecture to meet the storytelling need.

These are not full-scale reproductions of historic structures. The size of the buildings has been manipulated, and the unfolding of the spaces is purposefully staged to reinforce the overall narrative. Forced perspective also provided the Imagineers maximum flexibility in the design process. Forced perspective is the quality that makes buildings feel taller than they really are while making the environment more comfortable and intimate.

The physical space that the guest passes through is compressed, which aids in the storytelling process. This is why Disneyland seems cozy and friendly, particularly to children. In *Magic Lands*, John Findlay says, "The overall effect of the built environment was impressive but not intimidating." Hench noted, "It's one of the special charms of Disneyland that not only is the architecture related, but the ideas are related. You get the impression of ambience."

Architect John Kaliski observed, "The qualities that most impress me are intricacy, detail, and the ability to be constantly lost in the details, which are tactile and human scale." He feels that "the New Orleans street as well as some of the cul-de-sacs are places of imploded time that in effect are almost authentic. Understanding how to craft this and create this is part of the work of urban design and architecture and it is done to an exemplary state in portions of Disneyland." He did have some concerns. "The part for me [that] is claustrophobic is the relentless fantasy and lack of cultural complexity combined with the manipulation of too many experiences."

Karal Ann Marling saw it differently. "In the movies, the experience is continuous and unbroken, but in Disneyland, it is discontinuous and episodic, like watching television in the privacy of one's home, each ride a four- or five-minute segment, slotted in among snacks, trips to the rest room, and 'commercials' in the form of souvenir emporia. And it is always possible to change the channel."

Forced perspective plays tricks with the guest's perception of space and time. Walt knew that at the end of a long day, people did not want to feel like the exit was so far away. To slow people down, the first floor of the Main Street train depot was built at full scale, and the structure looks much larger than the buildings in the foreground. The scale of the depot contrasts with the rest of the Main Street façades, with the result that the street appears to be very short. The guests are now convinced that the exit is not far away, and they feel they can slow down and savor their last few moments in the park. They might even do a little bit of shopping along the way. To make the façades more personal, the storefront windows are lower than usual so that children have better access to view the displays.

Borrowing from the animation field again, the Imagineers enriched the guest experience with another visual trick. The animators called this tool the "inbetween". In the animation process, a scene is staged by a series of key drawings that highlight major points of motion. These drawings come to life because of a large number of 'inbetweens' that complete the scene.

According to Randy Bright in *Disneyland: Inside Story*, Walt did not believe that everything had to increase capacity, create publicity, or make money. He knew he had to create "remarkable pieces of out-of-the-way charm that doesn't shout or call attention to itself". Instead, "The visitor sort of stumbles upon it, experiencing all the surprise and delight that childhood discoveries bring." People instinctively want to decorate their spaces. Without such embellishments, a place will seem lifeless and dull. The inbetween ensures that a guest will never be without decoration within the theme parks. Some examples of inbetweens include Tarzan's Treehouse in Adventureland and the Frontierland petrified tree at Disneyland, and the Swiss Family Treehouse in the Magic Kingdom at Walt Disney World.

The architectural vocabulary developed at Disneyland has influenced other "invented" places. For an outstanding example, one has only to exit Disneyland and drive north along the freeway to The Grove in the Fairfax District of Los Angeles. Built in 2002, the Grove is one of the most successful shopping centers in the region. It was built adjacent to the historic and world-famous Farmer's Market (built in 1934) and was developed by Rick Caruso.[19] Caruso learned many lessons from Main Street, U.S.A. and creatively applied them, resulting in a dynamic urban space. Both Disneyland and The Grove are promenades between two activity nodes. Each has a mid-block street breaking down the scale of the corridor. Both of these "streets" have similar dimensional metrics: the linear distance and the roadway from curb to curb. The Grove main corridor has the same dimensions from the center intersection to the center of the hub park near the musical fountain. Like Disneyland, The Grove mall also features building façades framing a narrow corridor using forced perspective. However, there is a difference: at The Grove, the first floor is standard height for a retail establishment and the upper floor is taller than normal. The result is a highly energized space, not as laid back as Disneyland's Main Street.

The "Big River"

There are many other fascinating aspects of the Disneyland infrastructure. A hallmark of the Disney designers' capabilities is their ability to identify

---

19 Developer Rick Caruso considers Walt Disney a hero and said that he is "one of the true geniuses in the world." The Grove is what the *Los Angeles Times* described as a "wildly popular amusement park-like shopping center." He had already built other "lifestyle" centers in suburban locations such as The Commons at Calabasas and The Lakes at Thousand Oaks. The Grove was his first urban infill project of this type.

innovative solutions for technical engineering problems while exhibiting incredible place-making capabilities. For example, one of Disneyland's more understated design features is the use of water; the designers succeeded in using water to create a sense of place while at the same time keeping the water system infrastructure hidden from view.

Many parks feature streams and ponds, but the Imagineers were required to use water in a way that reinforces the storyline while providing visual relief. As Christopher Alexander explains, "People have a fundamental yearning for great bodies of water. But the very movement of the people toward the water can also destroy the water." Walt needed a durable, functional, and beautiful water system.

Disneyland has two different water systems. For the attractions—such as Splash Mountain, Pirates of the Caribbean, and it's a small world—the park uses a "clear" water system. The system of "natural" waterways that tie the park together and give it a special character is called the "dark" water system. *The "E" Ticket* magazine called this system "Disneyland's Big River". The headwater for the Disneyland Big River starts at the end of a pipe that pumps water from the Rivers of America. Near the Native American village is a 25-horsepower circulating pump that moves two million gallons of water a day. That water flows through a 21-inch pipe, 15 feet vertically from Frontierland and into Fantasyland. The water exits the pump and flows downhill in a pipe near Sleeping Beauty Castle toward two destinations: the Storybook Land Canal Boats and the pond surrounding the former Motor Boat Cruise loading area.

From there, the water flows downhill in a pipe that curves along the Tomorrowland side of the Matterhorn toward the moat in front of Sleeping Beauty Castle. The water enters the moat near the Snow White Garden and her Wishing Well. The flow of the water continues under the drawbridge and down the little river alongside of the Carnation Garden. The Big River passes underneath the faux-wooden bridge that leads to the gates of the stockade protecting Frontierland. As it approaches Adventureland, the water ducks into another pipe and reappears below the steps at the exit of Walt Disney's Enchanted Tiki Room. From there it flows into the rivers of the Jungle Cruise. Theoretically, as the water winds its way through the Jungle Cruise, it has traveled through the Irrawaddy, Mekong, Amazon, and Nile rivers. It exits the Jungle Cruise in a 37-inch pipe next to the base of Tarzan's Treehouse, travels under the walkway, and drains into the Rivers of America.

To keep the water circulating in the river, there are streams and waterfalls on Tom Sawyer Island. Inevitably, the water finds its way back toward the pump near the Native American village and the cycle begins all over again. According to *The "E" Ticket*, the system would lose as much as 30,000 gallons daily to evaporation on a hot day. To achieve a certain color, the park dumps in about twelve pounds of brown or green dye into the river and allows it to circulate for a few days. There is a well near Big Thunder Ranch. At every point in its journey, the Disneyland water travels via a complex, industrial-quality technological system; but to the Disneyland guest, the water is as pure and wondrous as any natural river.

Private Spaces

In any community, there need to be places that only a few can enter, where exclusivity is expected: homes, fellowship halls, members-only associations. In the case of Disneyland, those spaces included living quarters for Walt and his family plus a very exclusive club.

Considering the state of the regional freeway system at the time of Disneyland's construction, Burbank to Anaheim could easily be a two-hour drive. It made sense to have a place in both cities where Walt could rest. He certainly had enjoyed having an apartment next to his office suite on the third floor of the Burbank studio. Now he wanted the same thing at Disneyland. He picked the perfect location on top of the fire station facing Town Square. He could watch the guests walking about and get a great view of the train. Lillian worked with Emil Kuri to decorate the tiny 500-square-foot apartment. In addition to the apartment, there is an outdoor deck with wicker furniture overlooking Town Square. The mature eucalyptus trees that were the backdrop to Adventureland screened the rear deck. The apartment was Walt's escape from the public.

The apartment was comfortable for Walt and Lillian, but their family was growing. As part of the plans for New Orleans Square, Walt proposed to build a 2,200-square foot apartment to accommodate his many grandchildren. The location was specifically chosen on top of the Pirates of the Caribbean building to give the best possible view of the Rivers of America. Disney Legend Dorothea Redmond was picked to design the interior, and she incorporated a number of interesting features.[20]

---

20 Redmond's incredible career included contributions to movies such as Hitchcock's *Rear Window*, *Gone With the Wind*, Charlie Chaplin's *Limelight*, and *The Road to Bali* starring Bing Crosby, Bob Hope, and Dorothy Lamour. From there Redmond worked at an architectural firm for ten years before joining WED Enterprises. Her first project at Disneyland was the upscale Plaza Inn restaurant. Over the years she contributed concept sketches for the Magic Kingdom. Millions have admired her fifteen-foot by ten-foot mosaic murals that line the Cinderella Castle passageway. These huge panels are made up of thousands of small bits of Italian glass, real silver, and 14-karat gold. There is a matching set of panels in Tokyo. Ms. Redmond retired in 1974 and died in March 2009.

The living room and bedrooms face into a very private courtyard. A climate control system was installed in the courtyard to cool or heat the space as required. In the master bedroom, Walt had electrical sockets installed everywhere to undermine Lillian's efforts to keep him from reading late into the night. (It has been reported that Lillian had a tendency to move the furniture in the Holmby Hills residence so that Walt could not access the lights near the bed.) The apartment was to have a small kitchen and an inconspicuous stairwell entrance in the rear that would lead down to the antique shop below. Walt and Roy planned to call the new apartment The Royal Suite, named after the New Orleans Square street where the entrance is located. Walt died before the project was started; Roy felt that it would not be the same without his brother and suggested the space be put to another use.[21]

When Walt partnered with General Electric (GE) for the 1964–1965 New York World's Fair and designed the Progressland Pavilion featuring the Carousel of Progress, he was required to install a VIP lounge with bar facilities. This experience taught him the value of having a quiet, luxurious, very private spot to wine, dine, and entertain special clients and dignitaries. As the World's Fair was winding down, Disney and GE began negotiations to move the pavilion from the Fair and install it permanently in Tomorrowland at Disneyland. Again, one of GE's requirements was a functioning VIP lounge like the one in New York. Walt preferred not to have alcohol in his park and refused to build a bar. However, after much give and take, he agreed to build a restaurant that would only serve alcohol with food and put it somewhere other than Tomorrowland.

While Walt was working on the New Orleans Square expansion, he identified the perfect location for the hospitality suite adjacent to his private apartment. He wanted a place that blended the best in location, ambiance, and cuisine. The space became Club 33 and is named for the address of the front door: 33 Royal Street.[22]

It is a beautiful club. During their trips to New Orleans, Walt and Lillian

---

21   The space was turned into a hospitality suite for The Insurance Company of North America (INA), and later into executive offices for the Disneyland International team. It was finally opened to the public in July 1987 and served as The Disney Gallery. From its balcony, this much-loved art gallery provided one of the best views in the park as well as exclusive collectibles. By 2007, the suite was shuttered once again and rebuilt as the Disneyland Dream Suite, a tricked-out guest accommodation, as part of a promotion.

22   According to Jack Lindquist, Walt had a thing for the number 3 and reminds us that the park's address is 1313 Harbor Boulevard.

purchased many of the antiques on display in Club 33, and original artwork done by various Disney artists is displayed throughout the space. Much of the credit must be given to the creative talents of Dorothea Redmond and decorator Emil Kuri, who was a painter and illustrator at the Burbank Studio and who frequently worked with Lillian. In keeping with the New Orleans theme, Redmond chose to work in the First Empire style. This neoclassic style recalls the era of Napoleon and fits in perfectly with the early nineteenth century setting. Parquet floors, beautiful polished stone accents, and three huge chandeliers define the main dining room. A second, less-formal dining room is above the waiting area for the Blue Bayou Restaurant. The second dining room was to feature an Audio-Animatronics vulture that would "listen" in on conversations via microphones installed in the lighting fixtures. The bird would then talk back to the diners. However, it was felt that this might be an invasion of privacy and the plan was put aside. Club 33 opened on June 15, 1967. Sadly, Walt had passed away six months earlier.

A New Standard for Clean

Before Disneyland, most amusement parks were rather seedy places. The operators thought of the customers as "marks" and were not above a bit of shady play if it would earn a little more money. If somebody left with a dime in his pocket, the operator was not doing his job well enough. Trash was tossed anywhere and little attention was paid to the landscaping or architecture. "By 1952, amusement parks were often identified with the tarnished world of film noir, of scandal beneath the big top, and carnies," according to Norman Klein. Patrons felt unsafe in many areas of a traditional amusement park. Walt said that he wanted Disneyland to be different from the "dirty, phony places, run by tough-looking people". When Walt described the idea for the park to his wife, she asked, "Why would you want to build an amusement park? Amusement parks are dirty. They don't make any money." Walt's reply was, "That's the whole point. I want a clean one that will."

Walt sensed there was a change happening in the American culture. Families in the 1950s had begun to reset their expectations for what was meant by progress. There was a growing national consensus that proclaimed that cleanliness and uniformity was a sign of progress. With the spread of freeways, people preferred to patronize modern, familiar motel chains and eat in clean coffee shops housed in space-age Googie[23]-style

---

23 Googie was a popular architectural style in Los Angeles. The style grew out of the Streamline Moderne and features flashy buildings made of glass and steel, constructed in boomerang and trapezoid shapes, with sharp angles and zigzag roof-lines.

buildings. Walt assumed correctly that they would want to visit a different type of family amusement park as well. Karal Ann Marling noted, "If Disneyland was a place of amusement and escape, it was also, in its own way, a kind of pre-EPCOT utopia, a better, cleaner, more pleasant and resonant American place than 1955 afforded the average urbanite who drove to Anaheim on the Santa Ana Freeway." When Walt gave a tour of the park, a journalist commented that everything would soon be covered in litter. Walt curtly replied, "It'll never happen." "Why not?" asked the reporter. "Because, we're going to make it so clean people are going to be embarrassed to throw anything on the ground." Walt was right. Disneyland had validated people's expectations for cleanliness of public spaces, and the park would in time redefine the standard.

Disney Legend Marty Sklar said, "In the Disney theme parks, a dirty floor or an out-of-order facility may individually be of minor significance, but in the long run, they will diminish visitors' expectations of everything we do." Historian Judith Adams noticed, "Everything about the park, including the behavior of the 'guests', is engineered to promote a spirit of optimism, a belief in progressive improvement toward perfection." Walt's drive toward a spotless environment became legendary. Architect Charles Moore noted, "No raw edges spoil the picture at Disneyland; everything is as immaculate as in the musical comedy villages that Hollywood has provided for our viewing pleasure for the last three generations. Nice looking, handsomely costumed young people sweep away the gum wrappers almost before they fall to the spotless pavement."

Imagineer Bruce Gordon said, "At the time Walt was thinking about building a park, most amusement parks were not in a place you'd want to let your kids go on their own. The parks were kind of dirty, in seedy neighborhoods. You wouldn't want to drop off your kids there and meet them three or four hours later, the way you can in a Disney park today."

Today, virtually every commercial business district in every city goes out of its way to be as clean as Disneyland. This was not always so. Cultural historian Richard Francaviglia took a look at Marceline's Main Street during the time that Walt lived there as a young boy. "It was unpaved, rutted, and rilled, and horse manure helped turn it into a soupy quagmire." Walt did not accept his childhood experience as a given; he recreated the image of a traditional central business district and raised our expectations for quality, variety, and surprise.

The level of cleanliness was not the only change in the traditional central business district. By the early 1950s, many historic main streets in the United States had been threatened by shopping malls followed by suburban housing tracts to the suburbs. Downtowns had become run down and were considered irrelevant. New regional shopping malls—like Victor Gruen's Northland

Center in a Detroit suburb and his enclosed Southdale Center near Edina, Minneapolis—were the new center of commerce. To compete, many cities reinvented their historic central business districts by prohibiting automobile traffic and creating downtown pedestrian malls. Most of these conversions failed, furthering the decline of many downtowns.

Kenneth Jackson remarked, "While real trolleys in Newark, Philadelphia, Pittsburg and Boston languish for lack of patronage and government support, millions of people flock to Disneyland to ride fake trains that don't go anywhere." Because of their experience at Disneyland, many people wondered if the historic downtowns could be saved and preserved. As we will see later, this new cleaner, functional, and safe version of a historic downtown that was on display on Main Street in Disneyland would inspire others to rebuild existing central business districts. In many ways, Disneyland helped to save "downtown" from the wrecking ball and established a higher value for preservation and rehabilitation.

Trouble at the Border

By the early 1960s, the area around Disneyland had begun to deteriorate. What started out as a boom to the Anaheim economy was turning into a bust. Blight threatened not only Anaheim's well-being but also the long-term success of the park. Disney had dedicated massive capital to Disneyland. In 1980, June Rose Gader said, "Disneyland is not in Los Angeles. But to millions of people from every country in the world...Disneyland is Los Angeles— or vice versa." Similarly, Disney is Anaheim. The area around Disneyland was not making the best first impression, and Walt was frustrated that he could not easily improve the situation. While speaking to Cast Members at Disneyland's tenth anniversary in 1965, Walt said, "If we could have bought more land, we would have bought it; then we would have control of it, and it wouldn't look like a second-rate Las Vegas around here. But we ran out of money, and by the time we did have a little money, everybody got wise to what was going on. We couldn't buy anything around the place at all."

Former Disneyland President Jack Lindquist noted, "Harbor Boulevard, across from Disneyland, frustrated [Walt] tremendously. He was very disappointed in the city of Anaheim for not exercising greater control of the development that existed outside the park. Less than ten years after Disneyland opened, Harbor Boulevard was an example of ugly urban sprawl at its worst." Michael Sorkin added, "For Disney the frustration was double. First, at the millions lost to others who were housing his visitors. And second, the disorder of it all, the sullying of his vision by a sea of sleaze."

Even though Disneyland was the biggest game in town, the Anaheim business community was the real winner. In the first ten years, Disneyland took in $273 million while the rest of the Anaheim economy generated twice that, $555 million. Over time, the growth of South Orange County and other factors began to hinder the growth of Anaheim. Other businesses demanded improvements. In the early 1960s, as a way to combat the increasing deterioration of the area, 61 area business owners came together to form the Anaheim Visitor and Convention Bureau. The Bureau was responsible for the construction of the convention center adjacent to Disneyland and was instrumental in creating the Anaheim Commercial Recreation Area. Because of this public–private sector intervention, the city was able to develop a specific plan to control development within the resort district.

During the 1970s and the 1980s, the area surrounding the Disneyland Resort continued to suffer from blight, and this was a big concern for Disney. To find solutions, Disney began to develop a new master plan for the development of their property. The Disney Master Plan was based on guiding principles that included project unity. This meant a visit to the resort would create an "experience that is more powerful than its parts. Everything will support everything else. Visual contradictions will be eliminated."

In 1991, the plan was released to the public. It documented the Disney vision for a much larger facility, with a second theme park called WestCot and several resort hotels.[24] The project would represent a major financial commitment to the Anaheim community, with the hope that it would spur additional development and investment from others.

A well-done expansion would not only benefit Disney, but would also help the entire community. The plan suggested that transportation linkages with better connections to the region would be built. Guests would experience a dramatic entry sequence. Parking would be placed on the perimeter of the resort as a way to deal with the tens of thousands of cars that would be descending upon the project every day. Once inside the resort, the pedestrian orientation "would become a series of unfolding spaces that encourage walking". Finally, the resort would accommodate the diversity of guests "insisting on a wide variety of activities that appeal to a wide range of demographics". Disneyland would transform into a twenty-four-hour, seven-day-a-week urban resort experience.

---

24 The planned resort hotels included the original Disneyland Hotel, the New Disneyland Resort Hotel, The Magic Kingdom Hotel, and WestCot Lake Resort.

Chapter Eight

CalArts

Another aspect of Walt's desire to build a community was his interest in art education. By its very nature, animation is a collaborative art form. Like everything else, he wanted to control the environment to produce the best possible result.

One of Walt Disney's goals as the head of his own studio was to elevate the art of animation to a whole new level. He always wanted to show "those New York boys" and the others in Hollywood that he could do it better. This meant he needed to improve the skills of his artists. Very early, he became a big advocate of continuing art education for his team. By constantly improving the skills of his staff, Walt could achieve the quality that he demanded.

Art training for the Disney staff began in animator Art Babbitt's living room. Babbitt invited other animators over to his house and charged a small fee to cover the cost of the model. The classes were so popular that it was standing room only. Walt discovered the classes and invited Babbitt to move his classes to Walt's Hyperion studio. Once Walt gave his stamp of approval, the classes became an integral part of life at the studio.

As the studio continued to grow, Walt needed to find a better solution. He began to drive some of his artists to the Chouinard Art Institute, which had opened in downtown Los Angeles near MacArthur Park in 1921. Chouinard was so highly regarded that Walt even sent his daughter Diane there to study. Walt also brought one of the Chouinard instructors, Don Graham, to the studio to teach classes that focused on the study and analysis of movement. The quality that Walt was seeking was not to duplicate reality but to use it as a basis for a convincing two-dimensional fantasy. This intellectual interest would later evolve into the three-dimensional environments he would create at Disneyland.

In the late 1930s, Walt made a deal with Mrs. Nelbert Chouinard: he would pay her back in the future if she allowed his artists to train at her school. The founder, Nelbert Chouinard, had said, "Talent is more valuable than tuition." By 1941, Walt was paying as much as $100,000 a year on training. When Walt's studio became a success, he paid her back in full.

Mrs. Chouinard suffered a stroke in the early 1950s and was unable to take care of the school. Walt and Roy helped out by lending management resources. What the brothers discovered was that the school had been a victim of embezzlement to the tune of $75,000. Walt had a vision about a new way to teach the arts. His experience had taught him that everything was interrelated and that a multidisciplinary approach is the best way to achieve greatness. The curriculum would blend dance, art, music, film, and theater into a well-rounded experience.[25] In 1957, Walt directed Buzz Price to find a location for a community that combined an arts school, galleries, a theater, an international street with restaurants and shops, and a residential district called City of the Arts or City of the Seven Arts. The school would embrace the latest technologies, including a television broadcast studio and a Hall of Design with the latest in industrial prototypes. By 1958, Walt had revealed his vision for this new form of arts-based community to his staff at WED Enterprises. He even offered to partner with architect William Pereira. Walt hoped that he would be creating an environment that would be the American Bauhaus.

Animation legend Chuck Jones worked for Walt for four months in between jobs at Warner Brothers. In *Inside the Dream*, Katherine and Richard Greene quote Jones as saying, "Walt thought that a great art college would be one where people from the various branches would be able to observe other people at work. He said it would be a great thing if an animator could happen by a musician playing a fiddle. He could stand there and watch the musician for a while—study his positions, the way he puts the handkerchief over his shoulder and so on—and sketch him playing. And the musician could learn whatever it is the animator is trying to find out about musical instruments."

In 1961, Walt and Roy facilitated the merger of the Chouinard Art Institute and the Los Angeles Conservatory of Music, which was founded in 1883 and run by Lulu May Von Hagen. Walt hand-picked the Board of Trustees, which included Buzz Price, Marc and Alice Davis, animator Chuck Jones, and Millard Sheets. Walt intended that the new college be modeled after the California Institute of Technology (better known as Caltech) in Pasadena, California. Caltech is considered one of the finest crossover institutions in the world for engineering and science; Walt wanted

---

25   Walt's concept for an art college is similar to Margaret Mead's view of the benefits of "the city as a center where, any day in any year, there may be a fresh encounter with a new talent, a keen mind or a gifted specialist—this is essential to the life of a country. To play this role in our lives a city must have a soul—a university, a great art or music school, a cathedral or a great mosque or temple, a great laboratory or scientific center, as well as the libraries and museums and galleries that bring past and present together. A city must be a place where groups of women and men are seeking and developing the highest things they know."

a similarly interdisciplinary art school, which he called CalArts, short for the California Institute of the Arts. According to Buzz Price, the objective for Walt's art college would be "to create an inter-disciplinary professional art school where artists could be broadened by exposure to and study of different art forms—art, music, dance, theater, film, animation, and creative writing". The school would be designed "to offer students the opportunity of being taught by professionals, leading to employability. Employability was a unique new objective in the field of art education."

While most art schools focused on theory, CalArts would be similar to Columbia College Chicago, which stressed the practical application of the arts. This is the difference between Columbia College and its more famous neighbor, the Art Institute of Chicago. CalArts would become the first degree-granting institution of higher learning in the United States created specifically for students of both the visual and performing arts. Today, the school offers degree programs in art, design, music, dance, film, video, and theater. Urban planner Marsha V. Rood, FAICP, said, "Creativity is where diverse skills, diversity of population and a place to engage overlap." That was the type of environment that Walt had envisioned for his campus. Not only would students learn, they could also earn a living. An art gallery and performance spaces were included in the plan as a way to reduce the tuition costs. Each discipline would work with the other to carry out the artistic vision. It is easy to see how CalArts was meant to parallel Walt's animation studio at the height of its creativity in the 1930s. Walt was looking for that intimate camaraderie and spirit of adventure that existed in the early days.

Walt said, "Togetherness, for me, means teamwork. In my business of motion pictures and television entertainment, many minds and skillful hands must collaborate... The work seeks to comprehend the spiritual and material needs and yearnings of gregarious humanity. It makes us reflect how completely dependent we are upon one another in our social and commercial life. The more diversified our labors and interests have become in the modern world, the more surely we need to integrate our efforts to justify our individual selves and our civilization." He wanted the school to become a center of creativity to encourage famous artists to take up residency for limited periods and to teach courses. In *Inside the Dream*, animator Marc Davis recalled a conversation when Walt told him, "I'd kind of like to give a class at CalArts, too." Then he looked at Davis and added, "Oh, not drawing. I'm a pretty goddamn good storyman, you know."

To show their commitment to the CalArts project, the Disney brothers set aside 38 acres at the studio's Golden Oak Ranch. Roy stepped up the contributions from the studio; Walt's foundation gave another $1 million. The federal government loaned the school $4 million, and Walt was able to raise an additional $2 million from private donors. The brothers also looked at a 12-acre site next to the Hollywood Bowl. In the end, they selected a site in nearby Valencia due to seismic concerns at the Golden Oak Ranch. Although Walt died before ground broke for the project, he was so committed to the vision that he left fully half of his estate to CalArts. During the groundbreaking in 1969, animator Bob Clampett could be seen mugging behind Lillian Disney as she turned over the first shovel full of dirt. Dick Irvine was instrumental in raising funds for scholarships and student loans. Price said that CalArts turned out very much the way Walt wanted it to be.

The school campus was designed by architects Thornton Ladd and John Kelsey and opened in 1971. Ladd said, "I will build a building where everything interrelates. Six schools are going to be jacked around and communicating with each other." The main building housed a variety of functions: theater, art gallery, library, photo lab, ceramic and sculpture work room, practice and rehearsal rooms, and printing and lithography shops.

William Pereira, an architect and Walt's friend, consulted on the project. About the same time, Pereira created the master plan for the University of California Irvine (UCI) campus, which features a large central park encircled by a one-mile pedestrian ring road. The buildings face onto the open space. The roadways radiate out from the central park. The plan is based on a radial circulation system just like Disneyland.

As we learned in the final segment of "Magic Highways USA", anything is possible if there is the will. Why else would a man who rarely spent time in school want to build one? Why else would an animator want to build a model city (and actually did build a model of it)? Walt wanted to spark the imagination of others and give them the tools to work together to make things better than the sum of their parts.

Chapter Nine

Golden Oak Ranch

Not only did Walt and Roy Disney own property in Burbank and Anaheim, they also invested in a movie ranch: the Golden Oak Ranch in Placerita Canyon near Newhall, about 30 miles north of Los Angeles. Legend has it that in 1842, Francisco Lopez was taking a rest under an oak tree and spotted something shiny nearby. When he took a closer look, he discovered it was gold. Although this was the first major gold strike in California, it was too small to set off an immigration frenzy like the more famous gold rush of 1849 in northern California. Today, that oak tree is marked with a plaque as the "Golden Oak".

Film executive and producer Trem Carr began using the ranch as a setting for films in 1922. Many of the early movie studios have used the facility over the years. Walt leased the property for use as the background for the "Spin and Marty" segments of *The Mickey Mouse Club* in the mid-1950s. The Golden Oak Ranch's variety of natural settings turned out to be such an advantage that Disney purchased the 315-acre property on March 11, 1959, for $300,000. Over the years, the Disney Studio acquired additional Placerita Canyon land, bringing the total to just under 900 acres.[26]

The Ranch Plan

Once Disney took over the property, Marvin Davis and William Tuntke were assigned to develop a site plan. Davis had been responsible for the layout of Disneyland and for the preliminary master plan for Walt Disney World; Tuntke was an art director.[27] They designed an irrigation system to keep the property green, created two lakes that can be drained, and installed a waterfall that can be turned on and off. The sight lines were crafted to enhance the movie-making process. For example, at one spot along the banks

---

26 Many Disney productions have been shot at the Ranch, including *Old Yeller*, *Toby Tyler*, *The Parent Trap*, *The Shaggy Dog*, and *Follow Me Boys*—and, more recently, segments from *The Santa Clause*, *Pearl Harbor*, *Princess Diaries II*, and *Pirates of the Caribbean II* and *III*. Disney is not the only modern studio to use the Ranch; other productions include *The X-Files* (Twentieth Century-Fox), *Murder She Wrote* (Universal), and *Lassie* (Jack Wrather).

27 Tuntke was nominated for an Academy Award for his work on *Mary Poppins*.

of one of the lakes, the camera could be aimed in such a way that the lake looked like a river—a highly valued feature given the popularity of Westerns; directors could easily film a wagon train dramatically crossing a "river".[28]

New facilities were added to the ranch to meet the demands of new productions. A Western street was built for the 1978 television miniseries *Roots II*[29] with a covered wood bridge, the Golden Oak Hall from the movie *The Country Bears*, and barns, farmhouses, country roads, and a forest area. The ranch's Residential Street offers thirteen houses, each with a distinctive architectural style. The Urban Business District, with 42 varied storefronts, enables a production company to create a downtown from virtually any period. The ranch continues to grow with new soundstages under development.

The Golden Oak Ranch has played many roles in the Disney story. The Imagineers used the location to test some of their ideas. One oddity that remains at the ranch is the test track for the Rocketbike. The proposed attraction would have been featured in the Sci-Fi City section inside Tokyo Disneyland—a part of the park that was never built.

When Buzz Price started his feasibility study for the location of Disneyland, one of the first locations he mentioned to Walt was the Golden Oak Ranch. It was also considered as a potential location for CalArts. In fact, in 1965, Walt set aside 38 acres at the ranch to build his art school; however, a geological survey determined that the site had too many potential dangers, and the CalArts project was moved to nearby Valencia.

There were other dreams for Golden Oak Ranch. In *The Vault of Walt*, Jim Korkis revealed Walt's plans for a residential community in Valencia with an 18-hole golf course and a shopping village, all connected by—of course!—a train. He went so far as to engage Marvin Davis to design homes for himself and Lillian, their daughter Diane, and brother Roy Disney. However, Lillian squelched the idea when she said she did not want to live that far away from Los Angeles and her friends.

An Idea Reborn

It is said that ideas never really die at Imagineering and Disney. Today, a residential neighborhood called the Golden Oak Ranch exists on the other side of the continent, in Florida. Walt never built a community at the Golden

---

28   Sight lines have continued to be a careful consideration throughout the property. When the State of California proposed to extend the Antelope Freeway in 1962, Disney worked with the highway engineers to be sure that the roadway would not intrude into the view of the camera.

29   The *Roots II* set was removed in 2008.

Oak Ranch in California, but Disney decided that the story and history of the ranch was a wonderful image for a high-end residential community.

The subdivision is located at the northeast corner of Walt Disney World, with around 400 custom single-family homes priced from $1.8 million. It has access to shared facilities at another subdivision, the Four Seasons Resort, including a full-service spa, restaurants, golf course, and event space.

Disney has tried to build on the myth and legacy of the Disney Studios to sell residential units. The press materials tell us that when Walt was young and lived in Marceline, he would "lie beneath the spreading branches of his 'dreaming tree' and let his imagination run free. This is the symbolic Golden Oak. It was here that Walt's talents for storytelling and fantasy began to take shape into some of the world's most beloved characters."

The Florida Golden Oak development covers 980 acres, with half of the land set aside as a conservation area and bird sanctuary for migrating songbirds, ospreys, and wood storks. The subdivision includes four neighborhoods aimed at different price points. The largest homes will be in the Carolwood neighborhood, named after Walt's home in Holmby Hills, with each house sitting on a three-quarter acre. To enhance the value of the Carolwood neighborhood, the homes will feature water views or views of the golf course.

The Silverbrook neighborhood will feature homes set on one-half acre plots and will be closer to the Summerhouse, which is a private clubhouse for the exclusive use of the residents. The smallest neighborhood is called Kimball Trace, named after the famous animator and railfan. These homes are also closer to the Summerhouse and sit on one-quarter–acre lots. The final neighborhood, Marceline, named after the city in Missouri where Walt spent part of his childhood, has mid-sized homes and two parks.

Walt's vision for EPCOT was a community where the car was not essential. The Golden Oak subdivision is completely the opposite. The land use plan is an example of upscale suburban sprawl and—certainly by Walt's standards—a giant step backward.

Chapter Ten

New York

With the success of Disneyland and the positive impact that the park had on Anaheim's local economy, Walt had no shortage of suitors for a sequel—but, as we know, Walt did not like to repeat himself. There had to be an ever-new challenge. Although he started the next leg of his life's journey in New York, it was not long before Walt landed in Florida.

By 1960, the American Broadcasting Network (ABC) contract to broadcast *Disneyland* and other Disney-produced television shows was about to expire. The weekly show had premiered in 1954 and was hosted by Walt himself; ABC's cash and loan guarantees had made the Disneyland project possible. In exchange, ABC owned a significant piece of the theme park. Fortunately, the ABC deal included a clause that would allow Walt to buy ABC's share of Disneyland at cost. Walt took advantage of that clause and started to look for a better broadcasting and financial arrangement.

In his search for a new deal, one of Walt's first stops was at the National Broadcasting Company (NBC). When Walt first approached NBC in the early 1950s for money to fund Disneyland, the network turned him down. But things had changed over the succeeding years. At a Monday morning meeting in June 1959, the Disney team made a presentation to Robert Sarnoff, the head of NBC and—since the Radio Corporation of America (RCA) owned NBC—a leading advocate of color television. Never afraid of exploring the possibilities of new entertainment technologies, Walt understood the merits of color television. Once again, he would be ahead of the pack. Even though the early *Disneyland* programs were broadcast in black and white, Walt made sure from the start that the shows were produced in color in anticipation of new technologies.

Not only was Sarnoff enthusiastic about the television program, he also wanted to build an East Coast Disneyland in the New York area. The broadcasting network would help finance the park, just as ABC had done for the West Coast park, but Sarnoff in exchange wanted to own a piece of the new theme park—permanently. There would be no escape clause in the NBC contract. Walt was not so sure that he and his brother would benefit from adding another partner.

NBC hired SRI—Buzz Price's employer when he performed the first Disneyland site studies in the early 1950s—to conduct a feasibility study. The results of the SRI study made the project look like a win-win for everybody.

Naturally, Walt wanted to conduct his own study and turned to Price, who had founded his own company, ERA, in 1958. The ERA report was not so favorable to the project.

Price determined that year-round operation would be unfeasible in the New York climate. Traditionally, amusement parks operate about 120 days a year, the likely limit for a park in the northeast. Walt had learned from his California experience that operating all year maximized the investment in the facility and allowed him to build a professional staff.

The ERA study also showed that the New York tourism market was significantly different than the market on the West Coast or in Florida. Travelers were typically in New York on business, rather than for pleasure, and the duration of their trips tended to be short. Relatively few travelers came as tourists, so the park's market would be more dependent on local interest. Walt's impression of New York was, "That city is different. Its tourism is different."

Another factor was the lack of adequate sites. By the mid twentieth century, New York was a well-built-up region; large acreages of virgin land did not exist. Walt knew from the Anaheim experience that he not only needed a large site for the project, he needed significant acreage to buffer the park from adjacent development or the surrounding neighborhood. Whatever parcels could be cobbled together through public and private means would come at a very high price. Walt did not want to repeat the California mistake of too little land.

Walt's choice was clear: New York presented a number of problems, including the climate, the lack of affordable land, the nature of the tourism market, and the political environment. The New York project would not be good for Disney—a conclusion that was further validated by a different project, Freedomland, a short-lived history-based theme park in the Bronx financed by real estate developer William Zeckendorf. Freedomland opened in 1960—about the time Walt was exploring his own New York project—but was undercapitalized from the start, and it was closed in 1964. It was clear from the Freedomland experience that Walt had made the right choice to move on to Florida.[30]

---

30   Only 30 minutes from Times Square by subway, Freedomland's site plan was based on the map of the United States. It had 35 attractions, including an old-fashioned stern wheeler steam ship, a stage coach ride, a steam train, and a re-creation of the 1871 Chicago Fire where guests could participate by helping to put out the flames. There was the Tucson Mine Ore Car, which was an attraction similar to the Disneyland Skyway. C.V. Wood, Walt's construction manager for Disneyland, built Freedomland. Walt and Wood had had a falling out, and Walt fired him in 1956. Wood had by that time become well known because of his

Palm Beach

With New York but a memory, Walt traveled on to explore other possibilities. It took little time for another player to enter the picture, in the form of billionaire John D. MacArthur, and the Disney–NBC–RCA deal to build an East Coast Disneyland began to rise like the phoenix. More importantly, the project requirements demanded that Walt and his team create something that would not be a sequel to Anaheim. He would get a chance to solve the property adjacency issues that plagued Disneyland, because he would control what happened on the border. To accomplish this, Walt would become a city builder and surround his park with a new, futuristic community—a town of his own design that reflected his standards. Let's travel along with Walt to see what actually happened.

In 1959, MacArthur decided he wanted to develop 5000-6000 acres he owned north of Palm Beach for "a recreational enterprise". MacArthur had made his fortune as head of Banker's Life Insurance and RCA. The Palm Beach project would have been a four-way deal among Disney, NBC, RCA, and MacArthur.

Buzz Price was tasked to study the project. From Price's recollections, we can see that Walt was clearly pursuing his dream to build a community. "We put our effort together with WED in determining what kind of an interrelated park and city could be developed on that site. Walt wanted to emphasize future development in urban living. The park would take up 400 acres. A town base of 70,000 people would take up the rest." The ERA study looked to incorporate "advanced concepts of architectural design and technological improvements...in all phases of the town development". For this project, Walt first used the name EPCOT (Experimental Prototype Community of Tomorrow).

The project was to include an East Coast Disneyland, and the theme park would be part of a planned community. According to Price, the Palm Beach project represented the moment that Walt got fully obsessed by the idea of building a city. Walt saw an opportunity to do something truly grand; to take advantage of this golden opportunity, he began to learn more about urban planning.

You may recall that this notion of creating a city was not new to Walt. As early as 1957, Walt was toying with the idea of a City of the Arts,

---

contributions to Disneyland, and he used that notoriety to build other theme parks around the country. Part of the financial strain was the cost of doing business in the New York metropolitan area. Wood said that he had two working disbursement windows, "one for the staff payroll and one for building inspectors."

a community where artists would live, work, and play. He believed in this idea so strongly that he had a study commissioned in 1958. At the time, the idea grew and became CalArts. Palm Beach was to be a much larger project than CalArts. Walt already knew the proven formula for a family-based entertainment destination. He not only knew it, he had created it. The new theme park would incorporate all the best lessons from Disneyland, it would be bigger, and it would function even more effectively. Most important to Walt, he would get a chance to control the environment around his theme park. Nothing would be left to chance. Walt could design and build the surrounding community to his exacting standards. Building a city was just the kind of challenge Walt was looking for. This was not a sequel. This was a new production.

As the project grew, so did the demand for more land—and with it the need to justify a bigger investment. Price easily found the justification in his market research. Early in 1959, Price delivered to Disney a feasibility study that looked favorably on the Florida tourism market. On December 14, 1959, Price delivered another study for the Palm Beach project that solidified the justification. The study was described as "an economic and physical master plan for the City of Tomorrow at Palm Beach, Florida on 12,000 acres", and Price concluded that the "area offers a theme park attendance potential which equals or exceeds that experienced by Disneyland in southern California".

The study stated that an East Coast theme park would have no negative impact on the West Coast Disneyland. Price reported that "...Disneyland, in Anaheim—for all of its high penetration in the available southern California tourism—had a low rate of penetration each year in the Eastern populations". While Disneyland's market penetration in southern California was in excess of 25% in 1959, the penetration from East Coast markets was very, very low. Although awareness of the park was high due to the *Disneyland* television program, only 1% of residents in the Atlantic and New England states, 1.7% in the Great Lakes area, and 0.6% in the Southern markets had made the trek to the west coast. At the time, travel across the continent was neither easy nor inexpensive. Always working the numbers, Price determined that two-thirds of the U. S. population lived east of the Mississippi River, and it would take 100 years to saturate the market at the pace of the early 1960s. There was a huge opportunity to reach new guests with an East Coast park.

The Palm Beach prospect provided Walt an excuse to take a driving tour of Florida. He loved to go on car trips in any event; and after the Palm Beach excursion, he was even more convinced that the area held promise. As Walt had mentioned in 1959 to a reporter at the *Miami Herald*, "Florida would be better than California in many ways."

According to Buzz Price, Walt learned from MacArthur how to make beautiful lakes in Florida. During a visit to MacArthur's home, MacArthur had insisted that Walt and Price join him in one of his passions: skinny-dipping in one of his lakes. Walt declined but watched from the shore. Price said, "MacArthur then gave us a lecture on how you get that crystal clear water in the lakes of Florida, relating it to sand bottoms on the clean lakes and their percolating and filtering action. It sounded like a manageable technology and Walt was fascinated." Years later, the technology would be applied to the black water of Orlando's Bay Lake, and it led to the miracle of white sand beaches at the Walt Disney World resorts.

Even with the partners' enthusiasm and the strong market research, the Palm Beach project never made it past the study phase. RCA came on hard times, and there were contract issues between Roy Disney and MacArthur. There was a breakdown in the negotiations, and the deal fell through. By this point, only Walt was excited by the project, and his enthusiasm alone was not sufficient.

Still, Florida was now at the top of Walt's mind, and his dream would not die. He asked Price to conduct further studies, one in 1961 and another in 1963. A small group of Disney executives began to secretly look for locations on the East Coast. The primary focus was on central Florida, where the team was looking for five to ten thousand acres. Ocala and Orlando counties were prime candidates; it was in the second set of studies that the Orlando area rose to prominence in Walt's vision.

Chapter Eleven

On Location

One benefit of running a movie studio is the opportunity to travel. Walt frequently took advantage of visiting the sets of his live-action films when the production was on location. Always curious, Walt was frequently inspired by his trips abroad, and he brought back ideas that he would later integrate into Disneyland and his other projects. The trips expanded his vision; they got him away from the stress at the studio and gave him a chance to travel, to observe, and to think. Frequently, he would see something that would spark his imagination, and this in turn would result in new project ideas.

In 1958, Walt went to Switzerland to see the progress on the film *Third Man on the Mountain*. The film crew was working in Zermatt, a ski town where automobiles were banned and visitors arrived by train. The resort had both winter and summer activities, a rare feat for most ski resorts at that time. He was so inspired that he returned with not just one but two incredible concepts for his Imagineers. First, he wanted to build his own mountain—but it was not to be just a big pile of dirt. Walt wanted to build a scale model of the world-famous Matterhorn. Not only that, he wanted the Disneyland Matterhorn to contain his park's first real thrill attraction: an action-packed bobsled ride inside the mountain. His second idea was far grander: an all-season mountain resort. Had it come to fruition, it would have been even more revolutionary.

When Disneyland opened, there was a big mountain of dirt next to Sleeping Beauty Castle called Holiday Hill. The hill was created by fill when the construction crew dug out the moat in front of the castle. In 1956, the tower for the Skyway gondola was built on Holiday Hill. Although the operations folks at Disneyland had long thought a thrill ride would be a good addition to the park, they had tried nearly in vain to convince Walt of its merit; while he had early given the green light to making the Casey Jr. Circus Train the first rollercoaster at Disneyland, that idea ultimately did not work out. However, Walt's trip to Switzerland inspired him to think about ways he could use Holiday Hill. Would it be possible to reproduce the famous mountain and install a bobsled ride inside? That would be a fun experience and something you could not find anywhere else.

His team went to work to design, engineer, and build a 1/100th scale model of the Matterhorn right next to Sleeping Beauty Castle. The man-made mountain rose to 147 feet. Winding inside was the world's first two steel tube roller coasters. The use of tubular steel tracks would forever change the amusement park business; every steel coaster can trace its roots right back to the Matterhorn. As a bonus, Walt would finally be able to hide the unattractive Skyway support tower; the Skyway gondolas would travel right through the Matterhorn. In the end, Walt would be literally king of the mountain! The Matterhorn was the largest structure in Orange County at the time—a spectacular new icon for his guests that they could find nowhere else.

Winter Sports

Walt's trip to Switzerland also reignited an interest in winter sports, and he began to consider how to make winter activities more accessible. This renewed interest led to his participation in the VIII Olympic Winter Games, held in 1960 in Squaw Valley, California (near Lake Tahoe). As the chairman of Pageantry, Walt was responsible for the opening and closing ceremonies, which were a huge hit and which gave Walt the opportunity to experience how to present the best entertainment experience in winter weather conditions.

The success of the Winter Olympics kicked off a huge boom in the North American ski industry. Walt was intrigued with the idea of developing a mountain village in the United States that had all of the positive qualities of Zermatt. He knew that his experiences creating Disneyland could be applied to make his mountain village even better than Zermatt. He was very excited about building this retreat; as always, he turned to Buzz Price to look for possible locations.

Walt was not just being a dreamer. There were practical reasons for developing a ski resort. In the early 1960s—a time when most people traveled only in the summer and would never think to remove their child from school for a vacation to Disneyland—the off-peak winter season was very slow at Disneyland. The park would be busy all summer long, but very quiet other times of the year. A ski resort could balance the Disney portfolio, and it would generate considerable revenues when Disneyland was not busy. Freelance writer Peter Browning said, "The construction of a huge tourist resort" was "hardly a step at all. Rather it has been a natural linear progression: from cartoons to 'live' films; thence to the imitation of life cum amusement park at Disneyland; from there to the imitation more real than reality, the new, self-contained Disney World in Florida, a Tomorrowland with a vengeance."

The search for the perfect location for an all-season mountain village began. Price first looked on the north slope of Mt. San Gorgonio in southern California. Topping out at over 11,000-feet, the mountain had many advantages, including a gigantic north-facing bowl and proximity to both the Palm Springs community and Walt's vacation home at the Smoke Tree Ranch. The mountain was also a prime hiking location for the Boy Scouts of America, who surely would not give it up without a struggle. Walt decided to look elsewhere.

After conducting a study much like the one he did for Disneyland, Price recommended Mammoth Mountain. The location seemed ideal, so Walt entered negotiations with Andrew Hurley, who owned the Mammoth resort, and the McCoy family, who managed the ski slopes. All of the parties were close to signing a deal when, at the last minute, Hurley and the McCoys pulled out due to what they considered to be a lack of equity in the project. Once again, Price renewed his search for a good location.

Deep within the Sierra Nevada Mountains of California is a 15,000-acre sliver of land surrounded on three sides by the Sequoia National Park. Known as Mineral King, the area was a mining camp in 1873; when it went bust in 1882, Mineral King became a ghost town. Over time, with the lack of activity, nature started to reclaim the valley. When Sequoia was established as the country's second national park in 1890, Mineral King was not included in the boundaries; in 1908, the area was put under the jurisdiction of the United States Forest Service, and by the 1920s it was used as a summer camp and recreational area. The Sequoia National Park boundaries were expanded frequently over the years, but Mineral King was excluded due to the earlier development activities. Instead, it became part of the Sequoia Game Refuge—an important detail later in this story.

The resort area is located in an alpine terrain and at high altitude. In 1948, the Sierra Club became the first organization to recommend the area as suitable for a ski resort. In 1949, the Forest Service invited bids to develop the area. By 1953, a recommendation was made to make the area more accessible.

The conditions for a resort were ideal: Mineral King was an oval-shaped basin with three huge bowls, five-mile runs, and a five-thousand-foot drop. The area gave the State of California an opportunity to partner with the federal government to create a new winter recreational area—just the type of challenge that Walt was looking for. He could apply what he had learned at Disneyland and his experiences at Zermatt and create a new type of mountain retreat. Not only was this an exciting project, it was a way to redefine our relationship to the wilderness. The project became very near to his heart.

A Year-Round Ski Resort

In February 1965, the Forest Service released an updated prospectus with a development plan calling for overnight accommodations for 100 people, parking for 1,700 automobiles, and lifts with a capacity of 2,000 people per hour. The Forest Service awarded the contract to Disney in December. The original 30-year lease was for 80 acres with year-to-year leases on 300 acres. The development permit was for three years and authorized Disney to conduct survey and draft plans.

Buzz Price conducted multiple studies for Disney to determine the viability of the $35 million Mineral King ski and tourist project. The resort would have been a joint venture between Disney and the United States Forest Service, who had planned to lease the land to Walt Disney Productions with the expectation that Disney would develop the area with resorts like nearby Mammoth Mountain and Aspen and Vail (Colorado), and Sun Valley (Idaho). Walt Disney Productions was determined to position the Mineral King resort as a family-friendly destination, with ice skating, tobogganing, and sleigh and dogsled rides. The goal was to create a ski resort with a wide variety of activities that would appeal to all kinds of visitors. By targeting families, the resort would be set apart from the other ski areas in California.

Attracting overnight family visitors was given high priority. One study showed that because of this priority, Mineral King could realize higher spending per capita than other ski resorts.[31] Forecasters also predicted that the population growth would remain incredibly high in the southern California region, with a correspondingly high demand for locally accessible recreational areas. Mineral King was 271 miles from San Francisco and only 228 miles from Los Angeles.

Camping and skiing were recognized as increasingly popular recreational activities; since California had a lot of forests that held snow, this was considered a good thing for the state. Mineral King is located in an area that would be very attractive to residents of southern California. Although there were several ski resorts located in the San Bernardino Mountains near Los Angeles, Mineral King—with its more reliable snowfall—would be a bigger magnet for southern California skiers. As an ideal camping location as well, Mineral King was a prime candidate for full-year operation.

Forecasters also thought the property would be attractive to out-of-state guests. Research had shown that out-of-state visitors were strongly drawn to California because of the Sierra Nevada Mountains. One publication by the State of California reported that the mountains are "a topographic feature not duplicated in mountain ranges east of the Rockies". This included

---

31 Many years later, the Walt Disney Company would use this same strategy to enter the cruise line business. In spite of the ultimate outcome at Mineral King, that arm of Disney has proven to be very successful.

the extremely popular Yosemite, Sequoia, and Kings Canyon National Parks, which are located in the Sierra Nevada Mountains. In fact, initial projections claimed that the Disney resort would become as popular as Yosemite. Overcrowding would be more of a concern than lack of visitors; but just like the theme parks, the resort could be closed to additional visitors if it got overcrowded.

Walt knew there was another important benefit to year-round operation: a full-year facility could afford to develop a professional workforce. This had been a concern when Disney looked east for its next theme park project. Walt had always valued the contributions of his professional staff; he was reluctant to build a project that would be staffed primarily by less-committed seasonal workers.

Unlike Anything Else in America

Had it come to fruition, Walt's vision for the Mineral King resort would have created a first-rate development. Thornton Ladd and John Kelsey were selected as architects, with Marvin Davis providing direction. The designer for the ski facilities was Willie Schaeffler, a German-American skiing champion who worked on the 1960 Squaw Valley Winter Olympics; his innovative proposals included a trail system that used fourteen ski lifts.

Although the Mineral King development was originally intended to address winter recreational needs, Walt's vision included a full complement of activities to attract summer visitors. In fact, it was anticipated that 60 percent of visitors would come during the summer months, and the resort would make more money during the summer than in the winter—highly unusual for a skiing destination. To accomplish Walt's vision, the team's approach was to design a summer resort that had winter uses. For example, the ski lifts would operate in the summer and take people to trails and fishing lakes. Activities would be at all price points and would include cave exploration and wilderness lectures by Donald Duck. A showcase restaurant at the top of the lift would feature dances and entertainment. Other attractions would include a conference center as well as Disneyland-type attractions such as the Country Bear Jamboree.[32]

Disney's Mineral King resort would be much larger than the original program set forth by the Forest Service. The resort would be able to handle up to 14,000 visitors within the small valley. The "American Alpine" village would have two hotels—one deluxe and the other moderately priced—plus

---

32 Now at The Magic Kingdom, but originally designed for the Mineral King resort.

a dormitory for Cast Members. The plans called for accommodations for 7,200 people: 2,400 beds in permanent structures and an additional 4,800 beds in temporary structures. To support all of these guests and Cast Members, the resort would feature up to ten restaurants that covered the entire price spectrum. That number would grow to thirteen by the resort's fifth year of operation. A sandwich shop was proposed for the Midway Gondola Terminal 1,400 feet above the valley floor on Miner's Ridge.

There would be a wide variety of activities, including horseback riding, tennis, and swimming. Other facilities would include a hospital, an equestrian center, a gas station, a chapel, a power station, and an ice skating rink.

All of these activities would be contained in a high-density, compact, pedestrian-oriented village. The site plan was designed to minimize the impact on the surrounding valley. The three- to four-story buildings would be heavily themed and integrated into an Alpine village environment. Throughout the village, the architecture would resemble a Swiss chalet. There would be buildings with pitched roofs facing a "Main Street" with a protected plaza between the buildings. This would have created a very intimate and welcoming space, similar to Main Street, U.S.A. at Disneyland.

Walt said at the time, "When we go into a new project, we believe in it all the way. That's the way we feel about Mineral King. We have every faith that our plans will provide recreational opportunities for everyone. All of us promise that our effort now and in the future will be dedicated to making Mineral King grow to meet the ever-increasing public need. I guess you might say that it won't ever be finished." Of course, he famously said the same thing about Disneyland.

Access

Walt wanted to create a transition from the real world to this fantasy mountain village. At Disneyland, he used the tunnels under the railroad tracks; for the Mineral King resort, he proposed an access that was so unique it would become an attraction in itself. Automobile access would be limited and most guests would take a train from a large parking structure down in the valley. Visitors would park in a 3,600-stall parking structure that would soar eight to ten stories. Then they would take a "colorful excursion train" and slowly transcend the side of the mountain the last two-and-a-half miles until it stopped at a central station at the heart of the Mineral King resort. The automobile would become secondary to the visitor experience, just as it had at Disneyland. With this proposal, Walt was not only incorporating an approach that had been very successful Disneyland, he was also capturing a part of his wondrous experience in Zermatt, Switzerland.

One of the ways to raise operating revenues is to charge an admission to enter the resort area; at Mineral King, that would mean charging an admission to ride the train. Walt had ERA study the viability of a train and to research attendance patterns at other national parks. When they compared the costs of entering those facilities by car with the overall cost of using the train, the ERA researchers found that the resort would make substantially more money if they eliminated or severely restricted the automobile and provided train access only. The train option would have had the least impact on the resort facilities, and it was Walt's preference. The train had other benefits as well. The mix of visitors would skew more toward overnight visitors, and it was well known that they tend to spend more money per capita than day guests. Plus, something like an old-fashioned Cog stream train would become an attraction in its own right. There had even been talk about installing a monorail system.

One alternative included keeping the all-season highway as an alternative way to enter the resort, but it would require substantial improvements in order to expand the highway's low capacity. However, the study determined that this would threaten the viability of the fixed-rail system. When studies showed that the road was just not large enough, the highway was annexed into the California Department of Transportation (Caltrans) system, and in 1965, the state legislature approved a $30 million upgrade program. The next step in the process would be to widen and straighten the access road. Approvals for the project and the roadway were in place by December 1967.

Walt had died a year earlier, but Disney moved forward with the project. Disney hoped to have the first phase of the resort open by 1973 and fully completed by 1976. The initial estimate for the project was $35 million. Beyond the transportation network and the construction of the village, other infrastructure costs included the construction of dams on the mountainside to prevent debris from washing down into the valley, as well as the parking garage. The design for the project was considered so innovative that Walt and his team had won an American Forestry Association award for "Outstanding Service in Conservation of American Resources" in 1966. But Disney faced obstacles that even the best designers in the world could not overcome.

The Sierra Club

Although the Sierra Club first suggested Mineral King as an excellent place for a ski resort—and, ironically, had given Walt a citation to honor his wildlife films in 1955—they did not favor the Disney project. In 1972, the Sierra Club decided to contest the project; when the United States Forest

Service refused to hold public hearings, the Sierra Club filed the now-famous federal lawsuit (*Sierra Club v Rogers Clark Ballard Morton, Secretary of the Interior, et al.*) to stop the project.

The Sierra Club attorneys argued that the United States Forest Service did not follow its own rules with regard to lease terms. The organization reminded the court that roadways built within national parks, forests, and game refuges were meant to be limited in size and were intended for travel within the park; they were not to provide access links from one external destination to another. Since the access road had to cross through the national park property before entering Mineral King, it did not comply with the rules. The Sierra Club further argued that the size and scope of the Disney proposal were incompatible with the goals of a national game refuge—you will recall that Mineral King had been part of the Sequoia Game Refuge since 1926. The district court found the Sierra Club's arguments sufficiently substantial to justify a preliminary injunction against the project.

Disney and the government challenged the Sierra Club's legal standing to sue. The Sierra Club argued that as a conservation membership corporation, it did have standing to sue to protect the national parks, forests, and game refuges; if they didn't have standing, they asked the court, "then who speaks for the future generations for whose benefit Congress intended the fragile Sierra bowls and valleys to be preserved?" Although the district court had agreed that the Sierra Club had standing, the appellate court did not. However, the Sierra Club did not give up, and the case went all the way to the United States Supreme Court.

The Supreme Court determined that the Sierra Club did not have standing before the court on this issue, but the ruling kept the door open to the Sierra Club's filing an amended lawsuit, which is what the Sierra Club did. At the same time, the National Environmental Policy Act (NEPA), passed in 1970, adding requirements for environmental impact studies. As the case dragged on and more studies were completed, the project was scaled back by half. As the two sides prepared for another round in court, Disney declared it would not pay for the roadway improvements, and the state decided they would not pay for the upgrade either. After all of this effort, Disney determined that the Mineral King project was financially infeasible, and abandoned the development. The area was finally annexed into the National Park in 1978.

Critics and Fans

Mineral King had its share of critics, and they were pleased to see the project's demise. In *The Animated Man*, Walt Disney biographer Michael

Barrier was critical of the Mineral King project, calling it "a highly dubious use of a fragile valley". Peter Browning felt that the project's fatal flaw would be visitors who "will make the trip simply because it is there to be made; it will be a nice-day jaunt". Browning added, "Many would not make the drive if there was nothing at the end of the road." He suggests that the major attraction was not the Mineral King Valley but rather a Disney resort, and that resort "could just as well be located in the Mojave Desert or Los Angeles".

Buzz Price disagreed with Barrier and Browning's assessments. Price said, "Like everyone who had worked on this stunning project, we believed that Mineral King would have been the greatest winter resort in the world bar none." Speaking at Disneyland '55: A Birthday Celebration, a 2010 event at the Walt Disney Family Museum, Dick Nunis—who since the early 1970s had been part of the Disney leadership, including chairman of Walt Disney Attractions and a member of the Walt Disney Company's Board of Directors—echoed Price's sentiments. Nunis believed the Mineral King project would have redefined what a wilderness retreat could be, and it would have been a great year-round family attraction.

Some key concepts from the Mineral King project resurfaced many years later in an update to the National Park Service's draft Yosemite Valley Master Plan, released in November 2000. The plan shared Walt's desire to reduce automobile traffic, encourage walking and bicycling opportunities, and minimize the impacts on sensitive natural habitats. The Yosemite Valley Plan called for the construction of three new parking lots outside the valley and linked to a system of shuttle buses to bring in day guests. Overnight guests would still be able to drive to their accommodations, but the amount of land dedicated to parking would be reduced from 1,600 parking stalls to 550. The plans also proposed the removal of a 3.2-mile section of Northside Drive, a major thoroughfare through the valley floor, and replace it with a paved foot and bike trail. All in all, more than 180 acres would be restored to a natural state. Much of the 2000 plan has yet to be implemented due to significant reductions in the National Park's operating budget.

William Tweed of the Sequoia Parks Foundation wrote, "There can be little doubt that the wild plants and animals of Mineral King are better off today than had the area been developed, but let's not focus there. Instead, let's consider our larger community…in summary, if Mineral King had been developed, Tulare County would be more extensively urbanized, and Visalia would look more like Fresno." Would this be a good thing? In the absence of hard data, the answer probably depends upon how you look at the issue.

Independence Lake

Mineral King was not the only site on Disney's radar. According to Alpine Meadows operator Peter Kalussen, "Walt Disney was an avid skier who had helped start Sugar Bowl. He wanted very much to build a Disney-style ski resort somewhere in California. He first looked at Mineral King in Sequoia National Park, but then discovered the Independence Lake area." Kalussen outlined some of the benefits of building at Independence Lake. "The Sierra Pacific Land Company privately owned most of the area; it was a company [Kalussen] knew well. Having the land privately owned was a huge enticement because, as a result, federal permits weren't needed to develop the property."

Independence Lake is north of the City of Truckee near the 10,000-foot Mt. Lola. Because the north side of the lake is a protected flat area, Walt seemed to think that the location was ideal for a ski resort, and he hired Willy Schaeffler to look at the property to determine its viability. Kalussen helped in that survey. Kalussen reported that "[i]t had all the makings of a tremendous resort. Everything funneled back to the lake." The site had perfect conditions for all levels of the sport; Schaeffler and Kalussen identified intermediate and beginner slopes. Independence Lake could be a year-round operation like the vision for Mineral King.

After Walt's death, the ski resort concept was still considered viable by his successors. When Disney abandoned the Mineral King project, they entered into an agreement with the Southern Pacific Land Company and Sierra Pacific Power Company to develop a resort at Independence Lake. However, Independence Lake ultimately suffered the same fate as Mineral King— environmental concerns brought about opposition to the project. By March 1978, that project was also shelved.

Chapter Twelve

The World's Fairs

A century before there was Disneyland, there were World's Fairs. Walt was influenced by World's Fairs, and he in turn influenced a number of these major global events. His experience with World's Fairs helped feed his interest and understanding of city planning; many elements of the Disney theme park experience are rooted in these spectacular temporary international events.

There have been more than 300 international fairs since the first one in London, England, in 1851. Of these fairs, 90 have been classified as major events according to the Bureau International des Expositions (BIE). The combined attendance at all of the World's Fairs is more than one billion people.

Any World's Fair represents the ultimate "invented place". The best of the fairs captured the public's imagination like no other event. Many times the ideas on display were so powerful that community leaders would return home and commit vast sums of money, political capital, and land to transform their cities to reflect the latest trends. The biggest influence on city design has been the World's Columbian Exposition of 1893 in Chicago. The civic centers of Pasadena, Indianapolis, Washington DC, San Francisco, and dozens of other cities are its direct legacy. Perhaps as a child, Walt heard inspiring stories from his father, who had worked as a carpenter at one of the fairs.

The first event that Walt participated in was the 1939 New York World's Fair. Disney produced *Mickey's Surprise Party* for the National Biscuit Company, known as Nabisco. This 5-minute, 13-second Technicolor short featured Mickey and the gang enjoying Nabisco products. The audience was entertained and enjoyed the air-conditioned comfort of the theater. Walt did not personally visit the New York fair, according to Paul Anderson, who has written the definitive history of Disney's participation at World's Fairs. Walt did, however, visit the 1939 Golden Gate International Exposition in San Francisco. There he first saw the Thorne Collection of miniature building interiors, one of the inspirations that led to Disneyland.

The 1958 Brussels World's Fair

The 1958 Brussels World's Fair in Belgium was the first major postwar fair and the first held after television became readily available to public viewers. The fair turned into a prestige economic development event and a chance to successfully project the image of the host country to the world. The United States Pavilion featured the Disney production of *America the Beautiful*, a 19-minute Circle-Vision 360 film.

The film used breakthrough camera and projection technology that was developed by Walt's long-time collaborator, Ub Iwerks. Jim Korkis describes the technology as "eleven 16mm Cine Kodak Special cameras with 200 feet of pre-threaded film magazines mounted on a circular rig. The drive shafts of all the cameras were linked mechanically by means of a single sprocket chain." The rig can be mounted on the top of an automobile or boat, or hung below a helicopter or airplane. When shown on eleven screens, the film captured the guests' imaginations and put them right in the middle of the action. The film was a hit and became one of the fair's major attractions.

The Brussels fair was a huge success and attracted more than 42 million people—more than both years of the 1939–1940 New York World's Fair combined. On the final day, the Brussels fair attracted more than 1,000,000 people. Perhaps more importantly to our story, it was at the Brussels fair that Walt Disney viewed the exhibit Industrial Parks USA, which would influence his thinking about EPCOT.

The 1962 Century 21 Exposition

The 1962 Seattle World's Fair was called Century 21 Exposition. The fair, which focused on science and technology, ran from April 21, 1962, to October 21, 1962, and was considered small by World's Fair standards. Despite its modest size, it was a big success.

The architectural icon for the fair was the Space Needle and the theme was science and technology—in fact, the Science Pavilion was the most-visited attraction at the fair. Inside the Science Pavilion, guests visited a model of the World of Tomorrow—a projection of what our lives would be like in the year 2000. In many ways, the model mirrored what Walt wanted to see happen at EPCOT. As depicted in the display, the city of the future is zoned in concentric rings, described as an "archery target". The City Center is a domed downtown, surrounded by a greenbelt. The industrial and residential neighborhoods are located at the edge of the development, complete with parks, farms, and recreation areas.

Automobiles are not allowed in the City Center of the future. High-speed monorails connect the residential areas to the city core. To demonstrate, the World's Fair organizers commissioned Alweg—the German company known for development of the Disneyland monorail system in 1959—to build a full-size monorail system on a one-mile beam that connected Seattle's downtown to the fairgrounds. The system had many operational issues and was not as sleek as the Disneyland model; Bob Gurr described it as "big and ugly". However, the monorail continues to operate today, delighting riders visiting Seattle.

The 1964–1965 New York World's Fair

In 1959, Walt learned of a proposal for a 1964 World's Fair in New York, on the same site as the landmark 1939–1940 fair in Flushing Meadows, Queens, just off the Grand Central Parkway between La Guardia Airport and Manhattan. He told his Imagineers, "There's going to be a big fair in New York. All of the big corporations in the country are going to be spending a helluva lot of money building exhibits there." Walt explained, "They won't know what they want to do. They won't even know why they're doing it, except that the other corporations are doing it and they have to keep up with the Joneses. Now, they're all going to want something that will stand out from the others, and that's the kind of service we can offer them." In *Inside the Dream*, Marty Sklar wrote, "The World's Fair was, in fact, a great opportunity for Walt. He saw something that none of us realized at the time." Walt told his team, "This is a great opportunity for us to grow. We can use their financing to develop a lot of technology that will help us in the future." A Disney presence at this fair would give the company a chance to explore a number of other challenges and opportunities.

Walt suggested another benefit. "We'll be getting new attractions for Disneyland, too," he told his team. "That'll appeal to them: we can say that they'll be getting shows that won't be seen for just two six-month periods at the Fair; those shows can go on for five or ten years at Disneyland." Participating in the fair would be a chance for Walt to test the East Coast market with Disneyland-style attractions. There was no fear that an East Coast Disneyland would cannibalize the original park, since most Disneyland visitors came from cities west of the Mississippi. Marty Sklar said, "Getting into the World's Fair was a trial balloon for Walt. He wanted to see if his kind of entertainment would appeal to the more sophisticated eastern audience—'sophisticated' in that that's where the nation's leaders, the decision–makers were based." In *Realityland*, Jack Lindquist said, "The eastern media just totally pooh-poohed [Disneyland]. It was the old Lalaland routine: '[W]e're too sophisticated. It'll never fly here.'"

The Eastern media were wrong. Walt's participation in the 1964–1965 New York World's Fair was a turning point for the Disney Company. The fair was a chance to challenge the Imagineers. Walt wanted to prove to the world that his crew was better than any other group of designers. He had the chance to use other corporations' money to conduct research and development while benefiting Disneyland. It was also a chance to test the WED Enterprises administration and operations people and see if they could gear up and implement another major project while maintaining the expansion of Disneyland. Success would increase Walt's confidence that his team could build "Project X", which would later become Walt Disney World. Sklar added, "The Fair was one of the great stepping stones to Walt Disney World."

WED designed, built, and installed four attractions: Great Moments with Mr. Lincoln for the State of Illinois, it's a small world for Pepsi-Cola, the Carousel of Progress for General Electric, and Magic Skyway sponsored by Ford. Another Disney touch was the 120-foot Tower of the Four Winds kinetic sculpture by Rolly Crump. Harper Goff designed the signature Unisphere, although he was not working for Disney at the time. The Unisphere also echoed the Perisphere from the 1939 New York World's Fair.

The WED attractions became the hit of the fair. In a Gallup poll that asked people which exhibits they would recommend, three of the top four were from Disney. The scale was ten for a strongly recommend to zero for attractions people could "just skip seeing". General Electric tied with the General Motors Futurama at 9.1. Ford was right behind at 8.9, and it's a small world was 8.1. The small capacity for Great Moments with Mr. Lincoln was the primary reason it did not score higher. When the fair closed, three of the four exhibits were disassembled, shipped back to Disneyland, and reassembled. The dinosaurs of Magic Skyway became the finale to the Disneyland Railroad.

However successful the Disney attractions were with the public, they were not necessarily a success with some critics. In *Walt Disney: The Triumph of the American Imagination*, Neal Gabler noted that architectural educator Vincent Scully[33] was not impressed with the Disney attractions or, for that matter, with Disney's enthusiastic audience. Scully accused Walt to be a man who "so vulgarizes everything he touches that facts lose all force, living things their stature, and the 'history of the world' its meaning. Disney caters to the kind of phony reality—mostly horribly exemplified by the moving and talking figure of Lincoln elsewhere in the fair—that we all too readily accept in place of the true. Mr. Disney, I'm afraid, has our number."

Some 30 years later, Scully was still cautious about the impact of Disney's influence on the built environment. In an essay he wrote, "When you 'wish upon a star' you die like everybody else. This is a fundamental problem

---

33 Not to be confused with another mid-century southern California "landmark", sportscaster Vin Scully.

for Disney, dealing with American wish fulfillment—always, like it or not, the very stuff of dreams—as [Disney] invariably does." In *Building a Dream*, Beth Dunlop wrote, "There was a time, of course, when the name 'Disney' was considered little more than a pejorative term in the realm of architecture, a synonym for fake or cute."

In the end, Walt did achieve his objectives. He was now confident that his type of entertainment would work on the East Coast. He got a bunch of new attractions for Disneyland. He got other people to pay for his research and development, which created technologies like Audio-Animatronics—electronically controlled figures that act out motions that come from a series of signals on magnetic tapes. The corporations also paid for the development of high-capacity ride systems, including the boat systems for it's a small world, and a revolving theater. The fair produced the basic technology that would be used for the WEDway PeopleMover; Walt knew the PeopleMover would be a critical transportation system for his own city when the time came.

Highways in the Sky

The Monorail

One of the earliest sketches for Disneyland was Herb Ryman's proposed entrance to Tomorrowland; in the sketch, the entrance is framed by organically shaped buildings on the left and right, and a monorail hanging from a track. From the beginning, Walt was very interested in building a "highway in the sky" for his park.

In June 1958, Walt was on vacation with his wife, Lillian, and they visited the small mountain town of Wuppertal in Germany. Much to Walt's delight, there was a monorail train that had been operating for more than fifty years. The track rested on pylons built along the banks of a river. The train was suspended from the track and hung freely. It was like the one in the Tomorrowland drawing. As a railfan with "high iron" in his blood, Walt had to go for a ride. Although Walt liked the ride, Lillian did not care for the way it swayed back and forth during the curves. She became ill.

Later in the trip, Walt and Lillian were driving north along a major roadway near Cologne, Germany, when a monorail train suddenly crossed over their heads. This monorail was very different from the one in Wuppertal. This train rode on top of a steel-reinforced concrete beam. Walt was stunned. He wanted to learn more, so he drove right to the administrative building and asked for help. He learned that the Alweg Corporation, owned and named after the wealthy Dr. Axel Wenner Gren, was testing the monorail.

The company had been working on monorails since 1949. Walt was very excited because he had finally found his monorail for Disneyland.

Walt sent Joe Fowler and Roger Broggie to inspect the train and to report back. Both were impressed and felt it would fit right in at Disneyland. Joseph Corn said, "Being smaller than normal railroads, monorails would also lend a more human scale to the future." Roger Broggie and Bob Gurr modified the suspension technology so that the trains could climb the maximum grades and make it through tight turning radii. Not only did they want to showcase the technology, they also wanted to provide an interesting ride.

At first, the monorail trains were going to be built in Mannheim, Germany. However, due to the time it would take to ship the trains to Disneyland and other issues, it was decided to have Standard Carriage Works in Los Angeles build the Mark I version. In order to speed up the manufacture of the two monorails, construction was soon moved to Stage 3 at the Burbank studio. Gurr described the German trains as a "loaf of bread". As the train was built, Gurr significantly transformed the ugly box into a streamlined, bullet-shaped rocket like the ones he remembered from Buck Rogers films. As most things within Disneyland, the trains are 5/8th scale models.

Less than a year transpired between Walt's first sighting of the German monorail flying overhead and the televised grand opening at Disneyland.[34] In that short time span, the Imagineers engineered a functional suspension system, designed a beautiful train, installed the track, and tested the system so that it would be safe for the millions of passengers who would soon be riding.

Like the steam locomotives that circled the park, Walt personally owned the monorail through his company called Retlaw (Walter spelled backwards). One benefit for Walt of this arrangement, according to Michael Broggie, was his ability to "put on his bib overalls and kerchief, and go wait for the next train. When the train arrived, [Walt] would climb into the cab and tell the engineer [to take a] break." Since everybody at Retlaw was on Walt's own payroll, they did as the boss told them.

The attraction opened on June 14, 1959, and was originally called the Disneyland Alweg Monorail System. The initial track was a winding 0.8-mile loop. The Disneyland monorail became the first daily operating monorail in the western hemisphere—and the first to cross a public street when, in 1961, the beamway was extended to a total length of 2.5 miles and a station was built at the Disneyland Hotel. With a second stop, the theme park ride had transformed into a practical transportation system.

---

34 The grand opening featured Richard Nixon, Vice President of the United States, and family. The first Disneyland Monorail pilot was Disney Legend Bob Gurr.

Disney continually upgraded the technology, and soon the Mark II and Mark III versions of the monorail were in service. A major styling change came in 1987 with the introduction of the Mark V model. Instead of looking like Buck Rodgers, the trains resembled executive Learjets. In 2008, Disney introduced the retro-looking Mark VII model. The Disneyland system was granted a National Historic Mechanical Engineering Landmark rating by the American Society of Mechanical Engineers in December 1986.

When Walt Disney World opened, they had their own exclusive trains called the Mark IV. These trains featured air conditioning, and were wider and longer than the Disneyland trains. The Orlando trains were upgraded to the Mark VI model in 1989.

Although Walt was always interested in a monorail for Tomorrowland, he may have also been motivated to "one up" a major competitor. In 1956, CBS partnered with the Los Angeles Turf Club, owned by Charles Stubb, on a $10 million project to redevelop Pacific Ocean Park in Santa Monica. Inspired by the success of Disneyland,. the two companies hired set designers and ride system companies to develop a theme park over the ocean. The project was an immediate hit, and more people visited Pacific Ocean Park in 1958 than went to Disneyland. Never satisfied, Walt knew his team could do something that would top the competition. He said, "I can never stand still. I must explore and experiment." In 1959, the monorail brought the visitors back to Disneyland.

The Los Angeles region always had a thing for monorails. In 1953, the Los Angeles County Metropolitan Transit Authority (LAMTA) showed the alignment[35] for a 45.7-mile route for a monorail from Long Beach to Panorama City along the Los Angeles River. The trains would have been suspended below the tracks like the ones in Germany. An alternate plan was proposed in 1960, just one year after Walt's demonstration model at Disneyland. This system would have covered 74.9 miles, with 51 miles of beam overhead, 21.6 miles at grade, and 2.3 miles in tunnels. This system would have cost $529 million. This project was too ambitious and was scaled back to 22.7 miles, with 12 miles in a subway under Wilshire Boulevard, at a cost of $192 million. Monorail advocates argued that a side benefit to the project was the construction of a multi-mile bomb shelter. Officials were so confident that the project would be funded that they held a public groundbreaking in downtown Los Angeles and Beverly Hills in 1962. However, the funding did not materialize, and the project went nowhere.

Author Ray Bradbury was also a big fan of monorail technology. Bradbury tried to encourage the City of Los Angeles to build a system. He formed

---

35 The "alignment" for a transportation project is the path of the vehicle.

a citizen's group called Save Rapid Transit and Improve Metropolitan Environments. He had admired the multi-modal and successful transit network in San Francisco and thought a layered system like that would work in Los Angeles. He said, "Look, the psychology of the monorail is what makes it superior. First of all, it's not an elevated like the old trains in Chicago. It's up in the air, but it doesn't make noise…you hardly hear it." Bradbury added, "The important thing is that it's above the traffic, and would glide past the traffic."

The Alweg Monorail Company agreed with Bradbury on the merits of the technology and proposed a demonstration system for Los Angeles. After the success of the system at Disneyland and the experience gained at the 1962 Seattle Century 21 Exposition, Alweg was looking for a way to expand the business. So, on June 4, 1963, Sixten Holmquist, President of the Alweg Rapid Transit Systems, approached the Los Angeles County Board of Supervisors and the Metropolitan Transit Authority (MTA) and made them an offer.

The press release said, "We are pleased to submit this day a proposal to finance and construct an Alweg Monorail rapid transit system 43 miles in length, serving the San Fernando Valley, the Wilshire corridor, the San Bernardino corridor, and downtown Los Angeles." The offer was for "a turn-key proposal in which a group will share risk, finance the construction, and turn over to MTA a completed and operating system to be repaid from MTA revenues". The budget for the initial monorail network, including rolling stock, was estimated to be $187.5 million. Alweg would also conduct feasibility studies for expansion of the system to cover the entire Los Angeles region. In an interview with the *Los Angeles Times* in 1965, Walt said, "A monorail would be a natural attraction to thousands of people who would just ride it because it is something new and different. And it is needed. It's not something that would be scrapped after two years." A competitor company proposed a 75-mile suspended car system at a cost of $182.3 million.

In both proposals, the public agency would give the company all the fares collected for 40 years; that money would be used to pay for the bonds that would finance the projects. With either offer, the Los Angeles region could have had a fixed-rail transit backbone using revolutionary technology at no cost to the taxpayers. However, political pressure from Standard Oil Company dampened the Board of Supervisors' and the LAMTA's enthusiasm for the project.

In an interview in 2001, Bradbury said, "Telephone Alweg to accept their offer, made 30 years ago, to erect 12 crosstown monorails—free, gratis—if we let them run the traffic. I was there the afternoon our supervisors rejected that splendid offer, and I was thrown out of the meeting for making impolite noises. Remember, subways are for cold climes, snow and sleet in dead-winter London, Moscow or Toronto. Monorails are for high, free, open-air spirits, for our always-fair weather. Subways are Forest Lawn extensions. Let's bury our dead MTA and get on with life." To date, Los Angeles has spent billions of dollars to build 79 miles of fixed rail, much of it underground.

The WEDway PeopleMover

The PeopleMover is a by-product of Walt's involvement with the 1964–1965 New York World's Fair, where WED Enterprises developed a booster brake drive system to push Ford cars around a winding track with elevation changes.

Henry Ford II hired WED Enterprises in the summer of 1961 to design the Ford Motor Company Pavilion. The show was called Magic Skyway, and it featured Ford convertibles as the ride vehicles. The Ford Pavilion had a $30 million budget; at nearly 275,000 square feet, the building was the largest structure at the fair. Welton Becket was the architect. The Magic Skyway became one of the most popular attractions, with nearly 15 million visitors taking a spin behind the wheel of a Ford.

Ford wanted to give guests a chance to experience the new vehicles first hand. The Ford Mustang was introduced at this fair, and was the first chance that many people had to ride in one. This type of interaction is similar to what Ford did at the 1939 New York World's Fair. During that fair, drivers took guests on a ride along a short test track within the pavilion. This meant long hours in line for guests. A goal for the 1964 Fair was to provide a similar experience while increasing guest capacity and shortening the wait. Therefore, a new type of propulsion system was required to move the convertibles through the Magic Skyway.

"We discovered the idea for the New York World's Fair WEDway PeopleMover system while on a business trip to the Ford Motor Company in Detroit," John Hench said. "Walt and I were invited to visit the mill where Ford made steel for car bodies. We saw a device for handling steel ingots, masses of glowing red-hot metal. The ingots were moved around on tracks powered by rollers from one area to another while being transformed into sheet steel for making cars." Walt asked, "Do you think we could put some kind of seat on that type of conveyor, or some kind of arrangement for people to ride on...do you think this thing would handle it?" Hench replied, "Sure, look at the weight carried here. I bet that Roger Broggie would know how to do it."

The challenge was to find a way to push the Ford cars around a winding track with elevation changes. The solution was a technology called a booster brake drive system. This system was first used on the Matterhorn bobsleds at Disneyland. Broggie said, "Walt remembered the booster brakes on the Matterhorn, which were at the top of each hill. They were rolling tires that helped slow down the cars and get them going at the right speed."

As a result, the WEDway PeopleMover track has electric motors embedded every few feet to power the urethane wheels; the PeopleMover also has Masonite on the bottom of the vehicles.[36] Although the vehicles themselves do not have motors, the tires spinning below make contact with the plate mounted on the bottom, which pushes the tires along. The speed of the vehicles varies depending on how fast the rubber wheels are spinning. The EPCOT film claims one of the benefits of this technology is that "no single car can ever break down and cause a rush-hour traffic jam". Even if one of the motors breaks, it will not stop the system, as the other motors will pick up the slack.

To test the technology, a 300-foot oval track and loading ramp was built in the Burbank studio backlot. Ford sent over a white 1961 Lincoln Continental and a Thunderbird. The engines, transmissions, and much of the power train were then removed to make the vehicles lighter. Bob Gurr set up his conveyor system and it worked. Further refinements were made and the system was installed in New York.

In 1964, Walt had realized that he could adapt the World's Fair propulsion technology and create the WEDway PeopleMover system. Walt coined the term PeopleMover as a working title for the project and it stuck. In 1966, Walt had a chance to ride in a prototype of the attraction, but he passed away before the system could be installed in Disneyland. For Walt, the primary function for the Disneyland PeopleMover was to give guests an overview of Tomorrowland. After this "bird's eye-view" introduction, guests would know exactly where they wanted to go next and what to expect.

The WEDway PeopleMover made its public debut as a signature part of the new Tomorrowland when it opened in 1967. The Disneyland system was designed by Bob Gurr and Bill Watkins. What was not known to the general public was that the attraction was specifically designed as a prototype for the system that Walt wanted to install in his futuristic city of EPCOT. Just as he did with the monorail, Walt was using Disneyland as a way of testing the durability of the technology. It was one of the breakthrough technologies that helped spatially define Tomorrowland.

The Disneyland WEDway PeopleMover system consisted of 62 continuously moving, fully automated four-car trains. The attraction could host up to 4,885 guests per hour. The performance claim was that "on peak

---

36   Imagineer Bob Gurr said Masonite was "silent with a great grip."

days, it carries nearly 40,000 passengers". Guests would take a 16-minute journey through Tomorrowland. Sponsored by Goodyear Tire Company, the attraction opened in 1967 and closed in 1995.[37]

The loading platform is similar to a system that Walt spotted in Lausanne, Switzerland. Bob Gurr had already designed such a system, and Walt sent him to Switzerland to check out the Lausanne system. Gurr learned that the Lausanne version could not be used because of a number of safety concerns; Gurr's design was more suitable for the Disneyland project. In Gurr's system, guests would step onto a Speedramp, an escalator belt without steps that led up to the loading platform. The Speedramp had more carrying capacity than a traditional moving stairway. At the top of the ramp was a circular walkway that was moving at the same speed as the vehicles and that would "continue to move even while passengers are disembarking or stepping aboard". The vehicles ran continuously and "the next car is always ready". The doors opened and closed automatically; it did not take many attendants to manage very large crowds.

When the attraction opened at the Magic Kingdom, Disney used a different propulsion system, which in many ways was an improvement over the previous technology. Instead of using rubber tires—which were subject to wear and tear—to push the trains along, linear induction motors were installed. All of the moving parts were eliminated. Embedded in the track were powerful electro-magnets that were switched on and off in sequence. As the vehicle approached, the magnet pulsed on and the opposing magnetic field pushed the vehicle forward. Each motor was made up of a proximity sensor, speed sensor, and a motor unit. Unfortunately, one design constraint for systems powered by linear induction motors is that the track must be level; in this regard, there was no way to match one of the benefits of the older World's Fair and Disneyland technology, which allowed for elevation changes.

Two Giants

Urban planner and master builder Robert Moses was arguably the most powerful man in New York for 48 years, from the early 1920s through the better part of the 1960s. As the head of a number of semi-public agencies, including director of the New York City Public Works Department, Moses had created a power base that allowed him unprecedented power without having to be responsible to the public or to elected officials. Under his

---

37 The attraction has consistently polled at the top of the list as one of the most missed attractions at Disneyland.

leadership, New York built tunnels, bridges, parks, and parkways—all at the expense of mass transit. Moses did not hesitate to destroy existing neighborhoods in pursuit of what he considered "progress". He shaped New York's physical environment more than any other single person, and it reflected his vision of what that great city should be. Moses had been the force behind the influential 1939 New York World's Fair, and in 1964 he was interested in creating a sequel.

In an interview in 2010, Buzz Price recalled a story of two giants. He was on board the Disney-owned Grumman G-159 Gulfstream I airplane with Robert Moses and Walt Disney. His job was to pour the drinks while two men who had essentially reshaped the world discussed the site plan for the 1964–1965 New York World's Fair. The conversation was not going well.

Walt was drawing on a map and trying to tell Moses that the layout would lead to failure. In *Walt's Revolution!: By the Numbers*, Price wrote, "I poured Walt and Mr. Moses each a big scotch and then watched the two giants verbally spar with each other. They were two strong protagonists, each accustomed to being number one." Neither was listening to the other; "they were talking at the same time for about an hour". It was a test of wills and neither man was backing down.

The men were specifically arguing about the transportation planning for the fair. Walt did not like what he saw in the plans and had some suggestions. Walt knew he was an expert in how people moved about; he could see that Moses' plans would not encourage visitors to leave the main fairgrounds to go to the recreational area, a seven million–dollar investment from land developer Angus Wynne.[38] Walt knew that visitors need to have some "special inducement like a monorail or a PeopleMover". Price wrote, "Walt unsuccessfully tried to encourage Goodyear to install a people mover and even paid for a study." Walt thought a Disney-designed Alweg monorail system would become an attraction itself, just like at Disneyland, and would have the proper capacity to get the job done. It would also make for a fine legacy project and would remain operating after the fair closed.

Moses, however, had decided to go with a much cheaper system built by American Machine & Foundry Company, better known as AMF, the bowling alley equipment manufacturer. The two technologies differed in that the Disney version rides on top of the beamway, while the AMF configuration was an I-beam type, with the train suspended underneath the beamway. Walt disliked the hanging monorail technology because Lillian got ill on such a train during a visit to Germany.

---

38 Wynne would later go on to open the Six Flags theme parks.

Walt could not dissuade Moses from his plan, and in the end Walt was right and Moses was wrong. Just as Walt had predicted, the site plan for the fair and the transportation connections did not bring enough traffic to the recreational area. Wynne ended up bankrupted due to Moses' mistake. In fact, in spite of the success of the Disney exhibits, the 1964–1965 New York World's Fair as a whole lost money. The fair attracted 51 million visitors over two seasons, far less than the projected 70 million. The poor layout was cited as one of the reasons for the failure. Author and futurist Ray Bradbury wrote the script for the United States Pavilion's exhibit. He said the fair failed because "Walt did not design the whole thing". Bradbury said, "There were not enough benches, not enough trees, not enough restrooms…all the things that developers think are not necessary Walt would have provided."

In the end, the New York event was considered a "bandit fair" because it was not sanctioned by the BIE, thereby limiting the nations and members that could participate. There were several reasons why the BIE did not sanction the New York fair: For one, the BIE required that the fair take place within a single year; Robert Moses had insisted that the fair run for two years instead of the customary one. In addition, each country must be given 5,000 square feet of space rent-free for the run of the fair; New York refused to meet the real estate requirement, and this made it difficult to persuade foreign nations to build national pavilions. Most of the big names were missing. There would be no Britain, France, Italy, or Soviet Union. Moses made up for the lack of international participation by bumping up the number of state pavilions.[39]

After the Fair closed, Moses asked Walt to build a park in the New York area. However, Walt declined because he doubted that New Yorkers would embrace anything like the Anaheim Park. Buzz Price recalls, "He [Walt] said that audience is not responsive. That city is different." Walt was also concentrating on a new location to the south.

The 1964 Washington DC Plan

Although the 1964–1965 New York World's Fair was an important milestone for the Disney organization, it was a proposed alternative in Washington DC that would have the most influence on the design for EPCOT.

---

39 This is one reason why Walt was able to secure a spot at the Illinois Pavilion with Great Moments with Mr. Lincoln. Moses needed more "must-see" attractions and he proclaimed, "I won't open the fair without that exhibit!" As it turned out, there was always a multi-hour wait for Mr. Lincoln.

The proposal for the 1964 Washington DC fair had a number of innovations that would have revolutionized the World's Fair business. The event was pitched as a tool in the Cold War. A World's Fair in the nation's capital would be a powerful symbol. According to the proposal, "It would keep the United States on the psychological offensive." Washington DC is not just any city. "It represents instead America's essential spirit." The theme for the Washington DC World's Fair would be Science for Human Dignity.

The Washington DC region was a popular tourist destination for Americans, but it suffered from a relatively low foreign tourism visitation rate. The fair's advocates believed that the event could stimulate the economy with a projected attendance of 55 million visitors—more than 300,000 per day. It was expected that some days could top 700,000 people.

The Washington DC executives hired architect and planner Victor Gruen to draft an innovative site plan based on his concept of cellular urban organization.[40] Gruen was in charge of coordinating architecture and master planning for the Washington DC Fair. To support Gruen, the fair organizers drafted a review panel composed of leading names in the design field: Pietro Belluschi (Dean of the Architectural School at MIT), Walter Gropius (founder of the Bauhaus), and William Wurster (University of California Berkeley). Joining them were renowned architects Marcel Breuer, Philip Johnson, William L. Pereira, and Hugh Stubbins. In addition, Paul Rudolph of Yale and Jose Luis Sert of Harvard represented the Ivy League.

---

40   Victor Gruen (1903–1980) was born in Vienna, Austria. He was trained at the Vienna Academy of Fine Arts and was very active politically prior to World War II. Gruen left Austria when it was annexed by Germany in 1938. He immigrated to the United States and found his way to Los Angeles in 1941. He opened Victor Gruen Associates in 1951; the firm continues to practice today. Gruen had attended World's Fairs in Paris, New York, San Francisco, and Brussels. John Hench said that Disney had been a big fan of Victor Gruen for a long time and had studied his work. One of Gruen's landmark projects was the Northfield Mall near Detroit, opened in 1954, one year before Disneyland. This development is considered the first suburban open-air shopping mall and at the time was hailed as the next big trend in urban planning. It was as revolutionary and influential to urban design in 1954 as Disneyland would prove to be a year later. By 1956, Gruen had put a roof over his shopping mall with the opening of the Southdale Center in Edina, Minnesota. Gruen became known as the father of the modern shopping mall, a moniker that he came to loath. He grew tired of the cheap imitations of his work that destroyed communities instead of healing them. These experiences and more would lead Gruen to rethink the way urban centers could be formed. Gruen was striving for something much more important than just building shopping malls.

The Cellular Nature of Community

Gruen believed that there was an underlying cellular nature to a properly built community. If the basic unit of life is a cell, and millions of cells can come together to create an organism, he reasoned that an urban structure based on cells (clusters of mixed-use development) would be the healthiest system. Mixed use refers to a building or a cluster of buildings in the same general area through adjacency with multiple functions that coexist and can include residential, commercial, office, or live/work space. This blending of functions enhances pedestrian activity and safety, and it reduces the need for parking space. Think of the image of Main Street, U.S.A. Downstairs are the shops, and upstairs are the imaginary offices of important people. A crucial benefit of a cellular urban organization is that it can be scaled as small as a home or as large as a metropolis.

To illustrate the cellular concept, Gruen compared a city to the human body. In a person, a healthy heart is one that shows high cardiac output. For a city, the central business district is the heart, which must demonstrate "high vitality". Vitality is measured by the ability of primary functions to perform successfully and without strain. A healthy city is one with an "infinite variety whose buildings and structures form, between them, spaces of differing size and character, narrow or broad, serene or dynamic, modest or monumental, contrasting with each other by virtue of varied treatment of pavement, landscaping, and lighting". The only way to achieve "high vitality" is to ensure that the secondary or "utilitarian" functions are also working well. These utilitarian functions include sewer systems, the telecommunications networks, power supply, and transportation systems.

Gruen proposed two ways to objectively measure the success of urban spaces. He called those qualities "Appearance" and "Atmosphere". Appearance is the "sum total of the physical and psychological influence of an environment on human beings". Atmosphere is the "small-grained variety and diversity" that elevates a space from acceptable to exceptional. For Appearance, Gruen suggested that we measure the "degree [people] feel enabled to live undisturbed, unmolested, and free of interference". Think about this when you are traveling around your community; take note as you move through a space and pay attention to how comfortable you are, how you feel, and whether you are inspired. If you are, you are traveling in spaces that, as Alexander would describe, have a higher degree of life. They demonstrate wholeness.

Atmosphere is about function. As noted author Jane Jacobs said, the "main purpose is to enliven the streets with variety and detail". She added, "The whole point is to make the streets more surprising, more compact, more variegated and busier than before—not less so." Atmosphere does not come about because of showy architectural statements. As architect Mies van der Rohe said, "God is in the details"; for many people, this is what is referred to as the "Disney Difference".

Using Disney nomenclature, Walt called the public realm "onstage", where Appearance and Atmosphere would create a seamless show. "Backstage" are the utilitarian functions, hidden away from the guests.

Ray Bradbury said that Walt was in love with Paris, where he learned a great deal about what constituted a positive Atmosphere. He first visited Paris when he was only seventeen and joined a World War I ambulance brigade. Bradbury said, "[Walt had] learned that one of the great secrets of cities like Paris is that there are fountains everywhere, and flowers and more places to sit...and you surround people with beauty that isn't necessary."

Just like Walt Disney, Gruen would redefine the public's expectations for functional urban space. Mark Howard Moss said, "Both Gruen and Disney were in the dream business." They both knew how to create vibrant urban spaces that had the key ingredients of quality, variety, and surprise. Each man would influence the other.

Gruen analyzed what happened to the area surrounding Disneyland and knew the 1964–1965 fair sponsors needed to control the perimeter. After all, this would have been the first automobile-oriented World's Fair. Attendance projections were based on the assumption that 50 percent would be day visitors while the other half would need lodging nearby. They could be parking up to 100,000 automobiles per day, thereby requiring more land. A typical World's Fair would cover between 600 to 1,200 acres. For the Washington DC project, the project team was looking for 3,000 to 6,000 acres.

Integration with the surrounding highway network was central to the planning. The location was selected to follow existing development trends and to limit urban sprawl. Learning from previous fairs, the project team also proposed a large number of temporary housing units.

Gruen believed that "one of the main tenets of modern planning philosophy was the complete separation of various modes of traffic from each other and the separation of pedestrian traffic from all of them". In his proposal, the central core of the fair would be elevated on a raised platform constructed of pre-fabricated, reinforced concrete elements. Underneath the platform would be a network of utility corridors.[41]

---

41 This concept was later implemented with the famous "Utilidors" at the Magic Kingdom in 1971.

The Post-Fair Plan

The Washington DC World's Fair proposal may have been best remembered for its being the first totally air-conditioned international exposition. However, the biggest innovation in the proposal was the plan for the property once the event had ended. The vision was to build a new community that would grow out of the foundations of the fair. What was once temporary would become permanent. What Gruen proposed was to change the temporary dynamic of this type of event and leave a permanent legacy to the Washington DC area in the form of the infrastructure for a community of up to 200,000 people. It was the post-fair community plan that ultimately would have the most direct impact on Walt's thinking for EPCOT.

The Washington DC sponsors knew that most World's Fairs lose money. In fact, the only modern-era event to make money had been the 1933–1934 Chicago Exposition. This was due to a fair's limited lifespan: World's Fairs are designed to last six months.

As a way to amortize the huge upfront investment, the Washington DC plan emphasized the identification of permanent uses for the buildings and infrastructure. According to Gruen, "The destruction of the efforts of human ingenuity, of artistic talent, can be avoided." He said, "All facilities can be constructed for the World's Fair in a much more generous and convenient manner."... "The fact that many of the World's Fair buildings will later on become integral parts of a new city will permit the construction of facilities and structures which otherwise would be impractical."

Within the plan, there were two post-fair alternatives for the community-building component. Either alternative would house up to 200,000 people; the difference between the two alternatives was the residential densities. One alternative featured a robust average of 55 dwelling units per acre, while the other was an average of 35 dwelling units per acre. The denser alternative would have provided for more public spaces and a broader greenbelt. In both alternatives, roughly 295 acres of the fairground's former core would become the Town Center. The plans also called for almost a one-to-one ratio of residential acreage to recreational areas. More than 500 acres were to be dedicated to schools. There would be another 500 acres allotted to industrial uses. The post-fair community would be a full-service and balanced city.

Gruen said, "The World's Fair will be enriched by the inclusion of structures which will permit the visitor actually to experience elements of the CITY OF TOMORROW in accordance with the newest scientific, sociological and technological concepts." During the fair, "[t]his theme will be carried out by a special city planning exhibition and by a number of permanent structures which will form, later on, the core of a new satellite town". For example, a portion of the residential area would be opened prior to the fair and remain as a model village with "solutions found for many of our contemporary urban problems".

The permanent buildings at the fair's core would live two lives. According to the proposal, "[d]uring the World's Fair these buildings will contain national and international exhibits, and exhibits of industries from all parts of the world". Once the fair was over, "[t]hese structures will become the PERMANENT TRADE CENTER", which would provide a post-fair revenue stream because "those countries and those industries which are hesitant to make capital investments for their own buildings will be in a position to rent space in those structures".

In addition to the Permanent Trade Center, a large portion of the central core would be converted into a huge regional commercial center with shopping, hotels, and offices. The proposal included "clusters of buildings on platforms in a park", which would allow for trucks and other services to be hidden below. The main public areas would be under a climate-controlled roof or dome to protect the pedestrians from the brutal weather.

As part of the exhibits while the event was operating, visitors would be able to walk through FAIR CITY, an area that "will contain model apartments, model hospital rooms, model homes, etc., [that] will become apartment houses, row houses, detached houses, hotels, office buildings, stores, etc." Gruen pointed out, "The value of new transportation lines, of public utilities, of landscaping, fountains, sculptures, and other expressions of the arts will not be lost the day the Fair closes but will permanently serve not only the inhabitants of Fair City but the progress of city planning all over the world."

In Gruen's plan, construction would begin as soon as the fair ended on a ring of high-density residential units surrounding the commercial core. Beyond those homes would be another ring that would blend neighborhood services with lower-density attached residential units. Outside of this core, still lower-density attached residential units would be connected by greenways. Finally, the entire development would be "surrounded by parking and transportation facilities ringed, in turn, by an outer area of open land". He compared this urban form to a medieval castle and city. Also included in the post-fair plan was an international amusement park. "These facilities will be developed along the lines of the successfully operated Disneyland, near Los Angeles, California."

The post-fair project was meant to develop over time and grow organically. As the community developed, surrounding property values would rise and make the post-fair developer even more money. There was already a demand for more residential properties in the area; had Gruen's plan been selected, it would likely have been a fail-safe opportunity.

Out of a Fair

In May 1960, Ada Louise Huxtable, a Pulitzer Prize–winning architecture critic, wrote an intriguing—and, possibly for Walt, influential—article for *Horizon* magazine.[42] In the article, "Out of a Fair", she reviewed Victor Gruen's post-fair plan and noted that his vision called for a community that "promises comfort, convenience, and calculated visual pleasure". The article was published just about the same time that the Disney deal with John D. MacArthur in Palm Beach fell through.

Huxtable's article takes us through a brief history of World's Fairs and concludes that they are "a tired institution". She lamented that the proposal for the 1964 New York World's Fair was going to be more of the same. Nevertheless, she noted there was one proposal that would have been different, that really would capture international attention: the Gruen plan for Washington DC.

Although she praised the layout for the Washington DC fair, she said, "Its most remarkable feature is that it is in effect a re-usable plan." Impressed with Gruen's innovative thinking, Huxtable suggested, "Probably no man in America today has a more intimate acquaintance with the ills of cities and their possible cures than [Gruen]." So remarkable was the planning effort that "[a]ll of the familiar bugaboos of International Expositions have been anticipated and dealt with in this farsighted project".

In the article, Huxtable documented the process in which Washington DC lost the fair to New York. It was her feeling that Washington DC lost to New York's superior financial potential. The missed opportunity was that the Washington DC plans "offer[ed] a contribution of permanent value".

Huxtable outlined the features of the post-fair plan. Since many of the fair buildings would be retained, the city would have an immediate, vital commercial and cultural center. She admired how Gruen understood that the new city would develop over time and that each addition would enhance and embellish what was there before. She suggested that the plan was "a scheme that would be applicable for any city where sufficient open land is available".

According to Neal Gabler, Walt read Huxtable's article. He was already thinking about building a city on virgin land; could the Washington DC fair proposal and EPCOT be related? Maybe. They reflect many of the same values and solutions. Marty Sklar believes that Walt was influenced by Gruen's plan.

---

42 Ada Louise Huxtable began her career at the Museum of Modern Art in New York in 1946. From there, she worked at Progressive Architecture and Art in America. She is best known as *The New York Times* architecture critic from 1963 until 1982. She has also authored over ten books on the subject of architecture.

Chapter Thirteen

The Florida Project

What would motivate somebody as successful as Walt Disney to take on one of the most difficult challenges that anybody could tackle: the reinvention and renewal of our urban spaces? Could it be, after changing the world of animation and the amusement park industry, he felt he had a higher calling?

Walt Disney said, "I don't believe that there's a challenge anywhere in the world that's more important to people everywhere than finding solutions to the problems of our cities." Walt felt that something was wrong with the way cities were designed, and he believed that, with the proper application of new technologies and creative thinking, he could create a city that would demonstrate to others how they could solve their urban planning problems.

Walt was not a fan of cities, and he really could not understand why anybody would want to live in one. He felt that his growing up in the country had given him a sense of independence, individualism, and democratic character. Perhaps because he spent a lot of time on the streets of Kansas City as a boy, his image of city centers was that they were overcrowded, unclean, sometimes dangerous places, and always filled with visual chaos. Walt was especially disappointed with the way Los Angeles was becoming choked in urban sprawl. Walt sensed that many American cities and suburbs were disorienting and inefficient.

On the 1948 train trip to the Chicago Railroad Fair, Walt had told Ward Kimball, "I can't figure out why in the hell everybody lives in the city where they don't have any room and can't do anything. Why don't they come out here where they have this great empty land, filled with opportunity and silence?" Disney biographer Bob Thomas, author of *Building a Company*, speculated that Walt's interest in city planning could be "an outgrowth of his lifelong search for better ways of doing things: adding sound, color, full-length stories, and dimension (via the multiplane camera) to animation; revolutionizing outdoor entertainment". In *The Triumph of the American Imagination*, author Neal Gabler wrote that Walt wanted to "create an entire urban environment from scratch: a perfect city".

Science fiction author Ray Bradbury declared "that the first function of architecture is to make men over, make them wish to go on living, feed them fresh oxygen, grow them tall, delight their eyes, make them kind... Disneyland liberates men to their better selves. Here the wild brute is gently corralled, not squished and squashed, not put upon and harassed, not tromped on by real-estate operators, not exhausted by smog and traffic." In 1960, Bradbury suggested to Walt that he should run for mayor of Los Angeles because he was the only man who knew how things work. Bradbury really believed that Walt understood the issues, especially when it came to public transit. Bradbury said, "I'm all for making Walt Disney our next mayor…the only man in the city who can get a working rapid transit system built without any more surveys, and turn it into a real attraction so that people will want to ride it." Walt's reply was, "Why should I run for mayor when I am already king?" Again, in 1964, Bradbury suggested that Walt was the only person who could "save us from our own self-destruction". He added, "[Walt] Disney is a city builder. He has already proven his ability to construct an entire community, plus rivers, plus mountains, from the gas lines up. He has already solved most of the problems that beset Los Angeles."

Disney Legend John Hench said, "Disneyland was very courageous on Walt's part, and Florida shows the most guts of anything…to take a kind of civilization, make it ideal, and then to make it practical." With the success of Disneyland, Walt understood that there was a better way to organize and manage the urban environment. When done properly, this new thinking would create a world with the kind of places we want to return to again and again—because they are based on a "timeless way of building" and offer a higher quality of life for everyone. Walt also understood that he was the person best suited to take on the challenge.

The Anti-City

Urban planning policies and construction techniques after World War II had created lifeless, sprawling cities designed for the automobile and not for people. Victor Gruen called this type of development the Anti-City.[43]

Americans have long tried to bring order to our cities. The stringent use of Euclidean zoning—also called single-use pod zoning—has dominated land use regulations since the 1920s, gaining even broader acceptance after World War II. By design, single-use zoning began to separate where we live, work, and play. In order to justify every decision and to thwart litigation,

---

43 Gruen noted that this was what was happening around the front gates of Disneyland. In contrast, John Hench described the Disney theme park difference this way: "In modern cities you have to defend yourself constantly and you go counter to everything that we've learned from the past. You tend to isolate yourself from other people… You tend to be less aware. You tend to be more withdrawn. This is counter-life…you really die a little…I think we need something to counteract what modern society—cities have done to us." That was not the case, Hench pointed out, at Disneyland.

urban planners began to rely on precise statistical requirements; at the same time, planners relaxed physical design guidelines. Those practices led to disjointed public spaces.

Peter Katz, one of the founders of the Congress for the New Urbanism movement, said, "Cities have to move to a new system. [City planners] should look at the streets they like and the public spaces they like and then write the rules to get more of what they like and less of what they don't." He warned, "Conventional zoning doesn't do that. It just gives a use and a density and then you hope for the best." Federal and institutional financing programs only recognize certain standard development types. Federal road building programs with normative standards and public works practices are destroying the diversity of the countryside. Over time, there has become an insufficient variety between subdivisions, setback, lot size, and density. Because of all of this, there is a need to have ample parking everywhere, even at the cost of the pedestrian experience.

What about the professionals who can solve all of these problems? Just as Walt had observed in the arts world, there were no Renaissance people among city planners, no generalists. Every part of the process became its own discipline, and the segregation of the design, engineering, permitting authorities, construction professionals, and many other specialties resulted in places with no personality.

Why did Walt feel he could contribute to solving some of these problems? Maybe he realized he was one of the only people who could do what was necessary because he had done it before. He could contribute experience. Architect Peter Blake, the *New York* magazine architecture critic, said, "The truth of the matter is the only new towns of any significance built in America since World War II are Disneyland in Anaheim, California, and Disney World in Orlando, Florida. Both are 'new,' both are 'towns' and both are staggeringly successful."

A Practical Man

Walt was a visionary as well as a practical man. He knew he could not do everything. John Hench said that Walt did not want "to change people's lives...only the environment in which they lived". Imagineer Marvin Davis suggested, "It was his philosophy not to build a city that would solve all the urban problems all over the world, but to give a chance to American industry to experiment and show to the world just how the problems of traffic and housing could be solved..."

What Walt could do was to entertain and educate. A Chinese proverb says, "Tell me and I'll forget; show me and I may remember; involve me and

I'll understand." John Hench said, "Walt believed that the experience was most important. People could always read about ideas or see photographs of new concepts. They would find it more compelling if they went through it themselves. Once people experienced something first-hand, they could go home to their own communities and make changes." According to Hench, Walt said, "[E]xperiences were the only thing that you really own. They were yours."

Buzz Price said in *Inside the Dream*, "Walt wanted to try going beyond the park experience. He wanted to try improving the environment, the urban setting. He was full of ideas about what that place would be like. EPCOT would not be just a park, but an urban experiment where you could try to improve the way people live, creating alternatives to our frantic, automobile existence."

"It would be a place not only for testing physical things, but also educational developments and all forms of communication," according to Marvin Davis. "[Walt] was greatly interested in solving the young adult problem that faces everybody. If we can successfully show to the world an area in which teenagers are properly controlled and given an opportunity to express themselves and are kept occupied—this is something we really want to work on."

EPCOT was meant to be a showcase in American ingenuity just like Henry Ford's Greenfield Village. While Greenfield Village celebrated past achievements, Walt's city would be forward looking. Guests would be immersed in a real world "lab" testing the latest transportation, electronic, and infrastructure technologies.

Taking the Long View

In 1963, Walt had said, "Well, my greatest reward, I think, is that I've been able to build this wonderful organization." The Florida Project was meant to be a long-term project. It was Walt's hope that the project would keep his Imagineers busy for decades to come. His advice was, "Think beyond your lifetime if you want to accomplish something truly worthwhile." Walt estimated it would take him 15 years to complete Disney World, including EPCOT. He was so confident about the city building project that he turned over most of his studio responsibilities to other team members. He said to his core team, "You do a good job and I have confidence in you, and I have to concentrate on EPCOT." Walt was rightfully proud of his team.

"So the amusement park was really a secondary thing," according to Marvin Davis. "[Walt] was interested in solving the urban problem. It's a big scope, but that's exactly what he was thinking." When it came to the design of the East Coast Disneyland, the Magic Kingdom, Walt could not be bothered. When his artists would show him drawings, he would get irritated, make a quick decision, and then get back to what interested him. Roy set up a central committee to work on the amusement park; Walt was not included in the group.

Like a Sponge

In the late 1950s, spurred on by the CalArts project as well as the opportunity in Palm Beach, Walt began to learn everything he could about city planning. He read British author Ebenezer Howard's 1902 edition of Howard's *Garden Cities of To-morrow*[44]—for many people, the intellectual beginning of the move toward suburbia. Just like Walt, Howard was appalled at the condition of cities during his lifetime, and he proposed a new type of utopian community that would blend the best of cities with the best of the rural areas.

Howard's book was inspired by a Utopian novel, *Looking Backward 2000–1887* (originally published in 1888), in which author Edward Bellamy took a look at what life would be like in the United States in the year 2000. A cultural phenomenon, the book kicked off a new book genre that looked at utopian themes; it became popular to predict what the future would look like.

Howard proposed communities that would be divided into distinct neighborhoods, each with a balanced public life. Each neighborhood would be a standard size, self sufficient, and surrounded by a substantial greenbelt owned and shared by all of the residents. The neighborhoods would be connected by rapid transit to other such cities. Each neighborhood would specialize in certain industries and functions, with each part of the collection adding to a complete region.

Garden Cities suggested that vibrant and sustainable regions would be made up of "Rural Areas", "Corridors", "Neighborhoods", and "Districts". At the core of Howard's philosophy was an understanding of the nexus among those four land-use patterns and the best relationships among those uses. The book is persuasive and uses clear, simple graphics to illustrate how the author's land use and transportation solutions would work. For example, one drawing shows the organization of a region with 58,000 residents as concentric circles. At the center of the region is the "Central City" with

---

44 The book was originally released in 1898 as *To-morrow: a Peaceful Path to Real Reform*; a 1965 edition included an introductory essay by architectural historian Lewis Mumford.

"Inter-municipal Railway" lines radiating out from the center like spokes on a wheel. The railway lines lead to smaller towns with populations of 32,000. One node is called "Garden City" while the other is dubbed "Concord". Walt was strongly influenced by Howard's design; Disneyland is based, in part, on this radial model.

In the book, Howard described the design for a "social city" that attempted to create a bridge between the individualist (capitalist) system of the time and the ideals of socialism that were promoted by Trade Unions and Co-operatives. One socialist ideal in particular—communal land protection—was central to Howard's desire to create a higher quality of life.

One of the earliest and most successful examples of a community in the United States inspired by Howard's work was the town of Radburn, New Jersey, founded in 1929. Its designers, Clarence Stein and Henry Wright, created a suburban subdivision that accommodated the presence of the automobile, which they recognized was here to stay. Radburn is made up of smaller neighborhoods sharing a town center and high school. Each neighborhood was designed with the pedestrian in mind. The distance from one edge to another is only one-quarter mile, a reasonable walking distance for many people.

To overcome the conflict between pedestrians and the automobile, the community was designed with separate roadways for each transportation mode. Radburn features a short underpass that allows pedestrians to pass safely under a busy street. The design of the underpass is devoid of hiding places and is non-threatening. Walt had studied the Radburn community and incorporated its pedestrian paths in his own thinking. Within EPCOT Walt promised, "Children going to and from schools and playgrounds will use these paths, always completely safe and separated from the automobile." Other Radburn community design innovations would also appear in Walt's EPCOT design: residential neighborhoods placed around culs-de-sac, collector streets, and common open spaces within superblocks.

By the 1950s and 1960s, Americans—especially the growing middle class—once again started to look to the future. Stanford historian Joseph Corn said, "Their escape into the future was, at the same time, a nostalgic glance backward to a past of simplicity and common sense."

Robert Simon, Jr. took Howard's Garden City concept even further. Simon opened the new town of Reston, Virginia, in 1964—at the same time Walt was beginning to develop EPCOT. Simon built on Howard's common land vision and created a community connected by open spaces and pedestrian pathways. The original plan called for five villages that were less than a half-mile walk from edge-to-edge to encourage walking. Another innovation was the use of clustered housing, which allowed for higher densities and the preservation of more open space.

At the same time Walt was developing EPCOT, developer James Rouse was working on his new planned town in Maryland, which he called Columbia. The Columbia land-use plan featured ten self-contained "villages" that surrounded a regional shopping center and office district. Columbia would become known as a laboratory for education, recreation, religion, and health care. The physical design of the community encouraged social interaction.

According to Disney Legend Ray Watson,[45] Walt was also a big fan of Stockholm, Sweden. He kept a booklet about the city in his office. From 1950 to 1970, city planners had modernized Stockholm by building four new satellite towns. Each satellite town featured its own high-density center around the transit node and had a mix of uses including shopping, commercial, and residential. The satellite towns consisted of functional pods; each pod connected to the town center by a radial subway system and highways. Walt's EPCOT plans were clearly influenced by the Stockholm satellite design.

Looking for the Crossroads

The studies produced by Price's ERA showed that 40 percent of Florida tourists went to southern Florida, 40 percent to the central part of the state, and 20 percent visited the northern part of the state. Price figured that those who drove to the south had to pass through the central portion of the state, so that location presented the best opportunity for Walt's city. Price recalls, "In 1961, after rejecting some other alternatives, Walt asked us to look at the rest of Florida and figure out where the park should be. Late in 1963, we studied in depth a location in central Florida. The key conclusion was that central Florida (not Miami, as most people expected it would be) was the main point of maximum interception of Florida tourism, and that Orlando, centrally located, was the point of maximum access to the southerly flow of Florida tourism from both the east and west shores of the state. ... It was clear that we needed to be in the center of the state. Then we used the logic that we developed on Disneyland that we didn't want to be on the ocean and compete with the beach. We figured that the freeways that were coming from east and west were crisscrossing in Orlando."

Walt was beginning to narrow down the locations for his East Coast theme park. He and his team arrived in Tampa after visiting other potential expansion locations, including St. Louis, Niagara Falls, Washington DC, New Jersey, Colorado, and Baltimore. Walt was ready to make some

---

45 Ray Watson started as an architect, went on to serve as the president of the Irvine Company, and became the chairman of Disney. He served on the Disney Board of Directors for over 30 years. He was named a Disney Legend in 2011.

decisions. Traveling by private plane on November 22, 1963, Walt and his team instructed the pilot to fly over Orlando. They followed the Sunshine State Parkway toward the intersection of Interstate 4, then under construction. When Walt saw the construction site, he proclaimed, "That's it. The freeway bisects here." This trip was the first time that Walt saw the entire Florida property in person. Not everyone on Walt's team agreed with his assessment. Marvin Davis tried to describe what he saw. "Actually on a scale of ten, that property was a one-plus, maybe. It was just awful. It was a swamp. There was only one high spot in the whole thing." However, there was a lot of land; the problems of adjacent development that Walt had endured in Anaheim would not happen to him in Florida.

The team was not aware of the assassination of President John F. Kennedy in Dallas earlier that day until they landed in New Orleans for the night. The group was stunned. Even on the flight home the next day, nobody talked. It wasn't until the plane approached Burbank that Walt announced, "Well, that's the place—central Florida."

Property Acquisition

Five days after Walt's flight over Orlando, he and Roy gathered a very select group of executives to discuss "Project Winter". During that meeting, Buzz Price made a presentation about the "Central Florida Study" that would be a follow-up to the Florida flyover earlier that week. The group gave Price the go ahead to evaluate the site using the same successful formula that identified the site for Disneyland. Just like before, Price looked at highway and climate data, regional economic forecasts, and topographical conditions. He also looked for potential properties for purchase. He was given 60 days to complete this study.

The story of how Disney acquired that much property in a way that did not inflate the price of the land deserves a book of its own. Law professor Chad Emerson artfully tells that story in *Project Future*. According to Price, "He wanted it, he told Florida he wanted it, and he got it."

Disney set up five dummy corporations as a way to secretly purchase land. The colorful names for those companies are Tomahawk Properties, Reedy Creek Ranch, Latin American Development and Management Corporation, Bay Lake Properties, and the cleverly named AyeFour Corporation—a pun on Interstate 4. These companies were complemented by a system of subterfuge that disguised the travel patterns of the Disney staff. They wanted to hide Disney's intentions. According to Marvin Davis, "It was really classified stuff. It was CIA. His luggage was all [monogrammed] WED. So he called himself 'Walter E. Davis.' That was so cloak-and-dagger." Disney

World also went through many different names in order to protect the project's secrecy. At various points the project was known as Project X, Project Florida, Project Summer, and Project Future. In fact, the project was so secret only nine people within the Disney organization knew what was going on: Walt and Roy; executives Card Walker, Donn Tatum, Jack Sayers, Larry Tyron, Mel Melton, Joe Fowler, and attorney Bob Foster.

Card Walker, who became president of Walt Disney Productions after Walt's death, recalled one example of a close call on a trip to Florida that would have exposed the project. In *Inside the Dream*, he says, "One night we were having dinner in a small restaurant and this waitress spotted Walt and came over to the table, saying, 'I think I know who you are. You're Walt Disney.' At first he denied it—'Oh, no, I'm not Walt Disney'—but finally Walt said, 'Promise me you won't tell anybody who I am.' I think she wanted his autograph."

The team completed 47 transactions in order to acquire enough property. The largest parcel was the Demetree Tract (12,400 acres), which came with legal complications related to the underground mineral rights that were owned by Tufts University and Wilson Cypress Company.[46] Other large parcels included the Bronson Tract (8,380 acres), the Hamrick Tract (2,700 acres), the Hall Brother property (1,800 acres), and the Bay Lake Tract (1,300 acres). Also included were the Munger Subdivision, the Goldstein Property (37 acres), and others. Disney was able to purchase 27,443 acres—twice the total acreage of Manhattan Island, or about the size of Boston—for about $5 million. The cost was a modest $150 per acre. After all was said and done, Walt had all the property he needed.

The site featured a good transportation network near the intersection of Interstate 4 and the Sunshine State Parkway, two major highways. Imagineer Wathel Rogers said, "I remember going down to Florida with Walt, when they were first starting to develop all of that land. We stood out there in the middle of Interstate 4, right on the highway. Looking both ways, there wasn't a car in sight, and I said, 'Walt, are you sure this is the place you want to put this thing?' And he said, 'Yes, don't worry about it, Wathel. They'll come from all directions, and we're putting it right here, because it's in the middle.' What a visionary he was."

Project Goals

Marvin Davis, who was chosen once again to be Walt's key land-use planner on the Florida Project, said, "Walt was intrigued with solving the

---

46 The Demetree property would become home to the Magic Kingdom, Epcot, and Disney's Hollywood Studios.

problem of a central commercial area and a residential area co-existing and making the whole thing work for the moving of people and traffic in and out." He was not running away from existing cities, but decided to show them a better way using a clean canvas. Some of the other Imagineers who would also be instrumental in the early development of EPCOT were Herbert Ryman and George Rester.

Walt's intention was to use the experimental new town as a way to demonstrate the latest thinking in technology, service delivery, and governance. He wanted to build his city from scratch on virgin land, heeding Henry Ford's advice: "We shall solve the City Problem by leaving the City." Walt wanted to move away from the dominant model of suburban sprawl that was rapidly taking root throughout the United States. He wanted to demonstrate a different model that relied upon a mixed-use, transit-oriented development. John Hench said that EPCOT would "show how many of today's city problems can be solved through proper master planning".

The first site schematic for Disney World was hand drawn in 1965 by Walt on tissue paper. Although the site plan has changed many, many times over the years, it is remarkable how faithful it still is to Walt's original vision. In Walt's drawing, the north end of the property would be the East Coast Disneyland, resort hotels, and other tourist amenities. Not only would the theme park be a "wienie" to attract guests to travel the length of the property, it would also serve as the financial pump that would allow Walt to build the rest of the project. South of the theme park would be the centerpiece of the entire project, Walt's EPCOT. Continuing south, a visitor would pass by industrial parks, tourist trailer camps, motels, convention facilities, a swamp ride, and a golf course. The golf course would also be part of the drainage system. At the south end of the property would be the main entrance to the property, more motels, and an airport. The monorail would tie everything together: the beam would run the entire length of the property connecting all of the major land uses. Walt wanted the "truck route always under the monorail" as well as a separate lane for passenger vehicles.

When it came to designing the EPCOT city center, Walt asked his friend Welton Becket to draw up the first plans. Becket was the architect for Century City in Los Angeles (1957–1961), which was built on the former backlot of Twentieth-Century Fox. The 176-acre Century City development contained a hotel, office space, entertainment venues, a hospital, and a shopping center. It also contained the largest parking structure in the United States at the time. Pedestrian and automobile traffic were separated into distinct realms.

All of this was the type of development Walt envisioned for EPCOT; however, Marvin Davis said that Walt was disappointed in Becket's proposal. Walt felt that the architecture did not look inviting. Walt recalled Becket's advice when Walt had approached him to design Disneyland: to let his own people take on the challenge if he wanted it to get done right. So, Walt set up a secret project office at the WED headquarters in Glendale, California. The room featured a 16-foot aerial map of the Florida property.[47] The room was off-limits for most employees.

The Disney Secret Becomes Public

When the time came to build in Florida, one of Walt's highest priorities was to avoid the incompatible surrounding land uses that came with Disneyland in Anaheim. Walt was not going to repeat that mistake again. He wanted to control the edges. This time he had the resources and bought as much land as he could afford. The result was that Disney secretly gobbled up more than 43 square miles of central Florida. With this much land, spread over two counties, Disney knew they would need to find some way to govern the property in order to have maximum flexibility. They could not be limited to working through existing governmental agencies. The experimental nature of the EPCOT project demanded a new approach.

In 1965, the secret effort to acquire property for the Florida Project was coming to a close. Walt was forced to reveal his plans about one month earlier than he had planned. Emily Bavar—editor of *Florida Magazine* and on assignment for the *Orlando Sentinel*—had put the pieces together, and the story broke that Disney was coming to Florida. On October 24, 1965, the *Orlando Sentinel* banner headline was "We Say It's Disney". Governor Haydon Burns was at the Florida League of Municipalities Convention on October 25, 1965, when he made the official announcement.

Early on November 15, 1965, the Disney team flew around the property one more time. All reports were that Walt was very happy. Later that day, Walt and Roy conducted a press conference at the Cherry Plaza Hotel in Orlando and talked about their project. At the press conference, Governor Burns called Walt the "man of the decade" and Roy "the financial wizard of Walt Disney Productions". Walt commented on Roy's contribution by stating, "He's my big brother, and he's the one that when I was a little fellow I used to go to with some of my wild ideas, and he'd either straighten me out and put me on the right path—or if he didn't agree with me... .In this project, though, I'd just like to say that I didn't have to work very hard on him. He was with me from the start. Now whether that's good or bad, I don't know."[48]

---

47 The room was later reproduced for Project Florida, also known as the EPCOT film.

48 In a interview at a different time, architect William Pereira said, "Roy has a mission which he, better than anyone else, recognizes—and that's not to check Walt, but to see to it that he has the freedom."

Walt commented that there were a lot of "friendly faces in the audience". He had hoped that Disneyland would "command the respect of the community" and that he had the same goal for Disney World. He said that the Florida Project would be more than just an entertainment enterprise, but he was not very specific about the details. When asked how much Disney planned to invest in the project, Walt replied that he planned to top what he had spent at Disneyland, which was $75 million at the time; he expected to spend well over $100 million in Florida as a start.

During the question and answer period, Walt was asked if guests would be able to see the Orlando skyline. Walt chuckled and said that the reason he bought more than 27,000 acres was to make sure that did not happen. Even the name for the project was not totally settled at this point. When asked to confirm if the project would be called Disney World, he noted that Disney World was the name of the company's internal publication. They were still working on the name.

A question was raised about the theme park. Walt said, "The concept here will have to be something that is unique, and so that there is distinction between Disneyland in California and whatever Disney does—and notice I didn't say Disneyland in Florida—whatever Disney does in Florida."

One little nugget that Walt revealed was the possibility that he might build two different communities. One would be called Yesterday and would be based on a nostalgic vision of America, maybe similar to Greenfield Village in Dearborn or Colonial Williamsburg. The other community would be called Tomorrow. Walt joked that guests "might come one time and they stayed in Tomorrow, but their friends would say that they stayed in Yesterday and they will have to come back".

Walt said, "I would like to be part of building a model community, a City of Tomorrow, you might say, because I don't believe in going out to the extreme blue-sky stuff that some architects do. I believe that people still want to live like human beings. There's a lot of things that could be done." He added, "I'm not against the automobile, but I just feel that the automobile has moved into communities too much. I feel that you can design so that the automobile is there, but still put people back as pedestrians, you see. I'd love to work on a project like that." Walt was also excited about building the school of tomorrow. Walt wanted the school to be a pilot operation for teaching aids.

When Roy was asked about the finances, he felt confident that money would not be a problem. With the success of Disneyland, he stated, "[b]ankers realize what we can do".

A Federal Partner?

The Disney team tried to be creative in the financing of the Florida Project as well as the design. The team briefly looked at raising funds by taking advantage of a new federal program created to provide incentives for development of demonstration cities. In the early to mid-1960s, many civic leaders thought about urban renewal on a grand scale, which meant demolish what was already there and build something entirely new.

On November 3, 1966, President Lyndon Johnson signed the Demonstration Cities and Metropolitan Development Act of 1966. The program was administered by the Department of Housing and Urban Development (HUD). Later changed to the Model Cities Act, the legislation was a result of civil unrest in major American cities. The goals for the program were to "provide financial and technical assistance to develop 'new and imaginative proposals' and revitalize large slum and blighted areas; to expand housing, job, and income opportunities; to reduce dependence on welfare payments; to improve educational facilities; to combat disease and ill health; to reduce crime and delinquency; to enhance recreational and cultural opportunities; to establish better access between homes and jobs".

What may have caught the attention of the Disney team was the goal to "promote the...application of new and improved technologies and methods of constructing, rehabilitating, and maintaining housing, and the application of advances in technology to urban development activities". Disney had ERA prepare a report on the best way to seek federal funds. The conclusion was that Walt would have to give up a certain level of control to meet the reporting requirements. This was something he could not accept.

In October 1966, already very ill with lung cancer, Walt made *Project Florida* (the EPCOT film) to describe Disney World and promote EPCOT, "a living blueprint of the future". Art Linkletter reviewed the film about EPCOT and said, "Don't build another Disneyland." Walt said, "Art, it's not another Disneyland. I have learned things. I have a better plan and an idea of what to do. This will not be a sequel. This will be a city where people will live, work, and enjoy a better way of life." Linkletter approved and said, "Great Walt. Build it." He added, "He looked at me with sunken eyes, almost as if he knew he had little time left, and that was the last time I saw him."

Economic Impact Report

In January 1967, a month after Walt's death, Buzz Price and ERA produced an Economic Impact Report for the Disney World project. The objective for the study was to forecast the economic impacts of the Florida Project during the time period of 1968 to 1982.

The study introduced the project as "a unique and ambitious new type of development". Both the theme park as well as the new town of EPCOT would be "a model community representing the optimum living patterns of the future". The study described EPCOT as a mixed-use development with residential, office, commercial, and community services. The magnet that would draw visitors, residents, and office tenants would be the cultural-recreation complex plus the East Coast Disneyland. The theme park component was secondary to the demonstration city. EPCOT would also feature a showcase industrial complex leased to America's pioneering corporations.

As the ERA staff conducted the research, it quickly became obvious that the Disney World project would have a significant economic impact on the central Florida region, including Orange, Seminole, and Osceola counties. The report stated that the project would bring new wealth to the region and an increased benefit to the state from increased tourism and support industries. Opening day employment was estimated at 7,585 new jobs, with the resort payroll growing to 50,000 full-time "Cast Members" (Disney employees) by 1982.

The study found that the Disney World project would encourage tourists to extend their stays, spend more money, and give repeat visitors another reason to return. Most importantly, the resort would attract significantly more new visitors to the region. The forecasts showed that the greatest number of visitors would come from out of state. The project would not compete with other tourist destinations within Florida, but would incrementally add to the overall numbers. Disney World would become a named destination, much like Disneyland had become in southern California. Local tourist venues such as Silver Springs, Busch Gardens (Tampa), and Cypress Gardens (near Winter Haven) would also benefit from the Disney World development.[49]

There would be nothing else like it. The closest comparison to the proposed project would be a World's Fair. However, Disney World would be permanent and not fleeting like a traditional World's Fair. Just as Victor Gruen's proposal for the 1964 fair would have done for Washington DC, the Disney project would amortize the massive investment necessary for the infrastructure for Orlando.

---

49   Silver Springs continues to operate and is now owned by the state of Florida. Busch Gardens has evolved into a full-fledged theme park and continues to thrive. Silver Cypress Gardens theme park closed in September 2009; in 2010, the new owners announced the site would be transformed into the United States' second Legoland.

The ERA study also suggested that new tourism venues would be created to take advantage of the draw of Disney World. From the state's point of view, it would encourage even more repeat visits.[50] The state would benefit directly from the sales taxes that would be generated, and local jurisdictions would benefit from new revenues such as Transient-Occupancy Taxes (TOT), a tax paid by hotel visitors as a percentage of their bill to cover the demand for local infrastructure, maintenance, and service costs such as public safety. The study predicted that 60 percent of the construction materials would originate from within the state as well.

From the Walt Disney Productions point of view, the project addressed a real need in balancing the portfolio. Disneyland was primarily a West Coast phenomenon. Although the theme park was known throughout the nation based on the television show, East Coast market penetration was very low due to the travel distance. Only the Northeast–Central region had a West Coast market penetration of more than 1 percent—but most of the Northeast–Central residents who traveled also visited Florida.

The ERA study anticipated that the Florida Project would cost approximately $620 million over the first fifteen years. That budget would have included $100 million for the theme park; resort; the theme park infrastructure; and the initial commercial, residential, and tourist facilities for Walt Disney World. The other $520 million was for the city of EPCOT, remaining infrastructure, and other amenities. The project would be financed through a variety of means, including municipal bonds and federally subsidized municipal bonds to pay for infrastructure.[51]

Roy

When Walt died in December 1966, many people believed that his death would mark the end of the Florida Project. However, through the sheer will of his brother Roy, the project did live on. As a starting point, Roy decided to schedule screenings of *Project Florida*, the EPCOT film, to build civic interest in the project. The first screening of the 24-minute film took place at 2:00 p.m. on February 2, 1967, at the Park East Theater in Winter Park, Florida. Disney and the Orange and Osceola county delegations to

---

50   The study was correct. Sea World Orlando opened in 1973. Universal Studios opened two theme parks: Universal Studios Orlando opened in 1990 and Islands of Adventure in 1999. There is also CityWalk, an entertainment retail district, and three resort hotels.

51   By the time it opened in October 1971, the first phase had cost more than $400 million, significantly exceeding its budget.

the Florida legislature hosted the event. In the audience were over 900 business leaders, government officials, and members of the press. Their support would be necessary if the project was to become a reality. This would also be the first time the public saw images of Walt since his death. By all accounts, it was an emotional event.

According to the accompanying press release, "This film reviewed Walt Disney Productions' experience in the operation of Disneyland and outlined in detail the design concepts for Disney World's proposed Experimental Prototype Community of Tomorrow." In the film, Walt explained, "We call it EPCOT, spelled E-P-C-O-T: Experimental Prototype Community of Tomorrow." The basic land uses, such as an airport of the future and the Entrance Complex, would be "tied together by a high-speed rapid transit system running almost the full length of the property". According to Walt, the mission for EPCOT was to "always be a showcase to the world of the ingenuity and imagination of American free enterprise". The project "will take its cue from the new ideas and new technologies that are emerging from the forefront of American industry. It will be a community of tomorrow that will never be completed. It will always be showcasing and testing and demonstrating new materials and new systems." Most importantly, Walt reminded us, "There's enough land here to hold all the ideas and plans we can possibly imagine."

When the film ended, the audience learned the reason why they had been invited. Waiting for the audience to catch its breath, Roy stood before the crowd; then he began, "Wasn't that a dream? Doesn't that stagger you?" He continued, "Our Corporation is dedicated to making Walt Disney's dream a reality, but it cannot be done without the help of you people here in Florida." Roy laid down his challenge: "We must have a solid legal foundation before we can proceed with Disney World. This foundation can be assured by the legislative proposals we are presenting in the next session of the Florida legislature." He added, "If these requests are granted, I believe that we can make the new theme park a reality by 1971." At the screening, Roy released some additional project details from ERA and other studies to help convince the policymakers that Disney needed maximum flexibility with the least amount of constraints to accomplish the project. In return, Disney's success would benefit the Florida economy, with peak crowds in the resort's first year estimated at 50,000 guests per day.

The ERA study anticipated that the property needed to accommodate more than 12,000 automobiles per day. To mitigate the traffic impacts, Disney suggested that the state construct "a major interchange joining Interstate Highway I-4 and State Road 530, to provide adequate lanes from I-4 to an Entrance Interchange". Plus, Disney wanted the state to build another interchange that would connect State Road 530 to the Disney property. If the state did its part, Disney would build all the roads on the property.

The Reedy Creek Improvement District

From Roy's perspective, the most important objective for this film event was to make sure that the Florida legislature enacted the necessary ordinances to make the project happen. Disney wanted three things. In addition to the two interchanges, Disney wanted the state to create the Reedy Creek Improvement District (RCID) as the overall administrator for the entire property. Within the boundaries of the RCID would be the cities of Bay Lake and Lake Buena Vista.[52] Roy reminded the crowd, "We must have a solid legal foundation." Disney was not seeking public funds for a private enterprise. They were seeking unprecedented control over their property. They wanted flexibility, not red tape.

One of the most perplexing problems facing Walt in his effort to build a community was the conflict between his desire to fully control the project and the rights of residents to vote. Disney explored a number of creative ways to deal with the governance issue. It was Florida attorney Paul Helliwell, who was serving as lead legal counsel, who first suggested that Disney create its own municipality. Walt was not so sure. In *Project Future*, Chad Emerson writes, "Jules Stein, a friend who at the time was a lead executive of Universal Studios, had cautioned Walt against creating new cities as part of his Florida project. This caution resulted from trouble Stein had encountered after incorporating Universal City, a parcel of land the [Universal] Studios owned in the county outside the Los Angeles city limits." You can see the Disney Burbank studio from the upper lot at Universal City.

Helliwell convinced Walt and Roy that creating their own municipality would give them the greatest control over the property. A municipality would allow for ways to limit the review of other agencies, thereby providing the greatest flexibility. It would allow them to control the utilities. In *Married to the Mouse*, Richard Fogelsong summed up a 1966 ERA report, noting, "Both capitalism and democracy were problematic; each produced fragmentation of effort. The Disney solution was centralized administration—benign, paternalistic, based on expertise."

---

52 Attorney Bob Foster named Lake Buena Vista after the street where the Disney Studios were located in Burbank.

When the issue of voting rights was raised, Helliwell assured the brothers that Florida law had already been tested. Marvin Davis said, "Walt's thought was that in order to maintain the original philosophy of keeping this an experimental prototype, it would have to be something that was pretty much controlled by the company... This is something that we never really discuss very much publicly... In order to have the control that is necessary there, you would just about eliminate the possibility of having a voting community. Because the minute they start voting, then you lose control, and that's the end of the possibility of experimental development."

Walt and Roy agreed that the solution was to restrict voting rights to property owners. Using provisions provided under the Florida Drainage District Act, the landowners would elect a five-person Board of Supervisors. Each landowner would have one vote for every acre of land he owned above one-half acre. Since Disney was the sole property owner for much of the property, there would never be a conflict. Anybody who lived on the property would be leasing from Disney; therefore, they would not have voting rights with regard to land-use issues.

This solution had to be approved by the Florida Legislature, and the political climate was in Disney's favor. The Reedy Creek Improvement District (RCID) and the cities of Lake Buena Vista and Bay Lake were born on May 12, 1967, when Claude Kirk, Florida's new governor, signed the 481-page enabling bill. General Joe Potter said, "It gave us all the powers of the two counties in which we sit to the exclusion of their exercising any power." He added, "Of course it let us issue bonds." Potter noted that the only powers that still reside with bodies outside of Lake Buena Vista and Bay Lake "are the taxing power of Orange County, the sales tax of the state, and the inspection of elevators". The Florida Supreme Court ruled in 1968 that the RCID could issue tax-exempt bonds for public projects even though Disney was the sole beneficiary.

Richard Fogelsong described "a twin-tiered government, with two general-purpose local governments on the bottom and a special-purpose district on top". The benefit was that "the RCID controls both tiers: the forty-seven residents in the two cities are trusted, supervisory-level Disney employees, and the special-district government is controlled by the landowner, Disney". The purpose for having the two cities was to create an environment where all of the land was within the city limits of a municipality. The residents could not vote to incorporate those areas outside of any boundary. They already live within a municipal boundary. In Florida, only a popularly elected government could regulate building codes and land use. Since Disney controlled the cities, they controlled the planning and zoning authority. Fogelsong called the arrangement "a Vatican with mouse ears".

How unprecedented was this action? The governor turned to Roy and said, "Mr. Disney, I've studied the Reedy Creek Improvement District. It's very comprehensive. I noticed only one omission. You made no provision for the crown."

The RCID is the multi-jurisdictional organization responsible for the governance of the Walt Disney World Resort property. While the RCID is based on the legal foundation of a special utility district, it has morphed into something never seen before, a private/public agency with more powers than most elected governments in the United States.

When the *Project Florida* film was first shown to the public during the February 2, 1967, press event, Roy Disney first suggested the creation of this special agency. The Disney staff and Florida legislators drafted the formation papers for the RCID in 1967 to manage the property. According to Donn Tatum, "An essential ingredient of a Community of the Future is that it always remain in a state of becoming." Not only did the Florida Legislature create the RCID, they also incorporated the cities of Bay Lake and Lake Buena Vista under Chapter 298 of the Florida statutes. Matthew Arnold noted, "Chapter 298 required the circuit court to grant approval of this resource management district once the requesting landowners met certain rudimentary requirements. Once permitted, the new district, named for the major waterway that flowed through the property, encompassed not only Disney's property, but also those circumscribed areas still owned by holdout landowners."

Donn Tatum described the RCID: "In essence, a composite of special assessment, improvement and taxing districts already provided for under existing Florida laws, each of which now provides for a separate and independent district under separate governing bodies." The result is "the effect of combining the services these districts perform within a single District under a single governing body".

The legislation created three governmental agencies that would oversee the development of the 27,400-acre Disney property with the RCID in the lead. The RCID was originally created primarily to deal with flood control, drainage, and pest control issues. However, the unique agreement granted authority over a much broader range of issues, such as building and maintaining roadways, utility and sewer systems, public transit and public safety services, and regulating the zoning and building codes. Like other public agencies, the RCID could also issue bonds. They even had authority to approve a nuclear power reactor as long as it followed federal guidelines.

One of the few things the RCID cannot do is to regulate schools. Schools were not an issue in the first phase due to the very small permanent population. Nevertheless, Walt planned to build schools in EPCOT, and he was very interested in reinventing the educational system to "welcome new ideas so that everyone who grows up in EPCOT will have skills in pace with today's world".

All three governmental agencies, the RCID and the two cities, are required to comply with the Florida Local Government Comprehensive Planning and Development Regulation Act. In 1965, Marvin Davis and his team drafted the original development plan, which guided the development of the Magic Kingdom theme park, resorts, golf courses, plus a city that combines residential, commercial, and industrial uses along with the infrastructure to support all of this. That plan outlined how Disney World would be surrounded by a large greenbelt and protected from the outside world. This would not be a sequel to Anaheim. This would be a whole new production. It may be hard to believe today, but the RCID was more than 16 miles from the nearest major urban development at the time.

The RCID is governed by a document called a comprehensive plan, which is the primary document that regulates issues such as land use, conservation, urban design, infrastructure, and other factors that add to the character and quality of life within a community. This document is required by state law and is intended to ensure the local agency is protecting the quality of the environment and providing for the necessary infrastructure for a resort the size of a medium-sized city. Think of a comprehensive plan, or general plan as it is known in other parts of the country, as a blueprint for the future. Author Bill Fulton said, "The idea of the comprehensive plan is that the future physical form of a community should be envisioned and laid out in a forward-looking and wide-ranging document, often accompanied by maps and other graphic representations of the community's physical form." The fundamental purpose of land-use planning is resource allocation. Land has an intrinsic value that can be amplified through development or preservation. A comprehensive plan is a long-range policy planning tool that informs policymakers and all interested parties the best path to maximize those assets.

The 1965 Davis plan guided the development through the resort's opening in 1971. The RCID drafted its first comprehensive plan in 1974, when phase one of the project was completed. In keeping with the experimental nature of the Walt Disney World project, the RCID Comprehensive Plan predated the state's mandatory planning regulations, which were not put in effect until 1975.

The primary function for the comprehensive plan is to govern the location and intensity of land uses. In 1974, as it is now, the RCID was fortunate because there was little concern about conflicting land use like a government would have in a traditional city. Here, one entity owns much of the property and intergovernmental relationships have been firmly established. The planning process does take into consideration the impact of internal changes on the surrounding communities. The RCID planning process has always been meant to be a collaboration between regional and local agencies.

The RCID plan became the model for other Florida communities. At the time, the information would fit onto one map; today, the RCID plan uses more than 40 maps. The plan was modified in 1979 to meet the state's updated standards.

Throughout that first decade, the plan served the RCID and Disney; however, by the mid-1980s, the company was about to enter a period of very rapid growth with the opening of EPCOT and the arrival of Michael Eisner and Frank Wells. In 1988, consultants working with the RCID and Disney rewrote the plan with the expectation of having three theme parks and a much larger number of hotels, amenities, and second-tier attractions. Because of this effort, the state modified the land-use regulations in 1993. The success of the resort meant that urban development around the RCID property was starting to encroach. This was the motivation for another comprehensive plan update that started in 1996 and was completed in 1999.

In 2004, Comcast was interested in buying The Walt Disney Company. Concerned about what this could mean, the Florida legislature authorized a study to look at issues related to a change in ownership of the property. The state identified options for ensuring adequate governance of the RCID, including codifying a process to recall RCID board members as well as increased oversight of the RCID's operations. However, none of those changes were implemented when no deal was struck and the acquisition stalled.

A 2008 comprehensive plan update—still in effect in 2011—is based on nine goals, which are documented in the plan. The first goal is "to preserve the integrity of the natural environment; maintain convenient, efficient public services; minimize threats to health and safety; and control and direct future development through policies, principles and standards that support the potential for economic benefit". The RCID must continue to "maintain a safe, convenient, efficient, and balanced transportation system to meet the multi-modal capacity requirements of existing and future development".

Other goals include the RCID's original primary purpose, which was "to provide water, sewer, solid waste, and stormwater management services to existing and future development within its boundaries in the most efficient, cost-effective, and environmentally sound manner possible". They are also responsible for protecting and conserving the natural resources of the district. Since most of the property is tourist oriented, another goal is to "promote the creation of state-of-the-art vacation and recreational facilities; to maintain and expand access to these facilities; and to retain the visual, environmental, and psychological benefits provided by open space in the District" and "to promote intergovernmental coordination with the two cities within its boundaries; the two counties in which it is located; other local governments in the immediate vicinity; and regional, state and federal governmental entities for the mutual benefit of all involved parties". The RCID is also responsible for promoting "adequate public facilities to existing and planned development areas in a manner that is concurrent with the impacts of such development and [that is] efficient and consistent with available financial resources". It must also provide enough housing for "current and future permanent residents". Finally, the RCID must "facilitate the provision of an adequate supply of affordable housing for any unmet affordable housing need generated by employment growth within the district".

1969

On April 30, 1969, Roy took the project a giant leap forward at another press conference entitled Walt Disney World—Phase 1. To honor his brother and to remind everyone who was responsible for the development in Florida, Roy renamed the project Walt Disney World. This press conference was the first time that the general public got a look at what was proposed for the vast Disney property. Disney dwanted to put on a big show, so they rented out the entire Ramada Inn in Ocoee, Florida. In attendance was the new governor of Florida, Claude Kirk; Roy Disney; and Donn Tatum, Vice President of Walt Disney World Productions. Card Walker, who had been named executive vice president and chief operating officer when Walt died, hosted the show.

Throughout the evening, leaders from the various companies sponsoring the project touched on their contributions. Edwin Gott of United States Steel noted that the unitized modular construction for the Contemporary and Polynesian hotels was an experiment that could lead to lower construction costs for housing. Instead of each room weighing 30 tons, this modular process brought the weight down to 6 tons. With less load, everything from the foundation on up would cost less to build. Chase Morrissey of RCA pledged to develop the first completely computer-controlled telecommunications system.[53] Also making presentations were executives from Monsanto and Aerojet-General Corporation.

---

53   In a 1969 press release, RCA promised to develop "a dramatic preview of tomorrow's system technology at Walt Disney World." This would be the "first 21st century information-communications system as a total service for guests, residents, and management." It featured a "System of Systems" called WEDCOMM that linked the various communications technologies together.

Walt had found his ideal property in Florida. He had enough land to do anything he wanted, and the state had handed Disney a legal arrangement that gave the project complete control over the land use. Walt's team would carry on and gather the necessary entitlements to implement his dream. Everybody at Disney was on board for the first phase, which included the Magic Kingdom, a variety of resorts, and the infrastructure for long-term growth.

To describe Walt's power of persuasion, Edna Disney, Roy O. Disney's wife, told Richard Hubler in 1968, "Walt had a way of telling you about what he wanted to do and explaining it to you in a way that you fell right in line with him. You would go right along with him; you couldn't help it. He just had a way of telling it to you that way." She added, "Walt had very expressive brown eyes, and he used his eyes a lot. He'd use his eyes and hands and tell you all about everything and explain it all to you. That was his way of making you believe it all—and he was usually right." But Walt was gone.

What had happened to his vision for the City of Tomorrow? What would it have been like to visit? That is the next step in this journey.

Chapter Fourteen

The Promise of Progress City

The Carousel of Progress stage show was the centerpiece of the General Electric Pavilion at the 1964–1965 New York World's Fair. The show proved to be so popular that it was moved to Disneyland in 1967 as one of the major attractions in the newly remodeled Tomorrowland. Carousel of Progress used sophisticated Audio-Animatronics and a novel theater to take the audience on a light-hearted journey through time so the audience could witness how each new generation of electrical appliances had improved the quality of our life.[54] After the show's finale, the giant turntable would make one last turn; when it stopped, guests were invited to step on stage, ride the Speedramp to the second level, choose one of the three rows, and prepare to be dazzled. At the top of the ramp was the Progress City model. Let's revisit the model to learn how Walt's vision reflected the timeless principles for building vibrant communities.[55]

---

54   The Carousel of Progress theater was specially designed to handle very large crowds. The guest seating area was placed on a huge turntable that rotated around one of six stages. The show was broken down into six acts. The pace of the show was inspired by the Thornton Wilder play *Our Town*. Like the Magic Highways USA television program, Carousel of Progress offered a history lesson about home appliances and how they had impacted our lives. If you had been in the audience in 1967, this is what you would experience: During the first act, the audience's eyes are fixated on the dancing kaleidoscope light display while the stage is set for what is to come. The audience is treated to a dramatic orchestration of the Carousel of Progress theme song, the Sherman Brothers' "There's a Great Big Beautiful Tomorrow". (An updated version of the song is now performed at Disneyland's Innoventions attraction.) The platform under the seats begins to move as you enter the next scene. It is now the late 1800s. Scenes continue to roll, through the 1920s and into the 1940s. The final act finds the Audio-Animatronics hosts, Father and Mother, celebrating Christmas. The scene is set sometime in the near future, possibly within five years after the show was installed at Disneyland. The couple talks about the good life in Progress City. In the background, just beyond the floor-to-ceiling windows, is the EPCOT/Progress City skyline, which looks much like the drawings of EPCOT's city center.

55   The 1967 model was disassembled in 1973 and a small section was moved to Tomorrowland at the Magic Kingdom in Walt Disney World. Today, some of the

Progress City is an impressive scale model that reveals Walt's vision for EPCOT. Based on many of the drawings used during the EPCOT planning process, this huge model covers 6,900 square feet and measures 115 feet by 60 feet. Everything is built to the scale of one-eighth inch to the foot, and is incredibly detailed, with more than 4,500 structures, 22,000 scale shrubs and trees, and 1,400 working streetlights. Many of the buildings are lit from within. Some of the building interiors are even furnished. At the center of the model is a huge megastructure with a dome-like shape punctuated by skylights and a gleaming 30-story hotel tower.

The central city is surrounded by a greenbelt filled with a wide variety of structures: beautiful and sleek Mid-Century Modern civic buildings, an amusement park with spinning rides, and a lake with a Tiki restaurant on one edge. Surrounding this greenbelt are single-family homes and more parks. Way off in the distance is an atomic power plant. Look closely and you can see moving sidewalks and electric carts. Jet airplanes are seen leaving the Progress City airport.

The model is fully animated. The transportation network—monorails, automobiles, and WEDway PeopleMovers—has 2,450 vehicles in constant motion. According to one 1967 press release, this model is not fantasy; it could "be built today through applications of the most advanced technologies". Plus, you get to experience an entire day in a matter of minutes at Progress City. The lighting begins during the day, but slowly turns into night. At one magic moment, all of the lights in the model come alive and the city becomes "a sparkling jewel".

While we are viewing Progress City, Father and Mother from the Carousel of Progress narrate a four-minute tour of the model. Father proclaims, "Every time we think we have gone as far as we can, there is a springtime of progress." As they talk about the various community features, spotlights shine on that part of the model. Over there is the new General Electric nuclear power plant. On the other side is a local amusement park, which, Mother says, "[is] not exactly Disneyland, but it is clean and bright and lots of fun". Father tells us that the "heart of the city is the rapid transit system" and Mother tells us that "shopping is a breeze" and it is "not a chore to go downtown anymore". We learn that Grandma and Grandpa are leaving on a jet; and Father looks to the future and says, "Imagine how fast air travel will be when the SSTs [supersonic transporters] arrive." Father and Mother tell us how life in Progress City is convenient and rewarding, and we are

---

model can be seen from the Tomorrowland Transit Authority PeopleMover. Sadly, much of the detail has been removed, and none of the vehicles move anymore. In this tour, we revisit the model in its prime—the model I remember.

assured that everything we have witnessed is possible today, thanks to General Electric. Of course, the optimistic theme song that weaves its way into our heads continues to play in the background as we exit. "There's a great big beautiful tomorrow/Shining at the end of every day."

In a 1967 report issued by WED Enterprises, we learn that "the overall design of…Progress City is based on a concept developed by Walt Disney himself for the Experimental Prototype Community of Tomorrow, EPCOT, which he had planned for…Florida." In *The "E" Ticket*, Marty Sklar commented on the model: "I went through a lot of material with Marvin Davis, and with other people who were in the trenches on it… [A]s we began developing the model of the idea…we called it Progress City. That model almost exactly matched all our planning for EPCOT. I think Walt got a kick out of doing that model, without having to say that he was going to build this big city, but it was all there for anybody to see." Guests could view the model in the Carousel of Progress post-show or from the PeopleMover. Sklar estimated that during its Disneyland run, more than 31 million people saw the model.

Walt loved using models for all of his ideas. Maybe it had something to do with his passion for miniatures. He was heard to say that drawings lie, but models always tell the truth. Models can help the designer understand a project in new ways. A carefully crafted, highly detailed model can affirm the design direction or point out fatal flaws. This may explain why he required so many of his projects to go through modeling as part of the design process—even a project as large as a city.

The EPCOT Film

Possibly the most significant artifact that publicly discusses Walt's thinking about EPCOT is the 1967 film, *Project Florida*, better known as the EPCOT film. Sadly, Walt passed away two months after he recorded the film. This artifact provides us a bird's eye view of the project as described by Walt Disney himself.

Marty Sklar drafted the script; the set was designed to look like the Florida Room—featuring the same 16-foot aerial map of the Florida property—that was used by the project team at the WED headquarters in Glendale, California. Walt practiced before a select audience: actor Walter Pidgeon, Art Linkletter, and Welton Becket. When the film was ready, an accompanying press release explained, "This film reviewed Walt Disney Productions' experience in the operation of Disneyland and outlined in detail the design concepts for Disney World's proposed Experimental Prototype Community of Tomorrow." Let's "watch" Project Florida and see what we learn about EPCOT.

The film begins with a history of Disneyland and tells of the economic benefits the Orange County, California, region has reaped since the opening of the park. We are reminded that Walt built something unique and very special: an amusement park dedicated "to the happiness of the people who visit here" and functionally concerned primarily with meeting the public need. As proof of the validity of Walt's accomplishments, the announcer quotes extensively from James Rouse's 1963 speech to the Harvard Graduate School of Design, in which he explained why he believed "the greatest piece of urban design in the United States today is Disneyland". Then the film moves into truly exciting territory. We enter the secret Florida Project office, where Walt Disney is waiting to "bring you up to date about some of the plans for Disney World".

On every wall of the set are drawings of the proposed project in Florida. Walt starts by showing us exactly where the resort is located. We zoom down through a series of maps until we, too, are convinced that this is obviously the best location. It is apparent that the property is right at the center of the state and at the crossroads of major highways. Guests visiting Florida will not have to go out of their way to get to Disney World.

In dramatic fashion, Walt proudly demonstrates just how large the Disney World property is. Using himself as a scale, he is dwarfed by the map on the wall. "According to this scale, I am six miles tall!" With even greater pride he tells his audience, "The area we propose to develop is between the Reedy Creek swamp and the Bonnet Creek swamp. So one thing we don't need is a fence to protect us from trespassers." He reminds us, "Here in Florida we have something special we never enjoyed at Disneyland: the blessing of size."

In the film, Walt tells us, "I don't believe there is a challenge anywhere in the world that's more important to people everywhere than finding solutions to the problems of our cities." In order to implement this vision, he proclaims that "[we] start with the public need. And the need is not just curing the old ills of old cities. We think the need is for starting from scratch on virgin land and building a special kind of new community." He cautions us that "the sketches and plans you will see today are simply a starting point". We are warned that "everything in this room may change time and time again as we move ahead". But he promises, "The basic philosophy of what we're planning for Disney World is going to remain very much as it is right now."

Walt said, "[Disneyland is] something that will never be finished. Something that I can keep developing, keep 'plussing' and adding to. It will be a live, breathing thing that will need change." He made the same pledge for EPCOT. EPCOT would "[a]lways be in a state of becoming" and "never cease to be a living blueprint of the future where people actually live a life they can't find anyplace else in the world". This would be a city "dedicated to the happiness of the people who live, work, and play here, and those who come here from around the world to visit our living showcase". Welcome to Walt's technological utopia! And he is not going to do this alone. He is "counting on the cooperation of American industry to provide their very best thinking during the planning and the creation of our Experimental Prototype Community of Tomorrow".

As the film continues, we leave Walt and the announcer takes us on a tour of the EPCOT proposal. This will be a clean-sheet project; it will not resemble anything else that came before. EPCOT will demonstrate "to the world what American communities can accomplish through proper control of planning and design". Like Disneyland, EPCOT is based on the radial plan. Like Radburn and many post-war, master-planned communities, EPCOT also acknowledges that the automobile is here to stay. We learn that EPCOT will be a showcase to utilize and test new materials and ideas from American industry. It will be an opportunity to find solutions to urban problems and generate demand for new technologies.

At the end of the film, Walt gives a call to action; he wants to "bring together the technical know-how of American industry and the creative imagination of the Disney organization". The result will be "a showcase to the world of the American free enterprise system".[56]

John Hench said, "Walt saw building a city very much like a movie. You start with scene one, which relates to scene two and scene three. And you don't leave out any of the parts." He added, "There's a flow of relations that you must have so that their attention doesn't wander."

Heart of Our Cities— A Personal Reflection

The model of Progress City sparked my initial curiosity about EPCOT. I learned a lot more about the project after watching the EPCOT film many times. I also began to read everything I could find on the subject and that stoked my interest even more. But it was a chance meeting with Dave Smith when he was the chief archivist at Disney that really opened my eyes to the significance of Walt's vision.

I met Dave Smith while taking a tour of the Disney Archives. I asked him if Walt had been reading any urban planning books at the time of his death.

---

56 Walt actually filmed two different endings: one targeting the Florida legislature and the other aimed at the business community.

He told me, "Actually, on checking in [Walt's] office inventory, [I found that] he had only one book on the subject, *The Heart of Our Cities* by Victor Gruen." The book, published in 1964, is Gruen at his best as he explores ideas for city building based on his research and his experience. Let's explore some of his ideas to see how his book might have been of interest to Walt.

The Heart of Our Cities opens with Gruen on a cruise, reflecting upon the fate of our cities as the ship makes its way across the Atlantic. Gruen notices that a cruise ship is a city, with everything planned with an emphasis on function, comfort, and convenience. As Gruen suggests, "One of the primary purposes for a city is to bring together many people so that, through direct communication with each other, they may exchange goods and ideas without undue loss of energy and time." Gruen says a city that is functioning properly gives one "free choice" to be "sociable" or to be private—to express your "human gregariousness" while meeting others or "the chance to disappear".[57]

In *The Heart of Our Cities*, Gruen mentions Disneyland and finds the park to be an important urban space and an excellent example of cellular urban organization. He states that the park has become "a social center, a center of national and international tourism". Nevertheless, he is critical of what has happened to the area surrounding the park.

Although I could find no record of Walt and Gruen ever meeting, in separate interviews they each shared the same belief that television and the suburbs were sapping the vitality out of our city centers. They both figured that if you lose the center, the community is soon to be lost as well. Both men had major issues with Los Angeles, in particular. Gruen blasted the blight of billboards on Ventura Boulevard, while Walt battled the "second rate Las Vegas" developing around his park in Anaheim. By the 1960s, the area just outside of Disneyland's gates was becoming a hodgepodge of motels, restaurants, and other tourist-serving enterprises. The look was chaotic and threatening. Walt lamented, "We didn't create it, but we get blamed for it."

Gruen studies these "forces that threaten and destroy the city" and how they produce the Anti-City. Gruen argues that Disneyland was a great start, but that more land-use regulations would be needed. Anaheim's laissez-faire attitude toward planning of the public realm was destroying Walt's strong urban center.[58] Gruen also expresses frustration with the lack

---

57   The best of the Disney parks also exhibits this freedom. As John Hench said, "[People] feel more content here, in a way that they can't explain. You find strangers talking to each other without any fear."

58   Gruen's criticism and Walt's concerns went unheeded for many years; it was

of progress in the development of new public transportation technologies. He comments that millions of people go to Disneyland to ride a monorail that is being promoted as the transportation system of the future, but he is disappointed that the technology had been around since the 1890s.

It is revealing that the only urban planning book in Walt's collection was *Heart of Our Cities*; certainly he must have resonated with its message, especially with regard to solving the mobility issues. Technologies for transportation systems were among Walt's passions and specialties, and he made major improvements upon Gruen's designs. For EPCOT, Walt proposed to use monorails, PeopleMovers, and electric vehicles to move people around. Once again, Walt would synthesize the best of other people's ideas and create something not only better, but wholly unique.

Curiosity—What Did Walt Need to Know to Build His City?

The Progress City model piqued my curiosity and created within me a passion for urban planning history. Could such a city be built? Would it fulfill the promises made during the presentation? How does the city planning process aid or hinder the creation of great communities? Surely Walt would have asked these questions. Let's start with some basics about the profession of land-use planning to help us understand how Walt might have proceeded with designing his city.

Land is a valuable, limited resource. City planners manage the process that enhances that resource through development or preservation. According to planner and author Bill Fulton, a "city planner is a manager of a public process that determines the intensity and geographical arrangements of various land uses in a community". Many city planners work for local governments. Others work in the private sector and support the public process as consultants or technical specialists. City planners are also called urban planners, urban designers, land-use planners, and many other titles, depending on the specialty or focus. Planners "measure it, manage it, regulate it", and try to find the best possible use for the land. Sometimes they even get it right.

Good planning is dynamic. H. Stanley Judd said, "A good plan is like a road map; it shows the final destination and usually the best way to get there." Land is a precious resource, and it must be managed well or we will create places that are unlivable and do not reach their highest potential.

---

not until 2001 that a cohesive vision for the area was implemented through the Anaheim Resort Specific Plan.

City planners tend to look at the land differently than architects, just as city planners and architects tend to view the world differently. "Architecture is the thoughtful making of space," according to the great architect Louis Kahn. Many architects are focused on the object and how that object interacts within the context of the surrounding space. City planners, however, deal with the process. They provide direction for the application of the patterns that lead to good design, and they draft the policies that allow for creation of thoughtful spaces. Christopher Alexander said, "Process plays a more fundamental role determining the life and death of the building or city than does the 'design'." City planners understand what Walt meant when he said, "Happiness is spontaneous delight harmonized with circumstances." That is the type of environment they try to create every day.

Engineers play an important role in city planning, too; but they are an entirely different breed than either planners or architects. Matthew Frederick said, "Engineers tend to be concerned with physical things in and of themselves. Architects are more directly concerned with the human interface with physical things." He added, "An architect knows something about everything. An engineer knows everything about one thing." Walt well understood this tension between planners, architects, and engineers and with great pride coined the name for his team of designers that represents a blending of all of the disciplines: Imagineer.

Evolutionary, Not Revolutionary

According to Buzz Price, Walt wanted to learn everything he could about city building once he got that shot in Palm Beach. Even though the Palm Beach opportunity did not work out, Walt's interest in city planning continued to grow.

Urban planning in America has a long and proud tradition. We don't need to know the complete history of the profession to appreciate Walt's expertise; it is sufficient to learn a little bit about a few people who have had a strong influence on the trade. For example, both Christopher Alexander and William H. Whyte possessed enormous intuition and discipline, and they explored our built environment in mind-numbing detail. The results of their work are tools that help unlock the patterns that make up our built environment and help us create other beautiful and functional places.

Another genius and influence was Harrison "Buzz" Price, who figured out a way to measure virtually anything. He had a unique ability to take Walt's abstract dreams and translate them into algorithms that could count every potential dollar. This layer of discipline allowed Walt to focus even harder on creating the best possible experience, knowing all the while that with Price's contribution he would never stray too far from reality. After all, it was the money that he made on one project that helped to pay for the next new big idea. As we have seen, Walt was a dreamer, but Walt was also a practical man.

Probably one of the most inspirational city planners in America was Daniel Burnham. Burnham was the force behind the 1893 World's Columbian Exposition, the World's Fair along the Chicago shoreline that spawned the City Beautiful movement. Burnham drafted the 1909 Plan of Chicago, which to this day influences the way that city is developed. In the plan Burnham said, "Make no little plans; they have no magic to stir men's blood and probably themselves will not be realized." He added, "Make big plans; aim high in hope and work, remembering that noble, logical diagram once recorded will never die, but long after we are gone will be a living thing, asserting itself with ever-growing insistency." Anyone who has seen the few drawings of EPCOT that have been released to the public would agree that Burnham's concept might have resonated with Walt.

There were other larger-than-life characters in planning: for example, the all-too-powerful Robert Moses and his foe, writer Jane Jacobs, who wrote with such clarity that she changed the way we look at our existing neighborhoods and taught us how to understand, appreciate, and protect our shared vision.

Walt's approach toward city building was less revolutionary and more evolutionary. He learned from the best, reconfigured their ideas and qualities, and created something that was not only substantially better than what came before, but that would also continue to improve over time. What Walt wanted to get back to was the human-scale community. He wanted to return the public realm back to people. He knew that, for too long, we had been designing our public and private spaces for the convenience of the automobile. There had to be a better way. Had he known him, Walt would surely have agreed with Richard Bernhardt, a leader in the "New Urbanism" design movement that arose in the early 1980s.[59] Bernhardt identified seven principles that contribute to a human-scale community. He defined human-scale community as one that "maximizes pedestrian comfort and at the same time accommodates the automobile". Bernhardt said, "The basic building block of a community is the neighborhood." He advocated that a cluster of districts builds a true community.

---

59 Although the Walt Disney Company does not like the New Urbanism label for its town, Celebration—which opened in 1996—is possibly the best-known example of the movement.

We can easily see these principles in practice at Disneyland, which is divided up into many "lands". Each of the lands is limited in physical size, and each has a well-defined edge and center with a walking distance from edge to edge that is generally less than a quarter of a mile. Each land also has a fine-grained mix of uses, with something for everyone. Disneyland's corridors form boundaries between the lands that both connect and define them. The proportion of the buildings is carefully thought out, even more so than most urban spaces. There is a range of transportation options. All of the internal streets form a network with a large number of alternative routes. The civic buildings and gathering places are perfectly placed and provide orientation to the guests. Because Disneyland had been so successful in demonstrating all of these qualities, it gave Walt the confidence that he could apply many of the same lessons to his new town.

The Three Urban Development Patterns

Human habitats tend to develop along some very familiar patterns. Andres Duany, one of the founders of the New Urbanism movement, documented three such patterns. He called these models Urban Boundary, the Rural Boundary Model, and Transit-Oriented Development (TOD). Walt's EPCOT is a rare example of a community that could be successfully based on a blend of all three.

The Urban Boundary model is also known as Town and Country, and it was not exactly a new idea; this is the city-planning model that Ebenezer Howard advocated in his book, *Garden Cities of To-morrow* (1902). Howard first developed the Urban Boundary pattern in response to the railroads. Rail works best when stations are in well-defined development nodes with services and a variety of land uses nearby. This pattern is mostly influenced by the social structure of the community. It is not uncommon to see the development boundary move over time. In the mid-20th century, American planner Benton MacKaye[60] suggested that the Urban Boundary model is like building a dam around the city and allowing growth to rise within its boundaries. Over time, the city becomes increasingly denser, like a lake rising behind the dam. You can always build a higher dam if the market demands.

Basically, the Urban Boundary method of regulating growth looks at

---

60   Benton MacKaye is remembered primarily as the father of the Appalachian Trail.

the statistical needs of the city and projects a line on a map that delineates what is urban and what is rural. Sometimes this is called an urban growth boundary. Anything outside of that boundary is considered a different community. The goal is to protect the countryside from unwanted development. The City of Portland, Oregon, among others, has adopted this model. It is easy to identify a community based on the Urban Boundary model. The region typically has a dense urban core surrounded by neighborhoods. Each core is connected to other city cores by rail or highways. Between each city should be a greenbelt or open space. Sometimes, that open space has been spoiled by random development, diluting the benefit of the urban growth boundary.

The Rural Boundary model has also been called the Corridor and Wedge pattern. The development goal for cities planned according to this model is to safeguard valuable open space and channel urbanized areas along transportation corridors. The pattern of development is mostly influenced by ecological concerns. MacKaye, founder of the environmental movement in the United States in the 1910s, was the first to rationalize this model. In 1929, he suggested that highways be confined to the countryside and not be urbanized, saying that if you develop along the highways, you would damage the fabric of cities and destroy the countryside.

In the Rural Boundary model, planners start by setting aside specific sensitive areas and allowing development to reach those boundaries over time. MacKaye said this was like building a levee to protect special environmental areas and allowing the development stream to come right to the edge. In this process, planners design with nature. They determine the environmental assets that the community wants to protect from development and plan accordingly. The resulting plans allow development to encroach right to those boundaries, but it is not allowed to enter the sensitive area. The development takes on a more linear form, with growth developing along corridors. The wetlands protecting the Walt Disney World property are an excellent example of a sensitive area; development within the resort extends to the wetlands and tends to follow the various transit corridors.

Cities that were built during the time of streetcars were based on this development model. The streetcar (or, now, freeway) corridor could wind between the protected open space areas, extending development as far as the market would allow. Development becomes denser at transit stops and at intersections of major roadways. Sometimes these development nodes at intersections are bigger than central core cities, as documented in 1991 by Joel Garreau in *Edge City: Life on the New Frontier.*

A third way to organize the land use and transportation network for a community is TOD. Peter Calthorpe literally wrote the book on the subject—*The Next American Metropolis: Ecology, Community, and the American*

Dream (1993)—and he defines a TOD as a "mixed-use community within an average one-half mile pedestrian shed with a transit shop and core commercial development". This development pattern is similar to the railway suburbs of the 19th century. Mixed use refers to a building or a cluster of buildings with multiple functions that could include residential, commercial, office, or live/work space. This blending of functions enhances pedestrian activity and safety, and it reduces the need for parking space. Think of the image of Main Street, U.S.A. Downstairs are the shops, and upstairs are the imaginary offices of important people.

In the TOD model, transportation systems are the driving design force, with transit stations placed at regular intervals. Surrounding each transit station is a compact, walkable, mixed-use neighborhood. A successful TOD mixes residential, retail, office, and open space. Living in a community based on this model gives people options to commute using transit, bicycle, or on foot. Having these mobility options makes life convenient and functional for residents and employees.

When done correctly, a city organized around a network of TODs can benefit from the positive qualities of both the Rural Boundary and the Urban Boundary. In 1996, Michael Bernick and Robert Cervero said, "Transit-Oriented Development for the 21st Century must emphasize the role of the three Ds (density, diversity, design)." A properly designed TOD has a vibrancy and urbanity that is absent from most of suburbia. Architect and urban planner Léon Krier described the benefits of a TOD by comparing land-use zoning to the ingredients that it takes to bake a pie. Of course, you could consume each of the ingredients independently, but the pie-eating experience is far better when the ingredients are combined. It is the process of mixing the ingredients that creates something greater than the sum of the parts.

The power of the TOD development model is that each transit node can specialize in serving one or two functions; the transit node can itself become a true destination. Shopping and entertainment destinations could surround one stop while another stop is within the residential or industrial districts. The complete network within a region serves all of a community's needs. Since cars are still a necessity for some people, TOD parking is generally pushed behind buildings, within structures, placed in the interior of the block, or put below grade. The ground floor uses remain pedestrian-oriented, enlivening the street.

The Urban Boundary model works best when the property is under single ownership or when there is a system to transfer development rights from one landowner to another. Since Disney was the sole property owner in the Florida Project, they could set the boundaries as they saw fit. EPCOT would have demonstrated the viability of the TOD concept and could have possibly kick-started the retrofitting of our urban areas. Had EPCOT been built, Walt really could have changed the world.

The Rural Boundary model works best when there is a visionary like Walt, who instructed his team to "work with the land". The overall site plan for Disney World placed major destinations away from sensitive habitats, and the low-density residential fingers for EPCOT were determined by the existing topography and ecology. Walt's development process started with mapping the existing conditions and determining very early on which areas would be preserved and which would be developed. It is a nod to his genius that, although EPCOT was not built, the long-term Disney World development pattern has roughly mirrored his very first sketch.

The TOD model works best when the nexus transportation systems, land use, and destinations are addressed equally. Transportation technology was especially important to Walt. Perhaps he felt that a city, like a person, could solve many ills just by having a healthy circulation system. EPCOT was designed around the transit network. The major commercial center was to be located around the intersection with the most traffic. The rest of the uses were within the "pedestrian shed", the basic building block for pedestrian neighborhoods. With one set of pedestrian boulevards emanating from the central core and another pair as radials connecting the spokes, walking from one location to another would be convenient and logical. The pedestrian boulevards would come alive with shopping, dining, and other commercial activities.

The promise of Progress City was that EPCOT would become a laboratory to test new technologies, processes, and policies to create more livable urban environments. Walt said the purpose for EPCOT was to "build a living showcase that more people will talk about and come to look at than any other place in the world". EPCOT would have better access and less traffic than the traditional city. There would be a proper balance between public and private space. The community would enjoy many shared benefits and a logical relationship between the land uses and the connections that bind them together. The entire development would be very compact and would efficiently use the land, resources, and infrastructure in a thoughtful way. Walt wanted to build a city that was planned for people—not for the architecture magazines and the critics.

"More of this is true than you would believe."
– Jon Ronson, *The Men Who Stare at Goats*

Chapter Fifteen

EPCOT 1982—A Speculative Visit

Walt Disney said it would take fifteen years to build EPCOT. Alas, it was never to be built as he originally intended. Let's take what we know about the project and blend in what urban designers were thinking at that time about the development process, with the goal of peeking into what life might have been like living in EPCOT. We will also use the benefit of hindsight and utilize up-to-date urban planning tools to evaluate the strengths, weaknesses, constraints, and opportunities of the Disney World project. So, as Walt said in the EPCOT film, "By now, I'm sure you're wondering how people will live and work and move around in our community of tomorrow," but remember, "[a]s I said earlier, this is just the beginning!"

We started our journey to EPCOT by looking back at the "Magic Highway USA" television broadcast because this program was able to provide a foundation of knowledge and then add some speculation to make the impossible seem plausible. As we traveled toward EPCOT, we reviewed the timeless way of building and how Walt intuitively understood this concept and applied the timeless principles to the built environment in multiple projects, including his Burbank animation studio, his home in Holmby Hills, Disneyland, Mineral King, and CalArts.

If we follow the timeline that Walt first proposed and assume that EPCOT would have been ready for residents in fifteen years, then the groundbreaking would have been in 1967, which in fact it was—on May 30. The first phase included the theme park, resorts, a transportation network, and the necessary infrastructure for future expansion. That phase opened to the public on October 1, 1971. At that pace, the model city and industrial parks would have been completed by 1982. Disney did meet this time schedule (sort of) with the opening of Epcot Center theme park (without the industrial parks) on October 1, 1982. So far, so good, right?

It is valuable for us to learn what would have worked and what would not have worked in Walt's city and to identify if any of the timeless principles could be applied to our contemporary urban areas. As we explore the possibilities, we focus primarily on the planning and design aspects of EPCOT and Disney World as originally described by Walt Disney.

Planning is concerned with the public realm and how the city functions. Back in 1926, John Nolen described the role of urban planning in the Comprehensive Plan for San Diego. He said city planning is "an aide to the man in the street to visualize his city properly planned; a practical, sensible way of providing a place for everything with everything in its place; an instrument for uniting citizens to work for the city's future; and an efficient means of avoiding duplication and waste in public improvements".

Design refers to the city's architecture. If, as American architect Louis Sullivan presciently coined in 1896, "form ever follows function", what would the 1982 EPCOT and the rest of the Disney World resort look like?

With that, let us begin our speculative 1982 trip to Walt's EPCOT. In our fantasy visit, everything that Walt planned for Disney World, as revealed to us in the EPCOT film, is open and operational. Parenthetically, we'll also take a look at what really happened to some of the project elements as well as consider how EPCOT's timeless design is reflected in post–1982 urban planning principles.

A Bird's Eye View

The overall site plan for Disney World is basically a string of activity nodes placed along a south-to-north multi-modal transit corridor. The corridor is constrained on three sides—north, east, and west—by wilderness areas. Walt personally drew up the very first master plan; and as the planning process evolved, it did not stray very far from his initial concept. From Walt's initial schematic drawing to the final plan prepared just prior to his death, the basic alignment of land uses remained relatively the same. As Walt had said, "There's enough land here to hold all the ideas and plans we could possibly imagine."

At the southern end at the intersection of Interstate 4 and Florida's Turnpike (which was called the Sunshine State Parkway when Walt designed Disney World) is the Entrance Complex. At the northern end, drawing in visitors like a light bulb attracts moths, is the grandest wienie of them all—the Magic Kingdom theme park. In between are an industrial park and the city of EPCOT.

We learned in the EPCOT film that the string that holds all of these pearls together is the "high-speed rapid transit system (the monorail) running almost the full length of the property". Visitors flying into Orlando can land at the jetport, Disney World's own "airport of the future" in Osceola County. Guests driving to Disney World will most likely park at the Entrance Complex. Some will drive directly to their destination via a roadway system under the monorail beam.

Walt felt it was important to give people a preview of upcoming attractions—be it his movies, television show, or theme park. At Disney World, he aligned the roadways and the monorail to pass through all of the activity nodes on the way to the theme park. As we arrive at Disney World, we can see that this alignment gives all guests visibility into the Industrial Park, EPCOT, the Magic Kingdom, and other destinations.

When Walt started the Disney World design process, he first identified sensitive areas that he absolutely wanted to preserve. To define the development corridor, his engineers used the natural wetlands (Reedy Creek and Bonnet Creek) and turned them into landscaped buffers. Those areas were set aside from development in perpetuity. Next, the Imagineers selected additional open-space areas that may be a bit more subjective; they are not sensitive and could be developed but are not, because they provide other benefits to the project, including aesthetic value.

Within the open-space areas are pockets of land intended for controlled growth. Development areas are secondary to the areas worthy of preservation. In a hand-drawn sketch, Walt in 1965 marked the development areas and specified where he wanted to place the major activity nodes such as the theme park, the resorts, his city, industrial park, and other amenities like the golf course and a swamp ride.

Sometimes the function for a particular facility dictates its location. These structures cannot be located just anywhere. For example, Walt declared that the theme park would be at the north end of the property so that guests would be required to drive past the other land uses to get to it. He knew that the Entrance Complex had to be near the main highways. A Jetport, the regional airport, would work best if it were located at the southern edge of the property, away from where most of the people would be.

Once Walt located the major destinations, the street network was laid out to access all of the building sites. A trademark design element of Disney World is the network of wide curvilinear roadways. In 1934, Thomas Adams and Walter Baumgartner called this type of roadway pattern Topographical Informal. Andres Duany, founder of the Congress of New Urbanism, wrote in 2001 that the origin for the curved street "can be found in those pathways across the landscape that respond to steep topography by following the undulating patterns of the land". However, virtually all of Disney World is set on fairly level ground. Therefore, the curves are purely aesthetic. The slight bends in the roadways provide a pleasant, picturesque quality and are associated with a gentle hillside even though you are driving level. Monotony is interrupted by deflected views.

Although the curvilinear roadways may look nice, many guests find this type of road network disorienting. There is no intrinsic hierarchy. Since many visitors are unfamiliar with the basic layout of the resort and they are traveling at high speeds, Disney created special way-finding signs to increase awareness for motorists and to reduce accidents.[61]

The Disney World Jetport

Disney had the opportunity to build its own airport according to the entitlements granted as part of the Reedy Creek Improvement District legislation. From the earliest master plans, we can see that arriving by air will be a revolutionary experience. So, we decide to fly into Disney World Regional Airport for our 1982 fantasy visit; and, sure enough, landing and take offs are an "E" ticket ride. We are landing at the world's first operational radial jetport.[62]

About the early planning for the Jetport, Marvin Davis said, "The most interesting thing, I thought, was this airport, which was planned after the one in Cincinnati. We made a special trip to New York and met with the guy in charge of that airport, who said it worked like a charm. This circular plan cuts down the area that you need by half, instead of those long runways that you have now." Davis added, "They had a circular runway plan, and it worked on a banked curve for the takeoff. Walt and I had the early plan practically sold, but we ended up not doing it this way. Of course, we would have had to get all kinds of approvals from the F.A.A. [Federal Aviation Administration]." At the airport, this type of plan would be more efficient and get guests out of the air and through the facility faster. As the plans evolved, a second aviation facility was added to Disney World. The radial jetport would have been the primary airport. A second, smaller, more conventional facility would have handled general aviation. Over time, the radial airport idea went away and was replaced by a more conventional facility. The location for the airport on the Disney property moved as well. The radial facility was slated to take up most of the land

---

61   A curvilinear road network pattern is typical of master planned communities such as Irvine, California, where Ray Watson was the principal planner. Watson became the chairman of Walt Disney Productions in 1983–1984. Irvine is also on a relatively flat terrain.

62   If we had visited EPCOT earlier, we could have arrived in a Shawnee Airlines nineteen-seat de Havilland DHC-6 Twin Otter aircraft, which started service between Walt Disney World and the Orlando International Airport on October 22, 1971. Disney World was on the leading edge of air transportation technology with its STOLport, which was part of a regional network. (STOL is an acronym for Short Take-Off and Landings.) Unfortunately, that airport closed in November 1972; the runway still exists but it is no longer used as an airport.

south of Interstate 4. Instead, the facility we fly into is tucked in the wedge between the interstate and the Sunshine Parkway.

Although Walt never revealed the architecture for the Jetport, we can see that it mirrors the popular Theme Building at the Los Angeles International Airport. Built in 1961, that iconic Mid-Century Modern structure was designed by a team of architects who were all friendly to Walt Disney. William Pereira and Charles Luckman designed the Googie, or populuxe, structure with assistance from Welton Becket and Paul Williams. Walt would often turn to his friends like Becket when he knew they had special expertise. For example, Becket designed the Walt Disney World Contemporary and Polynesian resorts. This futuristic style of architecture was reflected in the redesign of Tomorrowland at Disneyland in 1967 as well.

The Entrance Complex

If we decide to drive to Disney World, we will park our automobile at the Entrance Complex and Registration Center. From there, we will rely on Disney transportation, just as Walt intended. Walt knew that Disney World and EPCOT would have to be designed to accommodate the realities of the automobile. His hope was that residents and visitors who arrive by car would be willing to park once if they are offered a superior, attractive, efficient form of mass travel as an option. After all, guests are like water; they will always search for the easiest path to get where they are going. At Disney World, there would be no traffic jams. It is hard to imagine as we visit in 1982, but when Disney World opened in 1971, the property was far away from the center of Orlando—more than sixteen miles southwest from the center of Orlando to the front gate, with a whole lot of nothing in between. Walt planned the Entrance Complex to be inviting, allow visitors to immediately decompress, and orient them so that they could be on their way toward their vacation destination.

The Entrance Complex is the sorting hub that helps guests determine which mode of travel will best get them where they want to go. We watch as many of the one-day guests pull into the 11,000-stall surface parking lot and head for the Registration Center. The parking lot is more than 141 acres.[63]

Some guests have permission to continue along a limited-access highway to the huge parking structure underneath the EPCOT Town Center or the

---

63 The proposed parking lot would be about the size of the current Epcot theme park parking lot.

surface lots adjacent to the Industrial Park buildings. Trucks are restricted to a separate roadway system. The automobile roadways run alongside the separate truck route. Both highways are under the monorail. By having different roadways for different types of vehicles, Disney is able to reduce conflicts between drivers who are not familiar with the resort and trucks in a hurry to their destination.

Other guests continue to drive directly to the Camping Area, the Trailer Park, one of the Magic Kingdom resorts, the golf course, or the nearby campgrounds and motels near Bay Lake. For the true adventurer, there is also a Wilderness camping area on one edge of the property.

Still other guests drive to one of the motel pods, each of which consists of four motels clustered around a common courtyard ringed by a road. Just as it is in Radburn and other planned communities, the common space between the structures is an amenity shared by all of the guests. Another "amenity" is that you do not need to have an automobile if you are staying at one of the motels. Whether it is by local bus service or by WEDway PeopleMover, the motel pods are conveniently connected to the Entrance Complex. As Walt had planned, guests park their cars once during the entire trip and enjoy Disney transportation the rest of the time. Like all successful TODs, Walt's design gives people options.

Once the main highway gets to the EPCOT Town Center, it dips below the massive building and divides into one-way couplets that eliminate left-turn delays, actually decreasing travel time through the area. As the EPCOT film suggested, the circulation pattern is a one-way road that circles the city center; in a sense, EPCOT is one giant roundabout. The Imagineers understood they had to control how much land was going to be dedicated to vehicles, and they knew that it costs a lot of money to park cars— money that could be put to better use elsewhere. It was futurist Glen Heimstra who said, "Trying to cure traffic congestion with more capacity is like trying to cure obesity by loosening your belt." The design team knew they could not afford to build massive freeways, but they could use the roadways smarter through technology.

Even in 1982, we can see that EPCOT is at the forefront of developing solutions that reduce vehicle miles of travel (VMT). VMT is a way to measure how much time vehicles are operating, and it is one indicator that helps to determine the level of greenhouse gases being released into the atmosphere. By providing multiple transit modes to get guests from one destination to another, Walt would have been able to control traffic congestion, thereby considerably reducing VMT.

The Transportation Lobby

At the heart of EPCOT is the Transportation Lobby. In the EPCOT film, our narrator tells us that the Transportation Lobby is a "vital center" and that the "transportation terminal will play a key role in the City of Tomorrow's ability to meet the needs of both visitor and resident". The Transportation Lobby is a multi-story terminal that is the crossroads for the various Disney World mobility systems. "Automobiles and trucks will not be barred from EPCOT," according to the film. "In fact, a vast armada of vehicles will continuously flow through the heart of the community, traveling below the pedestrian level on roadways reserved for specific types of vehicles." Most importantly, those vehicles will remain "out of sight to hotel guests".

The lowest level of the Transportation Lobby terminal is "reserved for supply vehicles". The "trucks will have easy access to all loading and service elevators for the delivery of commercial goods". The middle level is reserved for automobiles. Walt's promise was that, "for the motorist just driving through, no stoplight will ever slow the constant flow of traffic through the center of EPCOT". The plans show the use of one-way couplets, along with "parking areas for the convenience of hotel guests".[64]

The top level of the Transportation Lobby is the "heartbeat of EPCOT." This is the home base for the monorail and the WEDway PeopleMover network—both of which are elevated above the walkways. Like the Plaza Hub at Disneyland, the Transportation Lobby is the one spot where every pathway comes together; people can easily orient themselves, and then head toward a new destination.

The film said, "Two separate but interconnecting transit systems will move people into and out of EPCOT in speed, safety, and comfort through the central terminal." The monorail is "for rapid transit over longer distances" and the WEDway PeopleMover is "for shorter travel distances". Each transit system is the right scale and the right technology for the job. Both systems are powered electrically. According to Disney historian Paul Anderson, "Walt once said that in EPCOT the pedestrian would be king." Designed for the benefit of pedestrians and those using public transit, the EPCOT design intentionally discourages the use of the automobile. In

---

64 Architect and planner Peter Calthorpe has documented that one-way couplets are the best way to move automobile traffic through central cities. In *The Heart of Our Cities*, Victor Gruen suggested—based on his experience designing and building shopping malls—that truck and automobile traffic be organized in one-way couplets with convenient parking areas.

1966, Robert Moses claimed that EPCOT would be the "first accident free, noise free, pollution free city center in America".[65]

In designing EPCOT, Walt and his planners could explore how to mitigate the imbalance between vehicular traffic and pedestrians. They may have been influenced by French architect and pioneer of the Modern style Charles-Édouard Jeanneret, better known as Le Corbusier. He had proposed that cities be built with layers of transportation: automobiles on the top level, trains on the ground level, and three layers of subways below. There would be a separate pedestrian network that he called Streets in the Air. He wanted to create a pedestrian "freeway". This architectural concept was popular at the time of EPCOT's development. One example of a circulation system designed as a pedestrian freeway was the University of Illinois at Chicago, designed in 1965 by Walter Netsch of Skidmore, Owings & Merrill. Students could move anywhere on campus on wide sidewalks and rest in "council circles" carved out of the concrete. The intention was that the circulation pattern would foster informal conversations and the sharing of knowledge. However, for many people the campus felt hard and cold, and the pedestrian network was useless in the harsh Chicago winters. (Today, much of that structure has been torn down.) The hope was that Walt knew how to make such spaces more humane.

The battle between the automobile and the pedestrian had continued in the suburbs. The large regional shopping centers that gained popularity in the 1950s and 1960s typically consisted of a large structure surrounded by a giant parking field that acted like a moat. This moat "soaked up" automobiles while cutting off the center from the rest of the community. Inside the mall, the people were protected from those cars and the surrounding community and made to feel safe.

When downtown central business districts began to be threatened by these new suburban shopping centers, they countered with the pedestrian mall. Within a pedestrian mall, what had been a typical commercial boulevard would be closed off to traffic and transformed into a suburban outdoor shopping center. However, the results were not always positive, and in many instances the business district simply continued in its decline. With the lack of automobile traffic in these traditional downtowns, the malls began to

---

65   The idea of separating different transportation modes is not new. The idea is inherent in the Garden Cities approach of the late 19th century and was explicitly included in the 1929 designs for Radburn. In 1988, in his book *City: Rediscovering the Center*, William H. Whyte said, "One of the most hallowed of planning concepts is the separation of pedestrian from vehicular traffic. This is for the benefit of vehicles, so they get the prime space." Marsha Rood FAICP, a preeminent city planner, said recently, "Walkability is the soft under belly of livability."

feel deserted and unsafe, further accelerating the decline. Many pedestrian malls have been converted back into streets.[66]

In many respects, the 1967 redesign of Disneyland's Tomorrowland had been a trial run for many of the EPCOT transit initiatives. The theme for this part of Disneyland was "The World on the Move". The architecture for the new Tomorrowland was what John Hench later called "cartilaginous". In 1998, Karal Ann Marling defined the style as "an elegant way of describing a sinewy, flexible system of beamways and cantilevers connected at nodal points that were not quite buildings in the traditional sense". The beamway for the WEDway PeopleMover grew out of the ground on curved pylons that were very organic. The area featured clean, crisp Mid-Century Modern structures painted a stark white that spoke of flight and the American space program.

On display in Tomorrowland in 1967 were a wide variety of transportation technologies, each one capturing a specific space on the horizon. Way up high was the Astro Orbiter spinning rockets and the Skyway. Just below, on the second level, was the always-moving WEDway PeopleMover. At the same level was the sleek, futuristic monorail. On grade with the pedestrians was the Autopia. Below grade were the submarines, under water except for the top of their hulls and the masts. Even buildings moved in Tomorrowland, as we saw at the always-rotating Carousel of Progress. This was a world where the kinetic energy created by constant movement was an attraction in itself—and a world that suggested that Walt could succeed in creating a benevolent transportation system for EPCOT and Disney World.

When Walt decided to build a city, he figured a monorail system would become the transportation backbone for the entire project. At Disneyland, Walt had proven it could function reliably and provide a high level of service, and he wanted to integrate the technology into his city. The success of this transportation system is a principal reason why Walt thought that EPCOT could work as a city.

In EPCOT 1982, the monorail connects all of the major destinations. It starts at the airport, then heads north toward the Entrance Complex. The trains pass through the Industrial Parks and enter the Transportation Lobby below the mixed-use Cosmopolitan Hotel. From there they continue north and drop guests off at the Magic Kingdom. There are spur lines leading to the motel clusters and the low-density village projected for a later phase.

---

66 One of the most famous and successful examples of this process is State Street in Chicago, Illinois, based on a plan developed by Skidmore, Owings & Merrill (SOM).

The EPCOT WEDway PeopleMover is a "key system in [a] coordinated network" of transportation technologies and a critical piece of the puzzle. As touted in the EPCOT film, the WEDway PeopleMover is "a silent, all-electric system that never stops running". In designing EPCOT, Walt knew he needed a reliable intermediate transportation system to ferry guests from the Transportation Lobby out to the retail districts, the high-density apartments, the greenbelt with its recreational facilities, and the ring of low-density single-family homes. He also used the technology to connect the monorail to the industrial parks. As well as functioning as a transportation device, the WEDway PeopleMover also takes small detours, entering buildings to give guests a preview of what is going on inside.

Initial plans for EPCOT show a system of twenty WEDway PeopleMover lines "that radiate to and from the Transportation Lobby". In our 1982 visit, we can see that this system became the string that ties the various land-use pearls together. "From all over the community, residents going to their jobs converge by WEDway on the Center City. Many work downtown in offices, stores, and shops, but most employees go beyond the city core to their jobs." From the Transportation Lobby to the low-density residential zones at the far edge, the WEDway PeopleMover is the transportation system of choice for residents and visitors in EPCOT.

The EPCOT system features trains consisting of four attached cars, with each car seating up to four guests. The trains are much larger than either the Disneyland or Magic Kingdom versions. The "headway time", the waiting time until the next vehicle arrives, is a mere three minutes. If a train is not already at the station, a rider can press a button and it will signal one to come. If the demand decreases, surplus trains move back into the roundhouse.

This type of transportation system has an even deeper significance to the success of EPCOT. According to Michael Sorkin, "The driverless people-mover—its motions seemingly dictated by the invisible hand, mechanical creature of supply and demand—is a symbol of this economic fantasy of perfect self-government."[67]

---

67   The WEDway PeopleMover is the forerunner of another type of transportation technology called Personal Rapid Transit (PRT). At the theme parks, the custom has become one party riding in one vehicle. This is consistent with the PRT concept, whereby a guest is assigned to a private vehicle, not shared with strangers, for a nonstop, no-transfer trip from the origin station to the destination station. The WEDway PeopleMover provides an unprecedented level of privacy and security, which is a pleasant change from other forms of public transportation. It would be possible to provide users with key cards that limit access to certain stations. Disney tried to sell the PeopleMover solution to cities and shopping

The Urban Transect

One of the things that Walt was famous for was his keen eye for human behavior. He had an uncanny knack for understanding how people behave within a given environment. He was a big believer that the physical setting can impact people's behavior. Walt applied these same powers of observation to the design of his home, studio, and theme park. His first "view" of an idea was not its parts; rather, he saw the big picture and then drilled down into the tiniest of details, which intensified the locational character. That is how he was able to create such immersive environments. For any given environment, Walt made sure that all of the essential components were present.

A contemporary and powerful tool to analyze and understand how communities are organized is called the urban transect. The urban transect is useful to describe EPCOT because, according to The Lexicon of the New Urbanism, it is "a system of classification deploying the conceptual range rural-to-urban to arrange in useful order the typical elements of urbanism". As you will see, one of the most remarkable features about EPCOT from an urban planning perspective is how Walt's city followed this "natural ordering system, as every urban element easily finds a place within its continuum".

The concept for the urban transect is derived from ecological analysis. Andres Duany, one of the founders of the New Urbanism movement and the person central to the development of the urban transect, said, "Certain forms belong in certain environments. Ecologists use the transect to describe how each habitat supports symbiotic sets of mineral conditions, microclimate, flora, and fauna." An example of a transect is the progression through a sequence of natural habitats such as a shore-dune-upland to a wetland-woodland-prairie. The original idea for taking a geographical cross-section of a region and using it to reveal a sequence of environments goes back to Von Humboldt in 1790.

Only recently has the transect concept been applied to human settlements. This tool makes it easier to understand the organization of the components for city building. With this tool a community can regulate

---

mall developers. They set up a unit called the Community Transportation Services Division of Walt Disney Productions. The group offered modular systems that could be modified to meet the specific needs of its customers. In 1980, a 2.9-mile PeopleMover system was proposed for downtown Los Angeles, with 13 stops along its route from Union Station to the Convention Center. The Houston George Bush Intercontinental Airport installed a third-generation WEDway PeopleMover system in 1981.

buildings, lot size, land use, street configurations, the public realm, and everything else necessary for community living; the urban transect concept unleashes the creative talents of well-trained designers and enables them to build beautiful, functional places.

Duany says, "The transect arranges in useful order the elements of urbanism by classifying them from rural to urban." As an example, he suggests, "An apartment building fits in an urban setting and a ranch house belongs in a rural setting. A ranch house would undermine the immersive quality of a downtown district, whereas an apartment building is appropriate. Place either structure in the wrong environment and it just does not feel right." Duany had an even more poetic example: "A street is more urban than a road, a curb more urban than a swale, a brick wall more urban than a wooden one, and an allée of trees more urban than a cluster."

It is not important whether the transition between transect zones is gradual or abrupt. Take the relationship between Fifth Avenue and Central Park in New York, for example. What matters is that each zone is internally consistent. The SmartCode, a model zoning ordinance developed by Duany and many others, says the transect "organizes the natural, rural, suburban, and urban landscape into categories of density, complexity, and intensity in the same way the countryside relates to the traditional towns and villages we admire". The urban transect is meant to be a regulatory device, and it provides precise measurements to categorize different parts of our community.

We don't know if Walt or any of his designers consciously tried to achieve this goal; but we do know that if EPCOT had been built as Walt planned it, it would have been a very pure expression of the urban transect. Since it was to be built on a "clean sheet of paper"—in this case a greenfield site—the designers would not have had to incorporate pesky existing urban uses.

The urban transect is a good way to describe the design and function of EPCOT's various districts. Just like the transect described in the SmartCode, EPCOT is divided up into six zones plus a bonus. The highest-density activity node demonstrating the highest intensity of uses is the Core. The Core is supported by Centers. General Urban and Suburban zones support the Core and Centers. Beyond are Rural Reserves and Preserves. Whatever does not fit becomes a Special District.

In the EPCOT film, the transportation network circulates "to and through four primary spheres of activity surrounding the central core". The highest-density node is the center city with the resort hotel; Transportation Lobby; and the retail, dining, and office centers. "Many people who work in the offices and stores of EPCOT's city center board the WEDway here for their trip home." Next is the high-density residential urban zone that surrounds the core center city. Just outside the weather-protected enclosure is the greenbelt, which acts as the community's central park. Finally, there is a huge low-density residential zone. All of this is surrounded by a permanent environmental preserve. In addition to a central community, there are also Special Districts. At Disney World, special districts include the theme park, industrial areas, the Jetport, and the Entrance Complex.

Walt said that the initial EPCOT would be only the beginning, and some site plans do in fact anticipate future phases of development. One proposal shows low-density residential tracts adjacent to rural reserves, out on the exurban fringe at the very edge of the property. The EPCOT film even hints at more EPCOT-like domes and towers scattered throughout the region.

The Legible City

Walt wanted to create a city that would be more legible and easier for the guests to navigate, just like they could at Disneyland. What does it mean to say a city is legible? According to contemporary planners Nathan Cherry and Kurt Nagle, a legible city is a "more sustainable, balanced, and distinctive metropolis that works on all scales, from individual to regional". Kevin Lynch has said that "legibility works on many levels: individual understanding of a place and its functions needs to be as transparent as broad social and regional legibility".

To illustrate the point, let's compare a typical lifeless American city to a poorly written song. If this song has no rhythm or structure, it will have no identity. It will quickly be forgotten. What the song needs is a strong melody. That is what makes it memorable. For a city, that strong melody is its ability to be legible.

Although Walt was untrained in music, he had a miraculous ear for a memorable song. He seemed to have the same talent when it came to designing urban spaces; although he had no formal training in urban design, Walt had an extraordinary grasp of planning principles. EPCOT would be the model of the best of elements found elsewhere, but rearranged in such a way that it would become a brand-new thing. This is what happened when Walt started in animation, built the Burbank studio, and created his theme park.

In *Magic Lands*, John Findlay said Walt's goal was to create "readily identifiable, thoughtfully planned, distinctively western environments that, like a mental map, simplified land-use patterns". His use of the single entrance and the radial, or hub-and-spoke, site plan for Disneyland made all the difference. The Imagineers adopted this successful formula and applied it to the design for EPCOT.

Karal Ann Marling admired the order that came with the design of EPCOT. "Trucks enter the city through underground passageways; unseen and unheard, they discharge their cargo in a vast common basement corridor. Up above, all is rational, beautiful, and calm. Planes and factories keep their distance from houses and schools." She added, "The circles and ovals of the ground plan suggest a place with a center, or heart—a true community.

The Center City

As we tour Disney World in 1982, we can see that the most notable physical structure is the central structure of EPCOT with its skylight domes and hotel tower. Building on the success of Victor Gruen's indoor shopping centers, Walt wanted to enclose the "entire fifty acres of city streets and buildings" in the Center City so that he could protect his guests from the brutal Florida summers and give him complete control of the space. He promised, "In this climate-controlled environment, shoppers, theatergoers, and people just out for a stroll will enjoy ideal weather conditions, protected day and night from rain, heat and cold, and humidity." What is under the dome?

At the center of EPCOT is the fifty-acre elliptical Center City complex, which is a small part of the much larger 1,100-acre EPCOT project. Mike Lee described the aerial view of this structure as an "eyeball drawn by [Swiss Surrealist] H.R. Giger". Rising from the center is the 30-story Cosmopolitan Resort Hotel. Below the hotel is the Transportation Lobby.

The Hotel is surrounded by the Town Center. The Town Center is a "dynamic urban" destination that "offer[s] the excitement and variety of activities found only in the metropolitan cities: cultural, social, business, and entertainment". Along the outer rim of the enclosed structure is a ring of high-density residential apartments. The rest of EPCOT is outside of the enclosure.

Inside the enclosure, twenty-one and half acres (43%) of the space are dedicated to retail and hospitality areas.[68] The EPCOT transportation network and other public realm amenities account for sixteen acres (32%); the remaining twelve and one half acres (25%) contain non-retail uses such as office space, a television studio, banks, service shops, and warehouse space. Other non-retail uses include civic functions such as community administration, a fire station, post office, library, and a hospital.

From a distance, the central structure for EPCOT appears as a domed city with a tall central spire. However, the reality of construction costs suggests that the structure would be something far less exotic. Most likely,

---

68   As a point of comparison, the Mall of America in Bloomington, Minnesota, has over sixty-three acres of leasable retail and hospitality space.

the Center City is a series of arcades covering the pedestrian areas.[69]

The EPCOT Center City exhibits the five fundamental rules that distinguish it from urban sprawl. There is a center with identifiable neighborhoods. From most points, we would only have to walk five minutes to get to the center. The street network is legible and safe. Like the streets at the Burbank studio, the EPCOT streets are narrow, allowing the pedestrian to feel in charge. Land uses are blended and mixed; there are no large single-purpose developments.

In the EPCOT film, the announcer proclaims, "Here the pedestrian will be king, free to walk and browse without fear of motorized vehicles. Only electric-powered vehicles will travel above the streets of EPCOT's central city." The goal is to allow pedestrians to walk through the urban core without having to cross a major intersection. This is the same idea that was implemented in Radburn and is similar to a plan proposed by Victor Gruen for Fort Worth, Texas, in 1955.

Walt wanted to demonstrate how technology could enhance the interface between pedestrians and transportation systems. For example, when on a tour of a factory, he had spotted the use of a photoelectric sensor device for blind people. According to Marvin Davis, Walt said, "Gee, this is exactly what we need for our streetcars. We'll have one little village that will have an underground trolley like they have in France. We won't have a motorman, except one of these devices. This device will detect somebody in front and it will either slow down or stop the trolley."

The Cosmopolitan Resort Hotel

The "visual center of EPCOT" and "a shining jewel at the center of the city" is the futuristic 30-story Cosmopolitan Resort Hotel. It is the signature piece of architecture and the "beckoning hand" for the whole project. The hotel tower (designed by architect George Rester) is meant to be EPCOT's wienie, just as Sleeping Beauty or Cinderella Castle is for the theme parks.

As we stroll through the Center City, we see a 600-room hotel with "only the most modern guest rooms and convention facilities". It is located

---

69 In 1989, Johann Friedrich Geist defined an arcade as "a glass-covered passageway, which connects two busy streets and is lined on both sides with shops. Stores, offices, workshops, or dwellings may be located in the upper stories." Arcades have been around a long time, even in the United States. For example, the 1828 Providence (Rhode Island) Arcade is a covered passage with three stories of shops on either side. An arcade is simpler to design and less expensive to build than a dome. Arcades can be cost-competitive with stand-alone structures because they do not have to be burdened with a storm drain system.

directly above the Transportation Lobby. Other amenities at the hotel include spa facilities and "a seven-acre recreation deck located high above the pedestrian and shopping areas" with swimming pools, trees, and waterfalls. The facility has everything we expect from a first-class luxury hotel.

The Town Center Entertainment District surrounds the Cosmopolitan Resort Hotel. According to the urban transect, the hotel would be categorized as the Urban Core Zone. This area consists of the highest-density development with the greatest variety of uses, as well as civic buildings of regional importance.

The hotel tower has 30-stories, clearly the tallest structure at Disney World. Having a very tall structure as the centerpiece speaks to some of our basic needs. Christopher Alexander said, "We seem to have a need to climb up to high places. There is comfort in the ability to look down and size up the world below." From the hotel tower, guests have a grand view of the entire resort. No doubt the top couple of floors are dedicated to public areas like a signature restaurant, a lounge, and an observation deck. What a view!

Architect Louis Sullivan said tall buildings must be "lofty" and they "must be tall, every inch of it tall. The force and power of altitude must be in it." He concludes "it must be every inch a proud and soaring thing, rising in sheer exultation that from top to bottom it is a unit without a single dissenting line". Walt intended that The Cosmopolitan Hotel be tall enough to be seen for many miles. This is consistent with his other projects; for example, when describing how to design the castle in the Magic Kingdom, Walt had told his Imagineers that it was "critical that Cinderella Castle be seen from afar". In *Walt Disney's Railroad Story* by Michael Broggie, Walt reminded his Imagineers, "This is a magical place. The important thing is the castle. Make it tall enough to be seen from all around the park. It's got to keep people oriented." The same rule applied to the height of the Cosmopolitan structure, the beacon for EPCOT.

Early renderings for the hotel and the Progress City model show a Mid-Century Modern skyscraper in the International Style. In 1922, architect Phillip Johnson documented this then-new style of architecture that looks at volume rather than mass. Johnson said the form of the building would be driven by "regularity rather than axial symmetry". The smooth surface of the windows captures the sky and the asymmetrical setbacks animate the image. As Johnson stated, the design places "emphasis upon volume—space enclosed by thin planes or surfaces as opposed to the suggestion of mass and solidity". The drawings show a hotel tower that demonstrates "regularity as opposed to symmetry or other kinds of obvious balance". The tower's beauty is enhanced "upon the intrinsic elegance of materials, technical perfection, and fine proportions, as opposed to applied ornament".

In some ways, such as the extensive use of curved glass curtain walls and varied setbacks, the Cosmopolitan hotel tower is similar to the skyscrapers shown at the General Motors Futurama display at the 1939 New York World's Fair. The International Style dominated commercial architecture for decades, and we can see how the principles of the International Style were ultimately applied to the Contemporary Resort Hotel that was actually built adjacent to the Magic Kingdom.[70]

Town Center Entertainment District

Surrounding the Cosmopolitan Resort Hotel at its base is the Town Center Entertainment District. In the urban transect, this would be called the Urban Center Zone. Typically, the Urban Center consists of higher-density, mixed-use building types that can accommodate retail, offices, row houses, and apartments. Traditionally, there is a tight network of streets, with wide sidewalks, steady street tree planting, and buildings set close to the frontages. At EPCOT, the Town Center Entertainment District is organized like a daisy. At the center is the Cosmopolitan Resort Hotel.

---

70   Welton Becket was hired as the architect for the Contemporary Resort, along with Robert Tyler as lead designer. Marvin Davis managed the project for the Imagineering team. Design for the hotel began prior to Walt's death. John Portman's Hyatt Regency Atlanta (1967) inspired the Contemporary's soaring lobby. The lobby is also reminiscent of the interiors from the 1936 film *Things to Come*, directed by William Cameron Menzies and the Bauhaus artist Lazio Moholy-Nagy. The Contemporary was built in partnership with the United States Steel Reality Development, a subsidiary of the American Bridge Division (as was the Polynesian Village). The 400-foot-long structure resembles a bridge and consists of thirteen 150-foot steel trussed A-frames. The result is a soaring fourteen-story lobby space called the Grand Canyon Concourse. The monorail runs through the lobby and creates kinetic energy that enlivens an otherwise dull cavernous space. As one Imagineer said, without the monorail the lobby would resemble "a place where the Goodyear Blimp comes to mate." A 90-foot Southwestern themed ceramic tile mural by Mary Blair decorates the lobby. The mural is made with 1,800 tiles, took eighteen months to construct, and features a five-legged goat. The engineering breakthrough for the hotels was the innovative use of unitized modular construction. Each of the 1,450 "unitized" guest rooms for the Contemporary and the Polynesian weighs six tons. Each unit is fully outfitted in a factory about three miles from the hotel site—including the furniture, the interlocking plumbing, the utility fixtures, the carpeting, and the wall art. The units are so strong they could be stacked three high without external structural support. The only thing the builders had to do was slide the room into the frame and connect the utility lines. Every room is wrapped in a sun-resistant glass called Solar Bronze.

Radiating out like petals are sections that represent different parts of the world. Separating these petals are the elevated WEDway PeopleMover tracks. Guests can preview the various districts by train and then decide which one to explore.

When Buzz Price worked up a feasibility study for EPCOT, he noted that a covered town center would fail unless it became its own destination. Just being near the Magic Kingdom theme park would not be enough. To succeed, it needed to have its own drawing power, with enough throughput capacity to generate an adequate return on its giant investment.[71] To that end, EPCOT is the regional mall-sized, internationally themed shopping area. Imagine the World Showcase pavilions all under one roof. It features an unprecedented mix of carefully orchestrated signature retail, dining, and outstanding entertainment. The EPCOT Town Center Entertainment District has an ample supply of quality attractions, a variety of uses, and a few little surprises that make guests want to come back. As we saw in the EPCOT film, the Town Center Entertainment District has "shopping areas where stores and whole streets recreate the character and adventure of places 'round the world...theaters for dramatic and musical productions... restaurants and a variety of nightlife attractions". The EPCOT Town Center Entertainment District incorporates the best of Walt's ideas; its themed restaurants and nightclubs are similar to those included in the Mineral King plans, and the district also includes Disneyland-style attractions. There is a recreational retail area with destination specialty retailers and services. Also bringing people into the center are multiplex cinemas and the Circle Vision 360 large-format theaters. Plus, a Discovery Center that serves the community as a child-care center featuring hands-on learning experiences.

Walt always seemed to be toying with the idea of a multi-internationally themed village as a way of place making. For example, there was talk of an International Street for Disneyland on the east side of Main Street proposed as early as 1957. Bill Martin described the concept: "You go down the street—the houses are all designed to look at the street and you'd turn around and it was a different street on the way back. Same houses, but the juxtaposition of it and the designing, they were different types of international cities." Although it did not get far, Walt also had an opportunity to partner with Joyce C. Hall, founder of Hallmark greeting card company, to develop an internationally themed retail area that would have been a nature-based theme park in Signboard Hill, Kansas City.

---

71 This is not unusual in city planning. In *The New Civic Art* (2003), Andres Duany noted that pseudo-urbanism megastructures would fail unless there is a very large institution "such as a hospital or a university" and that the institution "requires internal connectivity through continuous corridors."

Walt's desire for an exotic, intimate, fully themed retail district based on a real world location was finally implemented with the opening of New Orleans Square at Disneyland in July 1966. The New Orleans Square project began in 1962. Originally, the planned centerpiece of the new land was a Pirate Wax Museum built in a basement-level show building. That project was delayed due to the Imagineers' focusing on the multiple projects for the 1964 New York World's Fair. Later on, the hole was filled with possibly the best theme park attraction ever created, Pirates of the Caribbean. John Hench said of the design for the area that "I think it tells something about New Orleans, the same way our Main Street tells something about Main Streets. It is like poetry. It condenses everything down to its essence."Along with the internationally themed areas, another big attraction for visitors to the EPCOT Town Center Entertainment District would be an indoor theme park, similar to a proposal Walt made to the City of St. Louis, Missouri, in 1965.[72]

---

72 St. Louis was riding on an urban renewal wave featuring huge projects such as Busch Memorial Stadium; the Jefferson National Expansion Memorial, featuring the soaring Gateway Arch; and the restored Old Courthouse and Old Cathedral. Large chunks of historic buildings were already demolished, waiting for the next big project. In 1963, like on so many other earlier occasions, city leaders asked Walt for his help. Walt had spent some of his finest years in Missouri and was interested in the challenge. He said, "Missouri and the history of Missouri are important to me." Walt was going to call the indoor theme park Riverfront Square. It would be two blocks north of Busch Stadium in downtown St. Louis. The project was designed to be inside a four-story building the size of a city block. The overall theme was the western expansion of America in honor of St. Louis as the primary starting point for many on that journey. Of course, Walt had Buzz Price do a feasibility study. Price suggested that the project could work and that it would make a modest profit. Most of the money would be made at the dining facilities. Retail would also be a big revenue generator. Walt wanted to use the St. Louis opportunity to educate as well as entertain. The indoor park would have included a Mike Fink ride (after the character who played opposite Davy Crockett in the ABC Disneyland *Davy Crockett* miniseries), a pirate ride, and an Audio-Animatronics spectacular called The Lewis and Clark Adventure. Another boat ride would be called the Blue Bayou Boat ride. There would be a Haunted Mansion, a Circle Vision 360 theater, even a Fantasyland with Peter Pan and Pinocchio dark rides. There would be a section of tight, winding retail streets that would resemble New Orleans Square at Disneyland. One theater would resemble the Golden Horseshoe Saloon while another would have been dressed up like a Mississippi River showboat. Planning for the St. Louis project was underway for two years. The project was ultimately killed when Disney and the civic leaders failed to agree on the financing, amongst other issues. Another distraction for Walt was he had the Florida Project on his mind by now.

The Projection of Place

To best appreciate our 1982 fantasy tour of EPCOT, we need to understand the concepts related to themed environments, so near and dear to Walt's heart. Matthew Frederick noted, "The more specific a design idea is, the greater its appeal is likely to be." He suggests that "drawing upon a specific observation, poignant statement, ironic point, witty reflection, intellectual connection, political argument, or idiosyncratic belief in a creative work can help you create environments others will identify with in their own way". That is how you create a place where the "there" is there.

John Hench said, "The concept of 'themed' environments—places designed so that every element contributes to telling a story—was developed and popularized by Walt Disney." Like the set of a movie, Walt created places that would tap the collective consciousness of guests and recreate a glamorous dreamlike vision of those impressions. Hench added that the use of these distinctive and familiar architectural styles gives the parks "archetypal truths". The stylized buildings are out of context and the scale is different, but you accept what you see because all the visual clues add up and create the underlying emotional appeal. It is the movie-making illusion of persistence of vision in three-dimensional terms, and it works.

Theme matters. Charles Moore commented on how "[p]lace is the projection of the image of civilization onto the environment". A vacant lot is just a vacant lot unless people imbue meaning on the site. It can then transform into a sacred space if that is the community's desire.

Walt loved nostalgia and knew others did as well. In *A Voice from the Attic*, Robertson Davies wrote, "The world is full of people whose notion of a satisfactory future is, in fact, a return to the idealized past." This grounding into a comfortable reality is what Walt was trying to achieve by avoiding all that "blue-sky stuff".

To squeeze in iconic architectural elements within the themed areas, the Imagineers used a cinematic design trick called "shrink and edit".[73] The designers take a real building for inspiration and then can change the scale, color, or detail to support the story. Each of the themed areas is distinct from the others. Like the World Showcase at Epcot, each pavilion captures the essence of one specific culture and creates a sense of place. Instead of being a collection of exact replicas of famous buildings, the Imagineers take well-known iconic buildings, change the scale and some

---

73   Examples of "shrink and edit" can be found throughout Walt Disney World today. The process was perfected at the World Showcase in Epcot Center and applied to the other parks, especially Disney's Hollywood Studios.

of the details, and then arrange the structures so that they can make the most compelling composition.

There are clear gateways. To make the experience more interesting, there are internal streets that meander, opening up around corners into hidden public spaces. Michael Sorkin says that "the coincidence is more than temporal. Television and Disneyland operate similarly, by means of extraction, reduction, and recombination, to create an entirely new, anti-geographical space." He says, "Disneyland, with its channel-turning mingle of history and fantasy, reality and simulation, invents a way of encountering the physical world that increasingly characterizes daily life."

Marvin Davis estimated that each "country" would occupy a long city block inside of EPCOT's iconic "dome", which is approximately 1,500 feet. To break these long corridors down and make them more relevant to the guests, the façades are designed at a pedestrian's perspective at a typical pace. That means the façades must have scale and rhythm. Designers do this by breaking the façade down into smaller sections, breaking the walls up with a large number of vertical rhythms like doors. When we walk along a façade that is primarily made up of vertical rhythms, it makes the walk more interesting and eye-catching. We move "column to column" and that makes the walk appear to be shorter than it really is. Long, horizontal walls are tiring. This technique is on display at Disneyland's Main Street, where the storefront façades are typically a mere twenty-two feet from edge to edge.

As we have seen by the success of Disneyland, there needs to be a diversity of functions visible from the street. Everybody gets a chance to be on the inside looking out and outside looking in. What is going on inside the buildings has a major impact on what is going on outside. The façades must have a sense of transparency. Main Street is designed with narrow units and many doors; there is a wealth of many different experiences inside, and the windows are custom designed to be low enough for a child to enjoy the displays.

We enjoy spaces best when they appeal to all of our senses. If we can look, listen, smell, taste, and touch the good things, we are more comfortable. Walt's solution throughout Disneyland was to pick the right surface materials and appropriate music, and to install Smellitzers, a special machine that pumps out the scent of cookies and candy. He applied the same solution for the themed areas inside of EPCOT.

The success of the façade starts with texture. Ground-level façades that offer texture with the use of good materials and carefully crafted details are an attraction in themselves, especially when you can reach out and touch the building and examine the smallest details. This is important to the illusion since the actual structures would be typical industrial buildings hidden by elaborate and highly detailed façades.

Learning from Las Vegas was the book that ushered in the Post-Modern architectural movement. In 1972, author and architect Robert Venturi opined that the use of vernacular architecture and iconography, masking the "ugly and ordinary" structures, would satisfy regular people even while it frustrated architects. Venturi called these structures the "decorated shed". A decorated shed is a conventional building that conveys meaning through signage or architectural ornament.[74] The interior spaces of EPCOT would be a "sprawling mega structure slip-covered in a period décor that makes the bleakest functional architecture look cozily quaint—hauntingly odd, all parabolic curves and weightless cantilevers, like some gleaming spaceport on Mars in the [year] 2000-something".

Andres Duany said, "Modern retail is conceived by the development industry in normative types that are designed, funded, marketed, and merchandised separately. Recently, however, it has been noted that retail types 'anchor' one another." One center embellishes and enhances other centers. For example, shopping malls are reinforced by the adjacency of entertainment centers, including restaurants, bookstores, and cinemas that remain open late. Duany adds, "All of these retail components are embedded into a continuous urban fabric forming town center. The retail streets demonstrate the high degree of visual harmony that is necessary for commercial uses to be compatible with the residential architecture nearby."

As we continue our EPCOT 1982 tour, we can see that the city is filled with street cafés under the climate-controlled roof. A street café has a special charm and rewards the guest who is dining as well as people passing by. It enlivens the promenade or the public squares. Cafés allow people to slow down, be on view, and be entertained by the passing parade.[75]

---

74   In *Designing Disney's Theme Parks* (1998), Karal Ann Marling suggested, "The stark geometry of the commercial shed, as Robert Venturi would later observe, could be redecorated at will." Marling added, "The buildings at Disneyland often fool you into thinking that they are turn-of-the-century business blocks or Third World trading posts, but actually are 1950s-style malls."

75   Throughout Disneyland, there are excellent examples of street cafés. They possess the essential qualities of a successful dining space such as multiple, intimate rooms and tables oriented toward a busy path. The best designs include an opening to the street and other features that contribute to a higher degree of life such as sitting walls, canvas roofs, and a place to wait. Guests are able to sit, dine, drink, and have conversations without feeling rushed. The tables reach right out into the street but are secure behind a permanent barrier. In some cases, the restaurants help to define a neighborhood. Notice how many restaurants were placed in New Orleans Square at Disneyland. Street cafés enliven small public squares by being activity nodes.

As we see as we walk through EPCOT, not only do the tourists visit the restaurants and shops, there are thousands of permanent residents living in apartments within steps of the shopping districts. This is a shopping center that automatically comes with the critical mass of visitors. In real estate, it is all about the numbers. EPCOT was not just a fantasy city. The project is rooted in the reality of the marketplace. William H. Whyte said, "What attracts people most is other people. Many urban spaces are being designed as though the opposite were true and what people like best are places they stay away from." Walt knew how to create places that could draw a crowd.

The Apartments

The urban transect describes the area at the edge of the central business district as a General Urban Zone. In most cities, this zone may have some mixed-use developments, but it is primarily made up of urban residential fabric. There is usually a wide range of building types: single, sideyard, and row houses. Setbacks and landscaping are variable. Streets are generally medium-sized blocks. In EPCOT, this is where we find "EPCOT's high-density apartments surrounding the metropolitan center." This is home to a large part of the residential population.

Life in the EPCOT Town Center apartments is very exciting. As part of the deal of living in a demonstration city, the homes are well-appointed with the latest gadgets. EPCOT residents participate in focus groups and user panels to evaluate the viability of the new technologies. Some of the residents work for one of the companies in the Industrial Park, designing or manufacturing such devices. These structures are mixed within the retail and dining areas and contain "services required by EPCOT's residents, but most of them designed especially to suit local and regional needs of major corporations". Some of the mid-rise office towers peek out of the enclosure.[76]

Because the apartments are located on the outer rim of the enclosed structure, residents are given a choice of views. Some residents' homes face into the enclosure and look down onto the highly themed pedestrian boulevards. Some of the apartments have balconies that allow the residents to enjoy the passing crowds. Having residents live along the edges makes it safer for pedestrians, as there are more eyes watching the street. Other residents face out of the enclosure with views of the surrounding greenbelt, the community service structures, the low-density homes, and the surrounding

---

76 Contemporary civil engineer Zev Cohen said, "People say they do not want to live near where they work, but they would like to work near where they live."

natural areas. The views are spectacular. Just steps from their front doors are internationally themed shopping areas or corporate office buildings.

The four- to six-story apartment blocks provide the Imagineers an opportunity to create a very large structure with a great deal of visual interest. Instead of solid monolithic walls along the outside edge, the apartments feature articulated outer walls. As guests approach the enclosed structure, they revel in the variety of surfaces and articulations made up from the apartment buildings. Some apartment buildings have step-back designs that help to mitigate the bulk. EPCOT presents the design opportunity to play with a variety of textures and to create more view opportunities for the residents.

If we lived in one of the apartment buildings, we most likely would not own an automobile—most of the time we would have no need for one. Because of the cost of parking spaces and the experimental nature of EPCOT, most apartment dwellers are not even allotted a space to park a vehicle in the large underground parking structure near the Transportation Lobby. Those living in apartments are for the most part required to rely solely on public transportation, short-range electric vehicles for on-property trips, or rental cars for longer journeys.[77]

In 1929, Clarence Perry identified a basic unit of measure that forms the fundamental human habitat and called it a neighborhood unit or a pedestrian shed. A typical pedestrian shed is only one-quarter mile. Within a pedestrian shed, you should find a range of services that meet ordinary human needs. There should be a balance of living, working, shopping, and recreational opportunities. Access to a convenient transit stop can extend the range of the pedestrian shed, and that is the secret to EPCOT's success. "Here and throughout the community, residents returning from work or shopping will disembark from the WEDway at stations located conveniently just a few steps from where they live," according to the film.

Victor Gruen built on Perry's work and described a way to measure the tolerance for walking within urban environments. He called this a Pedshed—the "desirable walking distance" that a "lazy walker" on a one-purpose trip without interruption will walk. If the walker can sit, shop, or eat, it distracts him; in that case, the walker is able to go longer distances. The length of a Pedshed is determined by factors such as appearance and atmosphere, as well as climate and topography. EPCOT as a whole has a large Pedshed because of the highly attractive and completely weather-protected environment. Within a Pedshed, there can be numerous environments, each with different walkability values.

---

77 Rideshare programs and companies like Zipcar are becoming more and more popular today.

As Buzz Price said, it all begins at the center. At the heart of EPCOT is a world-class resort hotel with conference facilities combined with the transportation center. This combination creates a critical mass of activity that energizes the edge uses. Within the Town Center, a typical guest may easily walk up to one mile, or 20 minutes, due to the careful design of the themed interiors. Imagine a network of storefronts along "very intriguing" little side streets like New Orleans Square in Disneyland or the World Showcase pavilions at Epcot Center—except that in EPCOT's case, a roof covers the streets and a simulated sky is projected onto the ceiling.[78]

A walking environment like the one found in the theme parks is the other environment variable within a Pedshed. Here, a person may walk up to a half-mile, or ten minutes, if they are provided with a highly attractive environment where the sidewalks are protected from sunshine and rain. If the central business district is attractive but not protected from the weather, such that people are exposed to the elements, the desirable walking range is limited to less than a quarter of a mile, or five minutes of walking. Degrade the environment even further with unattractive spaces like parking lots, garages, or a traffic-congested street, and the range is limited to only 600 feet, or two minutes of walking. This is typical of strip center development.

Within the Pedshed, Gruen suggested slow-moving people carriers such as moving sidewalks. Walt's solution to extend the Pedshed at Disneyland and enhance the experience was to use horse-trolleys, fire trucks, the omnibus, and other vehicles. Within EPCOT, it is likely that themed electric vehicles would have been used.

A city is best served when the transportation systems are scaled to their environment. When a pedestrian needs to move from one Pedshed to another, he or she will need to use some form of rapid transit. Gruen's solution was to align transportation technologies along a scale of gradation of movement. At each increment, there are certain transportation systems that can enhance the pedestrian experience or make the walker feel miserable. If the match is done right, the environment will "promise comfort, convenience, and calculated visual pleasure". The pedestrian will enjoy a positive experience. If the match is not right, the environment will feel unsafe, and the pedestrian will be on edge. This is when the messy vitality of a city becomes unbalanced. We might say it is the difference between walking in a theme park and walking through the parking lot on the way to the theme park.

---

78 Disney was at the forefront of innovative projection technology and would have been able to apply the system they pioneered for the Skydome Spectacular show that was displayed on the interior dome of the General Electric Pavilion at the 1964–1965 New York World's Fair.

Gruen struggled with a way to move people between one to two miles. That is a critical link in the scale of gradation of movement and the most difficult one for cities to deal with. For many people, this is too far to walk, but it is an inefficient trip in a car. He recommended electric mini-buses and taxis. At EPCOT, Walt solved this problem by using his revolutionary WEDway PeopleMover to connect the hotel complex and transit center to the retail and residential areas plus destinations outside of the enclosed structure. Most transportation planners would agree that a transit system based on a fixed rail connecting activity nodes with virtually no headway is a dream. The overhead PeopleMover tracks could also be used to define the edges of the themed retail districts. The trains would provide a preview of these areas to potential customers just as the PeopleMover provides an overview of Tomorrowland at the Magic Kingdom.

For trips of two to five miles, we need different transportation technologies. Gruen liked fixed-rail systems and larger buses. Walt preferred the monorail. The Disney World monorail system was to run south to north, with major destinations such as the Jetport, Transportation Lobby, the Entrance Complex, the Industrial Park district, EPCOT, and the Magic Kingdom. The monorail is perfectly suited for this challenge.

Areas that feature a compact form of urban development near transit are ideal. That is how the EPCOT center city is designed. One of the biggest benefits of living in these apartments is how well they fit within the pedestrian shed. Most residents have very little need to ever get into a car. Just the way Walt wanted it.

The Greenbelt

Just beyond the ring of high-density apartments we can see the community's most significant shared asset, the "sheltering" greenbelt.[79] As described in the EPCOT film, the "greenbelt is more than just a broad expanse of beautiful lawns and walks and trees. Here too are the communities' varied recreation facilities, its playgrounds for children, its churches, and its schools." The initial plans show a generous allotment of park space that is accessible to as many people as possible.

According to the National Recreation and Park Association (NRPA), the

---

79 Ebenezer Howard first described a greenbelt as the agricultural zone for the urban community. It is a permanent reservation of open space surrounding a community. According to the urban transect, greenbelt planting is generally naturalistic and building setbacks are relatively deep. Blocks may be large and the roads irregular.

amount of land that should be dedicated to parks is measured in acres per 1,000 residents. Current standards suggest that ten acres per 1,000 residents are ample, and four acres per 1,000 are the minimum. Many mature communities struggle with even that modest goal. The size of the greenbelt surrounding the 50-acre EPCOT dome is large enough to provide parklands well above the "ample" goal.

Strategically placed within the greenbelt are recreation centers. EPCOT offers indoor and outdoor recreational facilities for all age groups. From the Progress City model, we can see how the recreation centers are clustered with schools and other park areas. The park system features large parks, neighborhood parks, and supervised playgrounds.

It is likely that the larger EPCOT parks are based on lessons learned from Disneyland. With all of Walt's projects, the environment within the theme parks is highly structured, and we can see that it is the same way at EPCOT. Although it may appear that we have many options, the reality is much different. The spatial design, the attractions, and the circulation pattern all restrict choices. However, Walt clearly understood that not all play could be pre-programmed. Children would rebel; they needed a place to blow off some steam, a space where they can run free while allowing the parents to take a rest. When he realized that Disneyland needed a place dedicated to unstructured play, Walt used a piece of very valuable real estate inside of Disneyland, the island surrounded by the Rivers of America, to create a children's wonderland of beauty and imagination. The island was named Tom Sawyer Island. A brief detour to Tom Sawyer Island gives us a glimpse into the 1982 EPCOT parks for children.

It is important to remember that during the time that Disneyland was built, children's play areas were typically limited to a city park, the street, a private yard, or unsupervised "corner lots". Walt wanted to create something more memorable for Disneyland. He had his Imagineers apply a narrative to a children's play zone. The result is an immersive place where children can roam, explore, and be inspired by Mark Twain's stories of Tom Sawyer, Huckleberry Finn, Becky Thatcher, and the rest of the gang. The playground is loosely based on the fictional Jackson Island from Mark Twain's *Tom Sawyer*. At the time, this notion of creating a themed playground based on popular film and literary characters was unheard of.

A very innovative addition to Disneyland, Tom Sawyer Island was part of a $2 million expansion that included four other attractions. It opened to the public on June 16, 1956. It was one of the earliest examples of a highly themed children's playscape in America, and it became a model for others to follow. Marvin Davis, Disneyland's master planner, said, "The general shape of the island, the way it curves and so forth, was Walt's idea." Walt's daughter Diane said, "He kept on adding things until he felt that there weren't any missing parts." The island is approximately three acres and is twelve times longer than it is wide. Overall, the island measures about 800 feet from top to bottom. At the ends, the island measures approximately 250 feet to accommodate the turning radius of the *Mark Twain*. At the middle, it is approximately fifty feet to conserve space. Imagineers Vic Greene, Herb Ryman, Claude Coats, and Sam McKim worked on the project. Bill Evans created the landscaping plan. The island was built with the fill from the Rivers of America.

At the southern end is a hill called Lookout Point. According to press releases, Tom and Huck's Tree House was once the "highest landpoint in Disneyland". Just behind the tree house is Injun Joe's Cave. Its narrow passages and visual effects remind visitors that this is no ordinary playground.

To cross over to Smuggler's Cove there are two unusual bridges. Guests can choose between a suspension and a pontoon bridge. In between the bridges is a water pump, which feeds the waterfalls that circulate the river water. Many of the features of the middle of the island have changed considerably over the years. Even Fort Wilderness at the northern end of the island has been blocked from the guests.

What Walt did was build something specifically designed to spark a child's imagination. Yi-Fu Tuan noted that, "Playing and role playing are part of the 'fun' of being in a pleasure garden or in a Disney park. Play accommodates—indeed requires—illusion."

Tom Sawyer Island gives children opportunities to explore and to practice decision-making. From the very first moment children step off the raft, they have choices. "Should they take a pathway straight up the hill or turn right toward the shabby old grist mill? Should they head left up the trail along the river, or chance the dark entrance of the nearby cave?" asked *The "E" Ticket* magazine. The magazine concluded, "It's this fun combination... total freedom of movement within an adventure-packed environment."

Tom Sawyer Island provides opportunities for learning. This is not a passive environment. Children are asked to participate by making things happen. From a child's point of view, there are many paths to choose from. The island is just big enough to get mildly lost. The result is a more rewarding and richer experience. The parents experience a certain level of freedom and security as well, since there is only one point of entry or exit from the island.

When the island first opened, children had to figure out how to make Merry-go-round or Teeter-Totter Rock work (both now gone), find the cave that leads to the hidden treasure (still there), and search for the door in Fort Wilderness that leads to the escape tunnel (also gone). Children loved the opportunity to speed away from their parents due to the narrow passages and the "low bridge" places where adults would bump their heads. Entering Fort Wilderness was like walking on to a movie set for a Western. A child could peek into the Regimental Headquarters to see what Davy Crockett and Georgie Russell were up to. Then he could climb up the stairs to the towers and guard the fort with guns supplied.

Over the years, some of the trails, caves, and activities have been eliminated. The fort is closed. There are fewer options and details that encourage free play. An overlay of pirates has shifted the narrative to a more contemporary film franchise. Even so, Tom Sawyer Island is still a remarkable play environment. Even death is part of the experience. Along with the Tree House, the trails, the caves, and the Fort, Tom Sawyer Island has a cemetery. According to Christopher Alexander, "No people who turn their backs on death can be alive. The presence of the dead among the living will be a daily fact in any society which encourages its people to live."

There are also opportunities for motor skill development. The children can run, climb, and work their way across unusual rope bridges. When the island first opened to the public, they even had a chance to grab a pole and fish for catfish, perch, and bluegill. This is an open-ended experience where there are no time limits other than darkness.

Exploring the island creates opportunities for dramatic play. Here, children are in control of their own narrative. The design for the landscape architecture is based on the popular Westerns that dominated the television airwaves in the 1950s. It is a timeless setting. Robin Moore said, "The richness of physical elements in the setting and their relationship to each other should arouse curiosity and trigger imaginative associations." It is easy for a child to slip into role-playing. Moore adds, "If the environment is too literal, imagination will be limited; if too abstract, imagination will not be fully stimulated."

Another benefit is the opportunity for social development. This is the place where your children can interact with others. The island is filled with tiny, cave-like places. The entrances to these paths are low and difficult for adults to navigate. This creates a special realm that is only comfortable for those who fit. The environment helps in the selection process of who gets to play. In the course of play, ad hoc playgroups develop and new stories are created. For many children, this unfettered play may be more fun and more memorable than any other attraction in the park.

Along with play areas designed to foster unstructured play opportunities, EPCOT's park system offers a wide variety of experiences. The larger parks feature water displays and aquatic sports facilities. Some parks are wholly naturalistic and can be used for picnicking, group camping, hiking, riding, and nature study. Other parks include recreational facilities such as tennis courts, golf courses, and baseball fields.

Neighborhood parks are spread out in the greenbelt as well as in the low-density residential area. Each of these parks covers between ten and twenty acres. Some feature picnicking areas. Since these parks are so close to the homes, facilities such as restrooms and vending areas are limited.

There are also supervised playgrounds on school, park, and other public properties. This network of different-sized parks is a key ingredient to a successful recreation system plan. The greenbelt is also where we find other public uses such as churches, schools, a teen center, a senior center, and other recreational zones. The greenbelt is the community's gathering place to celebrate a healthy mind, body, and Earth.

For Walt's Friends

Walt knew that some people would prefer to live in a single-family home and have access to their automobile. After all, this project was conceived when the suburban lifestyle was booming. However, unlike other mid-century suburbs, EPCOT provides multiple transit options to lure residents out of those automobiles. Consistent with the Garden City concept and towns like Radburn, the streets run behind the houses, and the houses are organized around culs de-sac. Each home's front door is oriented toward the open space corridor, away from the area where the automobile is parked. As Walt's drawings seem to indicate, that open space is shared between the residents; there are no, or very small, private yards. In time, might community gardens also become part of the mix?

As we pass through the single-family neighborhood on our 1982 tour, we see that residents are not using their cars much. They are riding bicycles or small electronic scooters. Apparently, EPCOT is a perfect test environment for transportation devices that help us close the gap of the "last mile" between the home and the primary public transit lines.[80]

In traditional suburbs, the streets are designed at automobile scale. The pavement is wide and the setbacks are deep.[81] As you recall, Walt purposefully made the streets that ran through the Burbank studios narrow, which acts like a traffic-calming device. He made sure the pedestrian always felt in charge.

---

80   Walt Disney World was an early adopter of the Segway Personal Transporter; Karal Ann Marling noted that one goal for EPCOT had been to demonstrate "that it was possible, for example, to eliminate the automobile from the urban equation, or at least minimize its depredations by running service roads under and around city centers and providing cheap, efficient forms of mass transit."

81   In *Suburban Nation*, Andres Duany observed that many suburban streets are sized for "the jockeying of a pair of high-rise ladder trucks on a dead-end street" and "the most ambitious of maneuvers."

Although the spread-out nature of most suburban neighborhoods discourages the use of public transit, it is different at EPCOT. There are pathways leading to PeopleMover stations, where residents can use convenient storage spaces for the "last mile" vehicles.

The WEDway PeopleMover has stops throughout the low-density residential areas, at the greenbelt, the high-density residential zone, the retail zone, and the Transportation Lobby. EPCOT has fulfilled the promise that each home be within easy walking distance to the transit stations. If we lived in EPCOT, we would only need an automobile for trips off property. For example, residents might need a car to go shopping in Orlando for unusual items or services that they cannot find in the Town Center. Most of the services we typically expect to find in a residential neighborhood are not located in the EPCOT low-density residential zone. As much as we admire the neighborhood, we are not quite sure how we feel about the fact that, like the traditional suburbs, EPCOT has eliminated the corner grocery store.

One sharp contrast between Gruen's and Walt's thinking was the density of the outer core of residential units. Gruen stated that "the space-devouring detached single home was not considered as suitable"—he was an advocate of clustered attached homes that shared common open space. Walt was not convinced, and his EPCOT planning artwork shows large suburban-style single-family estate homes at the very edge. In one study, residential density in that area was estimated to be 18.2 persons per acre, with 6.6 dwelling units per acre. Buzz Price confided that "Walt wanted a place for his friends to live."

The Monsanto House of the Future

With up to 20,000 people living in EPCOT full time, what is life like in the private realm? Walt wanted the homes "built in ways that permit ease of change so that new products may continuously be demonstrated". Since we are tourists and not residents in our 1982 visit, we haven't been invited to go inside any of the homes. Although EPCOT homes likely have some significant differences, a look at Disneyland's Monsanto House of the Future may give us some clues about how the EPCOT residents live.

The House of the Future was an advanced demonstration home and one of the first truly futuristic attractions in Tomorrowland. Monsanto wanted to expand its presence in the home construction industry. By 1953, they contracted with a team from MIT that included architects Richard Hamilton and Marvin Goody from the Department of Architecture. The team wanted to demonstrate an affordable substitute for poorly designed, developer-driven tract houses. Voted one of the top 150 accomplishments at MIT, the house was a "prototype for low-cost, factory-built housing. As a building type—compact with fewer structural constraints than public or commercial buildings—the house form was an ideal laboratory for experimentation in design, materials, and construction."

The house was based on structural plastics research being conducted by engineer Albert G.H. Dietz from Plastic Research Laboratory at the MIT Department of Building Engineering and Construction. Monsanto's Plastics Division sponsored both Dietz's research and the installation of the model home in Disneyland. According to press materials, the goal was to design a house that would explore the maximum use of plastics as a material for home construction and demonstrate how "plastics [could be] used boldly [and] creatively as building materials." The challenge was not simply to replace wooden components with plastic ones but to find innovative ways to exploit the material's unique characteristics, structural integrity, and aesthetic qualities. Others had a similar interest; in 1954, Douglas Haskell of the American Institute of Architects asked, "In architecture, will atomic processes create a new 'plastic' order?" He thought homes of the future would not be mass-produced like automobiles but would come from scientific laboratories.

The house was a modular, polyester structure reinforced with fibrous glass. The materials and methodology were similar to those developed by Charles Eames for his 1950s' molded plastic chairs. The design was a white cruciform with four gracefully curved fiberglass wings cantilevered from a 256-square-foot central core. The central core also housed the air temperature control units. Each wing was 8 feet tall, 16 feet wide, and 16 feet long. Overall, the house was 1,280 square feet and had three bedrooms, two baths, a living room, a dining room, a family room, and a kitchen.

The Imagineers chose a cruciform because it "assures full daylight for every room, reduces inter-room noise, and provides added privacy for various family activities". The design also allowed for easy expansion. John Hench said, "The bottom was a 'compression member' and the top had a 'tension ring' that the modules hooked on to and hung from. You could hang more pairs of them as needed." John Hench added, "There was virtually no bad location for building it...in a rocky location or on a hillside, the 16' by 16' pedestal would have been easy to work with." You could even rotate it on the pedestal to change the views. Monsanto described the house as "strangely graceful".

Disneyland opened the front door of the Monsanto House of the Future to guests on June 12, 1957. To ensure a huge audience, the attraction was free and it was located at a prime spot off the Plaza Hub, adjacent to the Circarama Theater. At night, the glow of the home with all of the lights on added a special magic to the area. The attraction remained opened until 1967. It was estimated that more than 20 million guests walked through the house.

Disney proudly proclaimed, "Hardly a natural material appears anywhere in the House." Virtually every surface was synthetic. In 1953, MIT produced a report called *Plastics in Housing* to explore expanded uses of the material. The objective was "to develop plastics as a sound engineering material and help the construction industry utilize new designs and materials to achieve production line methods and facilities". The prefabricated demonstration house was a "dramatic attack" to increase the acceptance of plastics as a construction material. By the early 1960s, fifteen percent of plastic production was dedicated to home building.

The tour started in the dining and family room. All of the furniture was ultra-modern and made of plastic materials. The hope was the home would stimulate the guest's imagination. In fact, there was one spot just outside the front door that had to be repainted every night because visitors (usually male) would tap the side of the building just to see if it was really plastic.

For many, the highlight had to be the kitchen. The Kelvinator Division of American Motors Corporation designed the "step saver" kitchen, which was dubbed the "Atoms for Living Kitchen". Many of the appliances either dropped from cabinets or popped up from the counter. A pop-up dishwasher that used ultrasonic waves to clean would also be the storage unit for all of the plastic dishes. Instead of one large refrigerator freezer unit, this house featured three cooling units called "cold zones" that lowered from a ceiling cabinet: one zone for regular refrigeration, one for frozen, and one for irradiated foods. Even the storage shelves lowered from the ceiling unit with the push of a button. Rising from the counter was a microwave oven.

To light the rooms, Sylvania Electric Products Company provided adjustable lighting behind polarized plastic ceiling tiles. Bell Telephone installed the push-button speakerphone with "preset" dialing. The climate control system would allow for different temperatures in different zones within the house. There were even buttons to push to release the scent of roses or the ocean into any room.

The children's room was divided in two by a sliding panel, one side for the boy and one side for the girl. A benefit to using plastic was that it allowed for "tough durable materials that are easily washable". It was almost as if the designers were suggesting that the rooms could be washed down with a hose without damaging a thing. Both children shared a bathroom that featured a movable sink that rose and fell at the push of a button.

The next stop was the master bedroom and bathroom. For the lady, there was a vanity with a push-button speakerphone. The master bath was molded in two pieces. Along with the built-in electric razor and toothbrush was another hands-free push-button phone mounted on the wall—except this phone also contained a closed-circuit television so the family could see who was at the front door. The ceiling lighting was adjustable and had Sylvania Panelescent panels, which acted as a nightlight. There was even a sound system in the shower.

Finally, there was a spacious living room featuring a giant, futuristic, wall-mounted television screen and built-in stereo system. John Hench designed the "Alpha" chair, the first contoured chair that adjusts automatically and that includes a phone and music system with built in speakers. Facing Sleeping Beauty Castle were ceiling-to-floor thermal-paned picture windows featuring decorative laminated safety glass.

According to legend, the durability of the plastic was unexpectedly proven when Disney had to go through an extraordinary effort to remove the attraction. The original plan called for a one-day demolition. When the wrecking ball just bounced off the side, a new plan was drafted; for two weeks, the demolition crew resorted to hacksaws to take the house apart piece by piece, according to John Hench.

Another demonstration home that gives us a glimpse into what the EPCOT houses might be like was located at the Magic Kingdom, in the exit ramp at Space Mountain. RCA's Home of Future Living opened in 1975 and lasted until 1985. Guests got a chance to see cutting-edge technology such as a briefcase-size television with a videodisc player, closed-circuit television watching over the baby, telephones with screens, and a home shopping computer in the kitchen. It is easy to remember that a television manufacturer sponsored this display.

For EPCOT residential areas, the illustrations released by Disney show exteriors of low-density single-family residential architecture that was more traditional than the demonstration home at Disneyland. Instead of a neighborhood of space-age modular homes, the drawings suggest forward-looking Mid-Century ranch-style homes that resemble the very popular homes by Joseph Eichler, a trendy California home-builder. A look at Eichler's homes might tell us something about the EPCOT houses, too.

Eichler hired some of the best residential architects, such as A. Quincy Jones FAIA. Eichler's homes became known as "California Modern" and featured glass walls, post-and-beam construction, and open floor plans. The exteriors featured low-sloping A-framed roofs with simple, clean façades. Many of the homes had skylights and floor-to-ceiling glass windows. Some even had enclosed private courtyards. The houses were airy in comparison to the suburban homes being built at the time. Each home generated some of its own electricity. Solid waste was gathered and deposited in an automated vacuum collection system (AVAC).[82]

The Rural Zone

Surrounding EPCOT's low-density residential subdivision is a rural zone, which consists of lands in an open or cultivated state. Much of the land is dedicated to the complex drainage system that is a part of this zone. With an eye to the future, there is also land set aside for later phases in the project, including a very low-density residential subdivision and secondary town center.

Most communities in lightly urbanized areas have a controlled growth sector. This is land that has value as open space, but nevertheless is subject to development either because the zoning has already been granted or because there is no defensible reason in the long term to deny it. These areas may be slated for potential development. EPCOT is no exception.

The Swamps

After Walt's experience in Anaheim, he knew that he wanted to protect Disney World from adjacent development. At Disneyland, he hid the park behind a berm. At Disney World, he would be able to shield his city from the outside world by placing all of the development between two very large swamps.[83]

The urban transect contains a Natural Zone. The Lexicon of the New Urbanism defines these areas as "lands approximating or reverting to a wilderness condition". This includes lands unsuitable for settlement due to topographical, hydrology, or vegetation issues. These areas should be protected from development in perpetuity—as they are at Walt Disney World, where the activity areas are nestled between the protected Reedy Creek and Bonnet Creek wetlands.

Bay Lake is the natural water feature that Walt saw for the first time from his airplane. This beautiful lake with the little island caught his eye

---

82 Although not in a demonstration home, AVAC was installed at Walt Disney World in 1971; the technology allowed for garbage and soiled hotel linens to be collected at 17 collection points and sent to a central collection point every 15 minutes at speeds up to 60 miles per hour through 24-inch pneumatic tubes. The Walt Disney World system was designed by Aerojet-General and installed by Fluor. Today, more than 80 tons of garbage per day is removed via this system.

83 Today, most professionals prefer to call these natural areas "wetlands".

and was one of the reasons he wanted this property. Great care was taken during the acquisition process to purchase all of the land surrounding this asset. Early plans for EPCOT proposed expanding the lake to the west and building an extension to the south.

When it rains, the water has to go somewhere. The Disney World property is very flat, and it had very poor natural drainage when Walt purchased it. The water table is very high. The property has a lot of roads, parking lots, hotels, and theme parks that have hard, impervious surfaces. Those hard surfaces have traces of oil and other debris that can damage the environment if the stormwater runoff is not properly processed. The Reedy Creek Improvement District (RCID) was formed to develop and manage a storm water management system that serves the Walt Disney World resort and some of the adjacent land outside of the RCID boundary.

When laying out the resort, Walt said to his team, "We have to study the land." That team included Joe Potter, Joe Fowler, and Dick Irvine. They designed and built 44 miles of canals, 18 miles of levees, and 13 water-control structures. The stormwater system is capable of handling a 50-year storm event. That metric means there is a one in fifty chance of a significant storm event occurring in any given year. In this part of Florida, a typical summer storm event can drop 4 inches of rain in a very short period. The stormwater system is engineered to deal with this and much more. The RCID benefits by managing more than 10,000 acres that are used for runoff in lakes, waterways, and wetlands. The system was engineered so well that there has never been flooding in the adjacent properties.

The RCID crafted design guidelines that would minimize damage from any potential flood. All buildings must be at least one foot above the 100-year, 3-day storm elevation. The roadway standards must be above the 50-year, 3-day event. These infrastructure systems are very expensive to install and do not last forever. Constant maintenance is required, which is why maintenance is one of the primary missions of the RCID.

Walt was always trying to find the beauty that could grow from satisfying a functional need. The flood control canals are no exception. In an early engineering diagram, Joe Potter drafted a canal that ran straight from Bay Lake to the south edge of the property. When Walt saw the drawing he was very disappointed. Joe Fowler recalled the boss's reaction; "I was with Walt when he first saw it. Walt never raised his voice. The only way you could tell he was angry was when he raised his right eyebrow." Walt said to Potter, "Look, Joe, I don't want any more of those Corps of Engineers canals." General Joe Potter agreed and said of the final product, "They don't look like canals; they look more like rivers."

The Industrial Park

The urban transect also has a designation for areas that do not conform to one of the six existing normative zones due to their function, disposition, or configuration. These areas are called special districts. In most cities, special districts include "large parks, institutional campuses, refinery sites, airports, etc." We note as we review our 1982 tour map that, under this definition, Disney World has four special districts: the airport, the Entrance Complex, the Industrial Park, and the Magic Kingdom Resort Area. Some of the backstage functions related to public works could also fall into this category.

The 1,000-acre Industrial Park is connected to EPCOT by the monorail. Meant to be a showcase for American industry and ingenuity, the Industrial Park adds another dimension to the Disney World project. Walt wanted to "work with individual companies to create a showcase of industry at work". What would those companies get in return? "Six million people who visit Disney World each year will look behind the scenes at experimental prototype plants, research and development laboratories, and computer centers for major corporations." Imagine the good will and the ability to test-market products.

With the "hope that EPCOT will stimulate American industry to develop new solutions that will meet the needs of people expressed right here in this experimental community", companies could "find the need for technologies that don't even exist today". First came the theme park. Next came the city. What does the world of industry look like after Walt Disney has reimagined it?

Visitors to the United States Pavilion at the 1958 Brussels World's Fair were treated to a very special Disney treat: the 360 degree Circle-Vision film *America the Beautiful*. Just down the way from *America the Beautiful* was a more mundane display, but one that was critical to the development of EPCOT. That show was called *Industrial Parks USA* and was sponsored by the Society of Industrial Realtors of America.

The concept of the "industrial park" is a mid-century invention that reflects the postwar land-use development trends. After World War II, the population had moved out from the city centers and into the suburbs in large numbers—as did the jobs. While surveying the changing economic environment in the 1950s, William H. Whyte noticed that many companies that left the city center moved to within a few miles of the home of their chief executive officer. There was a growing demand by corporate America for a new kind of industrial complex that was clean, attractive, and functional. This was especially true for non-manufacturing activities such as research and development.

The Brussels World's Fair display featured the Stanford Industrial Park (1951) located in Palo Alto, California, which Stanford University had developed to exploit its intellectual activities in science and technology and enhance its reputation as a major research institution. The school combined two things that were antithetical: industry and a park, thereby inventing a new category of land use that would become known as an "industrial park". In *Magic Lands*, John Findlay said Stanford created "a landscape that acted as urban center for the Santa Clara Valley, looked both campus-like and suburban, and projected the values associated with university and suburban population". The Stanford Industrial Park blended good planning, extensive landscaping, and thoughtful architecture with a dedication to employee happiness. The display showed guests how the modern industrial park could live in harmony with residential neighborhoods. Walt thought that EPCOT would be the perfect opportunity to demonstrate this concept in a real city. An even earlier model of an industrial park that had influenced Walt's thinking was Thomas Edison's Menlo Park Laboratory. The laboratory was moved from New Jersey to Dearborn, Michigan, and rebuilt at Henry Ford's Greenfield Village in the 1920s. Thomas Hughes described Edison's original laboratory in New Jersey as "a retreat in rural settings that removed him from urban distractions without isolating him from big-city resources".[84] Walt had been to the museum and laboratory in 1940 and again after the 1948 Chicago Railroad Fair with Ward Kimball. Walt even met Henry Ford.

The industrial parks that Walt saw in Chicago and in Brussels had many of the same place-making qualities that Walt had implemented at his studio in Burbank. When he saw *Industrial Park U.S.A.*, he must have felt like he saw the second generation of his facility. Walt knew that

---

84   Walt Disney was a big fan of Thomas Edison. In 1963, he proposed an addition to Main Street, U.S.A. in Disneyland called Edison Square. The area would have been themed as a residential district set in a time period a few years later than Main Street. Each façade would represent a different part of the United States, including Boston, St. Louis, and Chicago. At Disneyland and the Magic Kingdom, Main Street, U.S.A. is set at the time when the gas lamp was slowly giving way to the electric lamp. The setting for Edison Square was the moment just after America had passed that point. The major draw would be an attraction called Harnessing the Lightning, which would have celebrated Edison's life. The concept was later reworked and implemented as the Carousel of Progress, which was created for the 1964–1965 New York World's Fair, moved to Disneyland, and has now ended up at the Magic Kingdom in Walt Disney World. As you recall, while it had its run at Disneyland, the Carousel of Progress show building was also the home to the Progress City model, Walt's mockup of EPCOT.

corporations would benefit from operating out of facilities that attract and retain the employees they needed, stimulate the creative process, and become a "worker's playground", just like his studio. It was only natural that he would incorporate this successful model in his EPCOT planning. "This industrial complex will provide employment for many people who live in EPCOT," said the film.

The way the EPCOT Industrial Park is connected to the rest of the community is an outstanding example of how TOD can work. This industrial park district is a desirable destination that will stimulate demand at the other destinations and transit stops. "At this complex, it was hoped that the Disney staff would work with individual corporations to help create a showcase of industry at work." Said Paul Anderson in *Persistence of Vision*, "Walt knew that the only way to pull off his dream of [EPCOT] was to involve American industry, and this complex was just one of many strategies to help entice this kind of involvement."

The typical worker or guest arrives at the Industrial Park using public transportation. As shown in the original Disney World plans, the 1,000-acre Industrial Park is strategically located between the Entrance Complex and the EPCOT Transportation Lobby. Walt knew this would encourage American corporations to participate, because it gives them positive exposure from the millions of visitors every year passing by on the monorail.

Like other parts of Disney World, the Industrial Park is set in a symmetrical radial circulation pattern. Once they arrive, "passengers disembark from the monorail and again board WEDway cars that radiate through each facility". Each transit line leads to one of the 160-acre Industrial Park clusters. The transit station is built on two levels; the upper level is the PeopleMover station with a rotating platform like the one at the Magic Kingdom. From there, workers and guests access the corporate buildings from either the upper-level pedestrian bridge or they go below to the public plaza.

Each Industrial Park cluster is made up of five or six large two-story industrial buildings facing an elevated PeopleMover station. Each building is shaped like a slice of pie, with the narrow end facing the station. The buildings range in size from 50,000 to 200,000 square feet. The loading docks are located on the long side of the wedges, while the workers who have arrived by car instead of WEDway or monorail park behind. The front entrance of each office building faces a well-designed public plaza that surrounds the base of the transit station. As the morning unfolds, the plaza comes alive with a blend of workers and visitors using the services and amenities, such as dining and shopping, located underneath the station. Each cluster has a conference center, and the warehouses are automated.

We 1982 visitors have reason to believe that tilt-up concrete construction was used for the Industrial Park buildings, because that was a technique that Thomas Edison was fond of using. Like the Stanford Industrial Park, use conditions prohibit smokestacks and any noises, odors, or emissions that might offend the workers. All of the buildings share the same climate control system, with a central refrigeration plant.[85]

The Far Horizon

In various master plans for Disney World, the Imagineers show a satellite community that would have been built at the northeast edge of the property. This area would have been a very low-density "residential municipality" with a central commercial center at the hub and residential roadways spreading out like spokes. Once again, the radial circulation pattern is the organizing principle for the community.

In between these residential fingers is open space and lakes. Nearby, a golf course was proposed for this area as well as on the other side of an extended Bay Lake south of the theme park district. The size of Bay Lake was proposed to double. Imagine today's Bay Lake and the Seven Seas Lagoon combined, and it would still be smaller than the proposed Bay Lake. A monorail spur would connect this neighborhood to the rest of Disney World.

Governance

As our 1982 visit to EPCOT comes to a close, we can't help but wonder what life is like for the 20,000 residents who live and work in EPCOT. By giving up some of their voting rights, what have the residents gained and what have they lost by following the rules that Disney has created and that are implemented by the RCID and the two municipalities?

Walt had said, "[EPCOT] will be a planned, controlled community; a showcase for American industry and research, schools, cultural, and educational opportunities. There will be no slums because we won't let them develop. There will be no landowners and therefore no voting control. People will rent houses instead of buying them, and at modest rentals." He added, "There will be no retirees, because everyone must be employed according to their ability. One of our requirements is that the people who live in EPCOT must help keep it alive. Everyone who lives here will have a responsibility to help keep this community an exciting living blueprint of the future." Just like the animation studio, everything would be a team effort working toward one man's dream.

---

85   Innovative when EPCOT would have opened, this technology has become more common in cities such as Chicago and even at the Disney theme parks.

Attorney Paul Helliwell sent Walt a memo to outline some of his concerns about "permanent residents". He pointed out that a permanent population would begin to demand a chance to participate in their local government. In Walt's reply to the memo, the line referring to "permanent residents" is crossed out and changed to "temporary residents/tourists". Clearly, Walt decided early on that the solution was that there would not be a permanent population. He suggested that nobody would be able to live there longer than approximately nine months. Living in EPCOT would be like being a crewmember on a ship. He said, "EPCOT will be a working community with employment for all." Residents would be working at EPCOT, the theme park, or any of the other facilities, and could include Disney Cast Members or representatives from participating companies.

In 2004, architect, professor, and director of graduate studies at the University of Notre Dame School of Architecture Philip Bess said, "The essence of traditional urbanism is entirely Aristotelian: the city [polis] is a community of communities that exists to promote the best life possible for its citizens, both individually and collectively. Hence, this view of cities assumes that the best human life necessarily entails both individual freedom and communal belonging and obligation, and recognizes both of these as goods necessary for the good life for human beings." He cautions, "Nevertheless, it has also been recognized that these goods also exist in tension, and each is subject to corruption: freedom can become license; communal belonging and obligation can become tyranny." Would people have enjoyed living in EPCOT? Ward Kimball did not believe that EPCOT could have worked. He suggested that "you can't experiment with people's lives".

As Disney discovered years later when they developed the new town of Celebration, neighborhoods could be managed through homeowner's associations made up of private property owners. Since World War II, more than 200,000 property owner associations have been created nationwide. The associations are municipal governments by contract. These private organizations manage the town in such a way as to act like a private government; they have very strict and effective rules with regards to regulation of the public realm. When people move in, they agree to live by a certain set of rules.

It is tempting to believe that Celebration might reveal something to us about EPCOT. However, we can't fully judge what life might have been like for EPCOT residents by looking at Celebration because it is a much different city than EPCOT. Much smaller than EPCOT and intended for "permanent" residents, Celebration began with 4,900 acres surrounded by 4,700 acres of protected greenbelts. Robert A.M. Stern and Cooper, Robertson & Partners designed the site plan. Although Disney does not agree with the label, many credit the town as one of the most visible examples of The New Urbanism or Traditional Neighborhood design.

Celebration was not an effort to fulfill Walt's dream; it was a result of pressure from the Bass Brothers, major stockholders in Disney during the early Eisner period, to squeeze more value out of the Florida property. Eisner hired an executive experienced in real estate, Peter Rummell, to come up with something that would be worthy of the Disney brand. Eisner was not completely sold on the project, but Rummell built a good case and was given the green light. The first residents moved to the city in 1996. Celebration is a small town that features a downtown designed by a collection of the world's great architects, state-of-the-art public facilities, and a walkable urban core integrated with a residential community.

As to the possibility that Eisner was finally fulfilling Walt's dream of building a city, Rummell said, "That was press copy stuff. One of the things [Eisner] and I were concerned about was that people would draw out the comparisons." But his boss disagreed—it was Eisner himself who made the comparison. In *Work in Progress*, he wrote that the creation of Celebration was "to make good on Walt's unrealized dream for a city of the future".

Epilogue

So What Happened?

After Walt's death, now came the problem he faced time and time again. This time it would test his team. What to do next? Do they do build a sequel, another theme park—or do they build the EPCOT that Walt imagined?

To say that EPCOT was an ambitious project would be an enormous understatement. It took every ounce of energy that Walt Disney had to get as far along with the project as he did. Shortly after Walt passed away, Roy convened a meeting that included Card Walker and Bill Anderson. Marvin Davis made a presentation outlining the latest thoughts from Walt about EPCOT. After Davis sat down, Roy turned to him and said, "Marvin... Walt's gone." That was the end to Walt Disney's experimental prototype city of tomorrow. What began in earnest in 1959 was no longer the plan. Although Walt's dream was bequeathed to the history books, Roy insisted that Disney World be renamed Walt Disney World to remind everyone who was the real inspiration for this project.

In mid-January 1970, Disney opened a preview center near the intersection of Interstate 4 and State Road 535. This was the first Disney building on property open to the public. On display were artwork, models, and aerials of the first phase of the project. Guests could make reservations for the hotels or purchase a souvenir. There was no mention of a city with residents or any displays that featured EPCOT. The preview center building still stands.

The first phase of Walt Disney World opened in October 1971 and included the Magic Kingdom theme park and two of the five proposed resorts. The Contemporary and the Polynesian Village resorts were built; but the Asian, the Venetian, and the Persian resorts were delayed and scheduled for a later part of phase one. The Asian resort project was so far along that the site was prepared on the western shore of the Seven Seas Lagoon. Even so, the site, with its distinct squared-off shoreline, remained vacant for fifteen years. Today, the Grand Floridian Resort and Spa is located on this spot. Other amenities completed during the first phase included golf courses, tennis, boating, camping, and other recreational facilities.

By the end of phase one, Disney had finished a third resort (the Golf Resort in 1973), a multi-modal transportation network, and the infrastructure to turn wetlands into a small city. They applied many of the lessons they learned in the operation of Disneyland to enhance guest comfort and increase capacity. The monorail system connected the theme park to the hotels just the way Walt had imagined.

Some of the advanced infrastructure technology did make it into the Walt Disney World resort. Michael Crawford, of the Progress City USA website, noted that Walt Disney World did "at least attempt to integrate some cutting edge prototype systems in its design. The AVAC trash disposal system is well known, and for a brief time a prototype pyrolysis plant sought to turn all that collected trash into power." There were two jet engines burning natural gas to provide power to the resort. The waste heat from the engines was used to heat water as well as to chill water for air conditioning. The resort featured a water hyacinth waste treatment program to filter sewage and waste. Crawford noted, "Some effluent eventually went to fertilize the backstage tree farm, and no wastewater was discharged into local rivers or streams."

The popular story for the genesis of the Epcot Center is that Imagineers John Hench and Marty Sklar pushed two models of two separate projects together—the already-announced World Showcase plus a new park called Future World. They turned the two projects into one massive 260-acre park. The combination would become something like a permanent World's Fair. In *Gaining Ground: The Renewal of America's Small Farms*, J. Tevere MacFadyen wrote, "With Epcot Center, Disney is marrying an international exposition to an industrial trade show, sending the happy couple off in a shower of technologically sophisticated amusements to set up housekeeping in an immense shopping mall." This project would be a win for Disney and for American industry. Marty Sklar said, "Industry has lost credibility with the public, the government has lost credibility, but people still have faith in Mickey Mouse and Donald Duck."

Phase two was announced in the 1972 Walt Disney Productions annual report, which listed Disney's "near future projects": the Lake Buena Vista townhouses as well as other apartments and condominiums. This was the first time since Walt had revealed his vision in the EPCOT film that the talk of housing surfaced to the public. By 1973, the company was suggesting that "WED Enterprises [will] do consulting work in transportation, recreational, and city planning". At the American Marketing Association meeting on May 15, 1974, Card Walker, then president and chief operating officer, announced that Disney would be moving ahead "in a phased program" with the concept for EPCOT. Disney was looking at EPCOT "from the point of view of economics, operations, technology, and market potential". The World Showcase concept was introduced as the next step in the development of the property; Disney was looking for "long-term commitments from industry and nations". However, Walker suggested that Disney was not quite ready to send out invitations for "the commitment of individuals and families to permanent residence".

A plan developed in 1976 proposed to turn the Lake Buena Vista area into a "new town" that would accommodate "transient residents". The plan proclaimed, "In a sense, it is the prototype of the prototype community that is being built at Walt Disney World." Residential clusters would be themed to activities such as boating, tennis, and equestrian. The development would feature "commercial, industrial, and institutional areas that will serve both local and regional demands" with "unifying transportation elements that tie the community together", including a multi-modal "intra-urban, inter-urban, and inter-state" transportation station. The Lake Buena Vista project would not be as ambitious as EPCOT. Disney intended to "build with distinctive, innovative designs to the extent possible within the limitations imposed by land development economics, financing, and marketing" and to "maintain a high degree of flexibility to respond to unforeseen opportunities inherent in these unique conditions".

The ground-breaking for the new theme park took place on October 1, 1979, and the park opened three years later. Epcot Center was more than twice as large as the Magic Kingdom and three times as large as Disneyland. The Imagineers working on Epcot Center had learned from Disneyland and the Magic Kingdom and followed many of the same positive design patterns that had made those parks so successful. To ensure that the lessons that Walt taught would not be lost on future generations of designers, Imagineer and Disney Legend Marty Sklar outlined the rules according to Walt—concepts that have taken their rightful place in the timeless way of building. Sklar suggested that you start by knowing your audience. You should wear your guest's shoes. Park design was meant to organize the flow of people and ideas. You need to create a "wienie", a visual magnet that acts like a beckoning hand. Disney communicates with visual literacy. They want to avoid overload and create turn-ons. Sklar cautioned us to tell one story at a time and to avoid visual contradictions. Each area must maintain its identity. The payoff is "every ounce of treatment provides a ton of treat". Finally, Sklar reminded us to "keep it up" and maintain what you have built. For many, this is the perfect description of the Disney difference. When all the principles are combined and applied to a project, the result is a place that demonstrates a higher degree of life that possesses that "quality without a name".

Nevertheless, Epcot Center was not EPCOT. In 1990, *Prime Time Live* reporter Chris Wallace interviewed Dick Nunis about the future of Walt Disney World. At the time, Nunis was the president of Walt Disney Attractions; he had been with the organization since the beginning of Disneyland and probably knew more about running a theme park than anybody else on Earth—even, perhaps, Walt Disney. Wallace asked Nunis about EPCOT and asked why Disney never built Walt's city of tomorrow.

Nunis tried to dodge the question by suggesting that the plans Walt left behind were sketchy at best. He suggested the city idea transformed itself into the vacation resort. After all, there are thousands of guests spending the night, and they will become the citizens of EPCOT. His evasiveness made it clear: in the end, only Walt and a few others had been genuinely excited about the city-building project. The rest of his team was satisfied with simply building another theme park and vacation destination.

Meeting the Public Need

Speaking before the 1963 Urban Design Conference at Harvard University, James W. Rouse summed it up best in his keynote speech when he said, "I hold a view that may be somewhat shocking to an audience as sophisticated as this: that the greatest piece of urban design in the United States today is Disneyland. If you think about Disneyland and think of its performance in relationship to its purpose, its meaning to people—more than that, its meaning to the process of development—you will find it the outstanding piece of urban design in the United States."

James Rouse was no amateur observer. He had been one of the most influential and successful real estate developers of the previous fifty years. Rouse created shopping centers from industrial sites that celebrated a very strong narrative theme. Not only did he advance the concept of the "festival marketplace" such as Faneuil Hall in Boston, Harborplace in Baltimore, and the South Street Seaport in New York City, he also had built the model communities of Columbia, Maryland, and Reston, Virginia.

Rouse went on to describe why he could make such a bold statement. He said, "[Walt] took an area of activity—the amusement park—and lifted it to a standard so high in its performance, in its respect for people, in its functioning for people, that it really does become a brand new thing. It fulfills all its functions it set out to accomplish, un-self-consciously, usefully, and profitably to its owners and developers." He told the audience that "I find more to learn in the standards that have been set and in the goals that have been achieved in the development of Disneyland than in any other piece of physical development in the country".

Rouse did get a chance to see how Walt worked first hand. Joyce C. Hall, founder of Hallmark Cards, wanted to build a new town called Crown Center, which was going to combine commercial and residential at a site adjacent to his card-making factory. Hall asked Rouse who could to teach him more about how to do this; Rouse suggested Walt. The three men got together at Hall's Malibu oceanfront home and talked about how to build a city. Hall said of the experience, "While I had not thought of our project as a city, it has since been described as a 'city within a city' many times. I believe it was enlarged and improved because of the creative thinking of these two master builders." According to Buzz Price, Rouse and Walt also worked on another proposed project called California Living, which was planned as Disneyland's second gate in what was then the parking lot.

Other intellectuals also took a close look at Disneyland and walked away impressed. In 1965, influential architect and teacher Charles Moore took a critical look about what it means to make a place. He turned his attention to the Los Angeles region and said this about Disneyland: "By almost any conceivable method of evaluation that does not exclude the public,...Disneyland must be regarded as the most important single piece of construction in the West in the past several decades." He adds, "Disney has created a place, indeed a whole public world, full of sequential occurrences, of big and little drama, full of hierarchies of importance and excitement, with opportunities to respond at the speed of rocketing bobsleds (or rocketing rockets, for all that) or of horse-drawn streetcars." Most importantly, "Everything works, the way it doesn't seem to any more in the world outside."

Regarding the positive public space in evidence at Disneyland, Andres Duany asks in *Suburban Nation*, "Why do so many people go there—for the rides? According to one Disney architect, the average visitor spends only 3 percent of his time on rides or at shows. The remaining time is spent enjoying the precise commodity that people so sorely lack in their suburban hometowns: pleasant, pedestrian-friendly, public space and the sociability it engenders."

Today, Disney design has evolved to a new understanding. Now the berm can be anywhere. Today, the berm is considered a threshold from one reality to another. Even something as mundane as a doorway can trigger this transformation. The doorframe acts like a proscenium arch in a movie theater separating the audience from the performers. Once you pass through that archway, you step on to the stage and play your role. It was an important development that has led to the basic design principles behind the Disney stores, the Disney cruise line, and other non-theme park properties.

The way we measure the authenticity of public spaces has changed as well. Tom Carson wrote in the *Village Voice* that "[n]othing looks fake. Fabricated, yes—fake, no. Disneyland isn't the mimicry of a thing. It's a thing." He states, "Disneyland is unilateral, literally a control freak's paradise." Nevertheless, he admits, "I know it's precisely this imminent abnegation of all independent will that thrills me each time I cross the parking lot to those heraldic ticket booths. The feeling's akin to the blissful relinquishing of responsibility I experience on airplanes, where I'm still happier than any place on Earth. I may die. But I won't be asked to live up to anything."

Even though EPCOT was never built as Walt imagined it, the Walt Disney World project has been influential in the way we design public spaces. Just like Disneyland, it has raised our expectations on how the built environment can meet the public need.

The New Urbanism

In 1996, a cross-disciplinary group of architects, planners, engineers, and deep thinkers came together and formed the Congress for the New Urbanism. They saw the threat of urban sprawl and the disinvestment of our central cities as a critical problem. Disney historian Karal Ann Marling suggests that New Urbanism is "a prettier, less corporate version of the 1965 and 1966 plans for the unbuilt EPCOT".

In many respects, members wanted to return to the positive design patterns inherent in traditional communities. They knew that the highly segregated neighborhoods common in America, both economically and socio-demographically, must be changed. They drafted a set of guiding principles known as the "The Charter of the New Urbanism" and went about trying to change the world.

The Charter of the New Urbanism clearly spells out the major issues confronting urban policy and design, and it also offers clear direction toward the solutions. Using a story-telling approach similar to Walt's, the Charter begins by providing an overview at the widest angle and zooms into the details. Similar to *A Pattern Language* by Christopher Alexander, the Charter starts with the region and works its way through the metropolis, the city, and the town. The focus continues to tighten to the neighborhood, the district, and the corridor. Finally, we get into the details of the block, the street, and the building. By following the Charter, developers would create communities that demonstrate a higher degree of life—communities based on the timeless way of building.

For many who believe in the New Urbanism, repairing, enhancing, and embellishing the public realm is a central responsibility for urban planners and designers. This is not unlike the way the Imagineers have tried to design the theme parks. In order to maintain the illusion, they have adopted the theatrical nomenclature of being "onstage" or "backstage" as a way of defining space.

Being "onstage" means the space is in the guest's view; it encompasses everything within the public realm, including distant vistas. Onstage, every design detail must be consistent and not create any visual contradictions that might upset the carefully planned story. When something is not right, it stands out. Being "backstage" implies that it is not to be seen by the guests. Those functions are hidden. Victor Gruen strongly believed that the "necessary" functions (such as utilities, waste disposal, and other infrastructure) be hidden and wrote about that extensively in *The Heart of Our Cities*. There is a different expectation for behavior from both the guests and the Cast Members, depending on where they are. That is the difference between being onstage or backstage.

How do you apply this level of regulation to the built environment when there are multiple landowners? To aid planning and design professionals and the public they serve, Andres Duany and his team developed a model zoning code called SmartCode. Remember, Duany stated that the goal for city building was to create "pleasant, pedestrian-friendly, public space and the sociability it engenders". The building code for the Disney theme parks is not the SmartCode, but it does share many of the same ideals.

The SmartCode is a regulatory device that allows for "smart growth" to flourish. Smart growth is a term used by many different organizations to describe a different, more efficient, and in many cases, more traditional, way of building communities. The SmartCode is different than the usual regulatory tools. Typically, a city is managed through a general (or comprehensive) plan, the zoning and development codes, and the building code. The general plan sets the stage for long-term policy decisions and acts like a blueprint for the community's development. The zoning and development codes are generally concerned with how a building relates to its surroundings. Building codes are primarily concerned with how a building works in and of itself.

The SmartCode is considered a form-based code, which is different than a traditional zoning code in that it does not describe buildings in terms of their use or simple statistical measures, but in terms of their form. The code is primarily focused on regulating the public realm or the onstage area. Many of the regulations deal with issues such as building setbacks from the edge of the street, the heights of buildings, proper layout of the roadways, and the proper use of landscaping. Although there is some discussion about land uses in the code, what happens beyond the view of the public realm, backstage, matters less than what the public sees.

The code is designed to be an implementation tool that encourages the community to develop a vision of where it wants to go during the planning process and then encourages growth to be consistent with that vision. The public is encouraged to participate, and the policies provide a level of clarity and certainty. When properly applied, the results are communities that are harmonious and that have avoided the physical and social monocultures prevalent in the typical post–World War II communities.

Form-based codes are meant to strengthen existing communities, preserve open space, and build compact, walkable neighborhoods with a variety of transportation. Smart growth tries to create housing choices and beautiful communities. What the SmartCode tries to accomplish is very similar to the goals that Walt had for EPCOT. He wanted to enhance neighborhood livability with better access and less traffic. Residents, businesses, and visitors would enjoy shared benefits. He wanted EPCOT to point the way toward thriving cities.

The Return of Main Street, U.S.A.

At a time when the traditional American downtown was beginning to become a relic, Disneyland came along and reminded people about what makes Main Street so special. That was the good news. The bad news was the old way of doing business was not going to work anymore because people had recalibrated their expectations of the experience of visiting the central business district. Disneyland was safe and clean, and now everybody expected downtown to be the same. However, the momentum had begun, and the desire to rebuild and reuse historic downtowns led to the creation of the National Trust for Historic Preservation's Main Streets program.

The American downtown had changed rapidly after World War II. What was originally the heart and soul of most communities was slowly dying out. The same retailers and services that seem to exist at the edge of every community were replacing the downtown gathering places: the same stores, the same buildings, and the same sprawl. Main Street was going the way of gas lamps. The success of Disneyland's Main Street reminded people of the special charm that comes with the traditional central business district. Disneyland was an invented place that became the inspiration to save the authentic thing all over the nation.

In 1977, the National Trust for Historic Preservation was concerned about this trend and decided to do something about it. They started a 3-year demonstration project that was designed to "study the reasons downtowns were dying, identify the many factors that have an impact on downtown health and, finally, develop a comprehensive revitalization strategy that would save historic commercial buildings". Out of seventy applicants for the pilot program, three communities were chosen: Galesburg, Illinois; Madison, Indiana; and Hot Springs, South Dakota.

The program required each community to hire a program manager; centralized management was a lesson learned from the regional shopping mall. The National Trust realized that single-owner facilities had an advantage over authentic downtowns. Shopping mall developers analyzed how people used their facilities and documented the findings to an almost unreal level. For example, in *Suburban Nation*, Andres Duany stated that "[m]all designers know that, upon entering, people tend to turn right, and walk counterclockwise. They know that visitors will most likely purchase sunglasses if they are near the rest rooms. They know that women's clothing stores will fare badly if placed near the food court." He asked, "How can Main Street possibly compete?"

A lot of research by the National Trust was done to understand how good design, organization, promotion, and economic restructuring can prove to be a winning formula. The pilot program was a success and the National Trust started to ramp up the program. The Trust established the National Main Street Center in 1980. By 1984, the organization had expanded once again; by 1990, there were more than 31 states and more than 600 communities participating in the program, including cities as large as Boston. Since that time, more than 1,200 communities have been revitalized using the principles and experience generated by the Center's client cities.

Technological Utopianism

America has a rich history in trying to create utopian communities: the Shakers, the Owenites, the Oneida community, Quakers, and the Church of Jesus Christ of Latter Day Saints. With the publication in 1888 of Edward Bellamy's *Looking Backward 2000–1887*, it became all the rage to talk about creating utopian communities. The financial crisis of the Great Depression and the spiritual reawakening in the 1960s contributed new ideas. The movement toward urban renewal after World War II also got people's creative juices flowing. How does Walt's version of utopia compare with other visions?

There was one utopian vision that did make a significant impact on the landscape for existing American cities. That event was the 1893 World's Columbian Exposition in Chicago. Daniel Burnham led a team of architects, engineers, and artists to create what many have called the greatest World's Fair of all time. Downtown Chicago was a dark, dirty, disgusting place at the time. Burnham decided to provide an uplifting contrast to the dingy urban core of Chicago and called his fair the "White City". Gigantic classic temples surrounded scenic lagoons filled with grand public sculptures. The fair's aesthetic was so influential it gave birth to the City Beautiful movement.

Joseph Corn and Brian Horrigan said the City Beautiful was a chance for "reformers to project the ideal values of beauty and order onto the corrupted cities of the nineteenth century". The City Beautiful movement spread and impacted the reconstruction of Washington DC, Indianapolis, Pasadena, Chicago, and many other cities. In fact, Burnham used the success of the 1893 fair to convince business owners to fund a new plan for Chicago in

1909. In an intriguing coincidence, Walt's father worked at the fair as a carpenter. As a boy growing up, Walt may have seen the elementary school–oriented *Wacker's Manual of the Plan of Chicago* by Walter Moody.[86]

In 1894, King Camp Gillette published a book called *The Human Drift*. He suggested that the future would consist of everybody living in huge skyscrapers with public areas covered under vast atriums and filled with light from the huge glass skylights. He suggested that there could be as many as 40,000 of these towers, and they would all be clustered together in a new town called Metropolis near Niagara Falls, New York. Although Gillette never built his city, he did go on to greater fame by inventing the safety razor.

While Ebenezer Howard wanted to wrap the city in nature, Swiss architect Le Corbusier wanted to do him one better. In 1922, he released a *City for Three Million*. He proposed a new city with widely spaced skyscrapers, huge parks, and a transit system hidden away under the ground. The scale and intensity of his city is almost unimaginable, and it was influential. Europe was looking for a new and different way to recover from the devastation left behind after World War I. Modernism was a cry to renounce the old society and to build a new world order. Like Walt, Le Corbusier was not interested in repairing traditional cities. Walt thought the best place to start was on virgin land. Le Corbusier wanted to wipe away the old city and start on a fresh clean canvas.

In 1935, Le Corbusier released *The Radiant City* and said, "The cities will be part of the country; I shall live 30 miles from office in one direction, under a pine tree; my secretary will live 30 miles away from it too, in the other direction, under another pine tree. We shall both have our own car." He added, "We shall use up tires, wear out road surfaces and gears, consume oil and gasoline. All of which will necessitate a great deal of work… enough for all."

What about trying to create a utopia out of an existing city incrementally? In 1916, New York implemented the first zoning law. City leaders further attempted to bring order out of chaos with the release of the New York Regional Plan of 1922. This was the first time that a local government put significant restrictions upon land use. To aid architects, Harvey Wiley Corbett and Hugh Ferriss published guidelines for the stepped-backed skyscrapers required under the new ordinances. Ferriss' drawings were very powerful and left a lasting impression. He expanded on these images in the landmark book, *The Metropolis of Tomorrow*. Ferriss made the future

---

86 Charles H. Wacker was the chairman of the Chicago Planning Commission at the time.

look romantic and beautiful, not the cold machine-age look envisioned by other planners. Corbett expanded on the separation between pedestrians and transit with his 1926 plans for "streets with separated traffic".

Richard Neutra also wanted to change the landscape. Already famous for his sleek modern houses in Los Angeles with flat roofs, ribbon windows, and sprayed concrete walls, Neutra published drawings that he described as "Rush City" in 1928. For him, efficient movement of vehicles would become the guiding principle for the city's organization. Neutra had practiced in Los Angeles; he took the transit corridors that are so common in the region and made them the central public space for the residents and businesses.

By 1929, Francisco Mujica had blended Le Corbusier and Neutra's thinking to create an incredibly dense "City of the Future" made up of 100-story-tall skyscrapers connected by elevated multi-level transit systems. Others had utopian visions based on the decentralization of our urban areas. In 1933, Ralph Borsodi was calling for everyone in America to abandon the cities and to move into carefully planned Garden City–type communities. Michael Sorkin said the 1933 Century of Progress Exposition in Chicago was based on the Garden City. The fair was "laid out along a meandering roadway meant to evoke an evolving incipient roadtown". Visitors to the 1933 fair had a chance to walk through the "Keck House of the Future", the first full-scale modern house to gain national prominence. Designed by George Fred Keck, it featured an all–glass and steel frame home plus a hanger for your own airplane. More than 750,000 guests walked through its doors.

Frank Lloyd Wright had proposed Broadacre City in 1936. His solution was to create an anti-urban utopia. Wright wanted to decentralize the city and return to our agrarian roots. He said, "When every man, woman, and child may be born to put his feet on his own acres, then democracy will have been realized." To facilitate his plan, Wright began to design and build moderately priced "Usonian" houses.

Another short-lived utopian trend started as part of the New Deal under Rexford Tugwell, chief of President Roosevelt's Resettlement Administration. Tugwell wanted to build a network of Greenbelt Towns based on the Garden City writings of Ebenezer Howard, who advocated that communities could become self-sustaining by farming their commonly shared open-space assets. Three American demonstration communities were developed: Greenbelt, Maryland; Greenhills, Ohio; and Greendale, Wisconsin. However, none of the communities could live up to the ambitious goal of being self-sustaining; in all three cases, the greenbelt was not big enough, and there was a lack of an industrial base.

In 1985, Howard P. Segal released *Technological Utopianism in American Culture*, which focused on futurist fiction between 1883 and 1933 and identified the major themes shared by the authors. In *Vinyl Leaves*, Stephen

Fjellman benchmarked Epcot Center against these themes and noted that many of these ideas were expressed in the theme park. Walt's vision for EPCOT also shared many of these same themes.

Segal said the future would be driven by technology and we would no longer be subject to "sooting smokestacks, clanging machines, and teeming streets". It would be as clean as Disneyland. "Wind, water, and other natural resources will be harnessed," Segal observed, and humans will have tamed nature. The circulation system would be based on separating pedestrians from vehicles. Agricultural production would be organized like a factory, and technology would take over the process of growing food. Everything would be electronically controlled: the climate, the transportation systems, our lives. This reliance on technology would extend to our homes. Even our workplaces would be transformed. We would all live in a world that is more efficient. Finally, in exchange for these technological wonders and a higher standard of living, we would be willing to give up some of our individual control in order to conform.

Although there is no record of Walt ever visiting the 1939 New York World's Fair, there is no doubt as to the important influence that event had on Disneyland, EPCOT, and Epcot Center. At the heart of the fair were the iconic Trylon and Perisphere; the Trylon was a 700 foot tall spire just above the Perisphere, a 180 foot diameter spherical building. Both signature structures become easily identifiable everywhere in the world.

When looking for a vision of the future for the new Epcot Center theme park, the Imagineers turned to the Perisphere globe for inspiration. Instead of placing the Spaceship Earth at the center of the theme park, they choose to place it right at the entrance. Stephen Fjellman noted, "Whereas the Magic Kingdom beckons visitors into its various lands, [Epcot Center] has a very different feel." He says, "Spaceship Earth seems to block people's access to whatever lies beyond."

Inside of the 1939 World's Fair Perisphere globe was the diorama of "Democracity". Henry Dreyfuss created the display to take visitors on a trip to see what American cities would be like in the future. Many of the qualities that Ebenezer Howard advocated in *Garden Cities of Tomorrow* were embedded in the model. At the center of "Democracity" was a central business district with a huge tower. In concentric rings around this core were retail businesses, residential neighborhoods, and light industry. All of this was contained within a greenbelt shared by everyone. Even pedestrian and vehicular traffic were separated.[87] Visitors rode in moving "sound

---

87 General Motors Futurama was the most visited attraction at the 1939 Fair. Norman Bel Geddes designed the exhibit, along with architect Albert Kahn. For

chairs" on a 15-minute journey over a "typical" 1960s American landscape. They witnessed modern office parks, farms under domes, an amusement park, and curved towers of steel and glass with ample parking. As the show ended, guests peered at a futuristic diorama of a typical 1960 roadway intersection. Then came the dramatic climax: once the show was over, guests walked out of the theater into a full-scale version of the intersection.

After World War II, the political will for more regional planning began to come into vogue. Bel Geddes was one of the first to tackle the issue of urban renewal with his 1946 Toledo Tomorrow plan. Victor Gruen also took on the challenge with his 1962 plan for Fort Worth, Texas. Gruen's intention was to knock down the historic downtown and replace it with a huge domed structure. Other projects that were actually built include the new towns of Reston and Columbia.

By the late 1960s and early 1970s, the vision of utopia took the form of the megastructure. Joseph Corn described this as "a single, vast, unified structure, encompassing all areas of human activity". As he said, the future would "no longer [be] sprawling or various in its form, the city of the future would be remarkably neat, compact and mechanistic". These structures truly would be, as Richard Neutra described them, a "machine for living".

Buckminster Fuller was one of the first to jump on this bandwagon with his 1964 New York City Harlem River Project, which featured fifteen 100-story towers connected together and housing 45,000 people. In 1971, Fuller proposed a domed central city for East St. Louis, Illinois, called the Old Man River's City project. More than 125,000 people would live, work, and play in this one structure. Fuller said, "I have never engaged in a development that I have felt to have such promise for all humanity, while being, at the same time, so certain of its realization, because its time is imminently at hand." In spite of his confidence, Fuller's project never got off the drawing boards.

In 1967, the Ford Foundation hired Paul Rudolph to study the implications of the Lower Manhattan Expressway in New York. Rudolph was most famous for his Art and Architecture Building at Yale, built in 1963. Robert Moses was determined to plow down much of SoHo and Tribeca and replace the neighborhoods with a highway that connected the Holland Tunnel to the Williamsburg Bridge. What Rudolph envisioned was, in effect, a megastructure extending all the way across Manhattan with

---

many visitors, this was the first time they saw a community that was designed with the automobile specifically in mind. The American urban landscape we find so familiar today was much different in 1939, when "What was good for General Motors was good for America." General Motors promised that "transportation progress is but a symbol of future progress in every activity made possible by constant striving toward new and better horizons."

a whole series of buildings that stretched, nearly unbroken, from river to river. This would be an urban renewal project at an unprecedented scale.

Rudolph was fascinated with seeing the city as a system—a huge, interconnected web of physical structures and transportation modes, all of which he wanted to weave together into a beautiful object. Truck, trains, and automobiles would be relegated to underground roadways, while the public lived above, enjoying their balconies along the terraced structure. The buildings were designed as gigantic frames holding prefabricated apartment units that would simply be slipped into the structures. This was an ambitious project like EPCOT and would use some of the same construction technology and techniques that were implemented at the Contemporary and Polynesian resorts.

The avant-garde group known as Archigram also proposed megastructures with lighthearted names such as Plug-in City, Walking City, and Blow-out Village. "Visual Futurist" Syd Mead produced a series of renderings for U.S. Steel; his vision of the future suggested that nature could be tamed.[88] However, Mead ultimately painted a darker picture of the future of urban living with his set design for the movie *Blade Runner*.

Paolo Soleri added to the megastructures literature with his proposal for gigantic structures called arcologies, a combination of architecture and ecology. The residential density of an arcology is so high that nothing like one currently exists. For example, Soleri's 1969 Babel Canyon project was designed to house 250,000 in a structure one-half mile high. Industry and services would have been hidden in the basement.

Walt thought a lot of this was nonsense. As you recall, at the Florida press conference Walt said, "I don't believe in going out to the extreme blue-sky stuff that some architects do. I believe that people still want to live like human beings." When you peel back the layers, we find that Walt's utopia was rather conventional with regard to existing construction technology; as an urban transect, virtually everything about it was tied one way or another to already existing communities.

Walt said, "The automobile has moved into communities too much. I feel that you can design so that the automobile is there, but still put people back as pedestrians, you see. I'd love to work on a project like that." Once again, Walt was taking the best of the existing technology, packaging it with a heavy dose of human-scale design—a timeless way of building with a higher degree of life, thereby creating something entirely new.

---

88 For those of you who rode the now-demolished Horizons pavilion at Epcot Center and experienced the opportunity to choose which future you wished to visit, the ideas behind Mead's drawings may sound very familiar.

While Walt really did not like to repeat himself, perhaps EPCOT was to be the beginning of many such cities. At the end of the EPCOT film, a suggestion was made that "a community the size of this prototype could become part of an entire city complex composed of many such communities, planned and built a few miles apart". Maybe, just maybe, if a city such as EPCOT had been successful, it would have been the first time Walt planned in advance to produce a sequel.

EPCOT: A Product of Its Time

According to Matthew Frederick, "All design endeavors express the zeitgeist." Zeitgeist is a German word meaning, roughly, the spirit of an age. EPCOT and the Disney World project were no exception. Over the centuries, we have seen at least six different intellectual trends. In the Ancient era, there was a tendency to accept myth-based truths. Next came the Classical era, which valued order, rationality, and democracy. When that broke down, we entered the Medieval era, during which the truth primarily came from organized religion. The reaction to the repression of the Medieval era was the beginning of the Renaissance, when there was a holistic embracing of science and art. The Modern era came next, during which truths were revealed by the scientific method. Today, we have entered the Post-Modern era; now we are inclined to hold that truth is relative or impossible to know.

Matthew Arnold called Walt Disney World a "wholly commodified utopia" because "Disney has been able to construct and infuse its urban environment with technologies, efficiencies, and philosophies unknown in either the wholly public or wholly private sectors. Disney has combined all of these factors into the type of liberating, comforting, safe, and fun environment of which Americans dream."

Although we have for the most part taken a positive and optimistic look at Walt's efforts to create a community, EPCOT has its fair share of critics. Matthew Arnold said, "Disney felt that the corporation and not traditional government could best create jobs, prevent poverty, improve education, and provide for the common good. In fact, he believed that a corporate structure should replace democracy itself in EPCOT." Susan Willis was critical of the influence of the theme parks. She said, "The erasure of spontaneity has largely to do with the totality of the built and themed environment. Visitors are inducted into the park's program, their every need predefined and presented to them as a packaged routine and set of choices."

Walt's version of Disney World and EPCOT is a thoroughly Modern-era project. In contrast, Stephen Fjellman argues that the current version of Walt Disney World is a Post-Modern place: "[Walt Disney World] is a seemingly endless mélange of discreet, bounded informational packets plopped down next to each other willy-nilly—Liberty next to Fantasy, Japan next to Morocco. It is so rife with differences and strange borders that the very concept of difference is obliterated."

Maybe one of the most cynical critics has been Michael Sorkin. In *See You at Disneyland*, he showed a picture of a cloud and said, "This is the sky above Disney World, which here substitutes for an image of the place itself. Disney World is the first copyrighted urban environment in history, a Forbidden City for post-modernity." His fears are not idle: "Renowned for its litigiousness, the Walt Disney Company will permit no photograph of its property without prior approval of its use." He suggested, "Disneyland less redeems Los Angeles than inverts it." He pointed out that the "central experience, by anyone's empirical calculation, is neither walking nor riding but waiting in line. Most of a typical Disney day is thus spent in the very traffic jam one has putatively escaped, simply without benefit of car." Sorkin concluded that a visit to Disneyland is "brief, thrilling, and utterly controlled, a traffic engineer's wet dream".

Would Walt's EPCOT have been as relevant in a post-modern world? Or would it look like a giant dinosaur, a product of a much different time?

Would It Have Worked?

Ever since I first saw the Progress City model as a little boy, I always have asked myself: would this actually work? Could Walt Disney have built a city like the one on display filled with 20,000 residents and millions of visitors? Walt certainly knew it could work.

In the EPCOT film, Walt said, "I believe we can build a community that more people will talk about and come to look at than any other area in the world." He added, "We know what our goals are. We know what we hope to accomplish." EPCOT was not a sequel, but "the most exciting and challenging assignment we've ever tackled at Walt Disney Productions". He reminded us, "It's an exciting challenge; a once-in-a-lifetime opportunity for everyone who participates ... Speaking for myself and the entire Disney Organization, we're ready to go right now!" Walt knew where he wanted to go. Too bad he could not stick around long enough to take us there.

The reality was that the group who worked on the project was very small. There was a lot of risk and a lot of unanswered questions. During my conversation with Buzz Price, I asked him if the project would have worked. After all, very few people knew as much about the EPCOT project as Price. He was in the room with Walt and Roy. Without hesitation he said, "Absolutely yes." Buzz added, "Walt would obsess over a problem."

Price reminded me that the concept and design for EPCOT was not revolutionary but evolutionary, based on tried-and-true architectural technologies, a creative and thoughtful blend of the land uses, arranged in a way where the hotel and day guests are coming from one direction to meet the residents coming from another direction in the middle. This would be a community with the built-in critical mass necessary for sustainable economic success. In EPCOT, everyone could interact in a beautiful, comfortable, and inspiring public setting.

Would it have worked?

Buzz's conclusion was unequivocal: "EPCOT would have been more famous than Walt Disney World."

Bibliography

Alexander, Christopher. *The Nature of Order: The Phenomenon of Life.* Berkeley, Center for Environmental Structure, 2002.

Alexander, Christopher. *The Timeless Way of Building.* New York: Oxford University Press, 1979.

Alexander, Christopher with Sara Ishikawa and Murray Silverstein. *A Pattern Language: Town, Buildings, Construction.* New York: Oxford University Press, 1977.

Anderson, Paul. "A Great Big Beautiful Tomorrow." *Persistence of Vision* 6/7, 1995.

Barrier, Michael. *The Animated Man: A Life of Walt Disney.* Berkeley: University of California University Press, 2007.

Beard, Richard. *Walt Disney's EPCOT.* New York: Abrams, 1982.

Bright, Randy. *Disneyland: Inside Story.* New York: Abrams, 1987.

Broggie, Michael. *Walt Disney's Railroad Story.* Pasadena, California: Pentrix, 1998.

Browning, Peter. "Mickey Mouse in the Mountains" *Harper's*, March 1972: 65–71.

Burnes, Brian, Robert Butler, and Dan Viets. *Walt Disney's Missouri.* Kansas City: Kansas City Star, 2002.

Calthorpe, Peter. *The Next American Metropolis: Ecology, Community, and the American Dream.* Princeton: Princeton AP, 1993.

Cherry, Nathan. *Grid/Street/Place: Essential Elements of Sustainable Urban Districts.* Chicago: APA Press, 2009.

Corn, Joseph J. and Brian Horrigan. *Yesterday's Tomorrows.* New York: Summit Books, 1984.

DeGaetano, Steve. *Welcome Aboard the Disneyland Railroad.* Winnetka: Steam Passages, 2004.

Disney Miller, Diane with Pete Martin. *The Story of Walt Disney.* New York: Disney, 2005.

Donaldson, John Stanley. *Warp and Weft: Life Canvas of Herbert Ryman.* Los Angeles: Incanio 2010.

Duany, Andres with Elizabeth Plater-Zyberk and Jeff Speck. *Suburban Nation.* New York: North Point, 2000.

Duany Plater-Zyberk & Co. *The Lexicon of the New Urbanism*. Miami, 2002.

Dunlop, Beth. *Building a Dream: The Art of Disney Architecture*. New York: Abrams, 1996.

Emerson, Chad Denver, ed. *Four Decades of Magic*. Montgomery: Ayefour, 2011.

Emerson, Chad Denver. *Project Future*. Montgomery: Ayefour, 2010.

Findlay, John. *Magic Lands*. Berkeley: University of California, 1992.

Fjellman, Stephen. *Vinyl Leaves*. Boulder: Westview, 1992.

Foglesong, Richard E. *Married to the Mouse*. New Haven: Yale University Press, 2001.

Frederick, Matthew. *101 Things I Learned in Architecture School*. Cambridge: MIT University Press, 2007.

Fulton, William and Paul Shigley. *Guide to California Planning*. Point Arena: Solano, 2005.

Gabler, Neal. Walt Disney: *The Triumph of the American Imagination*. New York: Knopf, 2006.

Gordon, Bruce and David Mumford. *The Nickel Tour*. Santa Clarita: Camphor, 2000.

Greene, Katherine and Richard Greene. *Inside the Dream: The Personal Story of Walt Disney*. New York: Roundtable, 2001.

Gruen, Victor. *The Heart of Our Cities*. New York: Simon and Schuster, 1964.

Hench, John. *Designing Disney*. New York: Disney, 2003.

Hitchcock, Henry-Russell and Philip Johnson. *The International Style*. New York: Norton, 1922.

Howard, Ebenezer. *Garden Cities of To-morrow*. 1902. Available as a facsimile reprint, Kessinger Publishing, 2008.

Jacobs, Jane. *The Death and Life of Great American Cities*. New York: Random House, 1961.

Imagineers. *Walt Disney Imagineering: A Behind the Dream Look at Making the Magic Real*. New York: Hyperion, 1996.

Janzen, Leon and Jack Janzen. *The "E" Ticket*. 1986–2009.

Klein, Norman. *The Vatican to Vegas*. New York: New Press, 2004.

Korkis, Jim. *The Vault of Walt*. Orlando: Theme Park Press, 2012.

Kurtti, Jeff. *Disneyland Through the Decades*. New York: Disney, 2010.

Kurtti, Jeff. *Since the World Began*. New York: Hyperion, 1996.

Kurtti, Jeff. *Walt Disney's Imagineering Legends*. New York: Disney, 2008.

Kurtti, Jeff and Bruce Gordon. *The Art of Disneyland*. New York: Disney, 2005.

Kurtti, Jeff and Bruce Gordon. *The Art of Walt Disney World*. New York: Disney, 2009.

Lark, Max. "Walt's Dream Factory Turns 70." *Disney twenty-three*, Spring 2010: 18–24.

Lassell, Michael. *Celebration: The Story of a Town*. New York: Roundtable, 2004.

Lindquist, Jack with Melinda J. Combs. *In Service to the Mouse*. Orange: Chapman University Press, 2010.

Malmberg, Melody. *The Making of Disney's Animal Kingdom Theme Park*. New York: Hyperion, 1998.

Malmberg, Melody. *Walt Disney Imagineering: A Behind the Dreams Look at Making More Magic Real*. New York: Disney, 2009.

Mannheim, Steve. *Walt Disney and the Quest for Community*. Burlington: Ashgate, 2002.

Marling, Karal Ann. *Behind the Magic: 50 Years of Disneyland*. Dearborn: The Henry Ford, 2005.

Marling, Karal Ann, ed. *Designing Disney's Theme Parks: The Architecture of Reassurance*. New York: Flammarion, 1997.

Moody, Walter Dwight. *Wacker's Manual of the Plan of Chicago*. 1912. Available as a replication of the 1923 edition, Nabu Press, 2010.

Moore, Charles W. *You Have to Pay for the Public Life*. Cambridge: MIT University Press, 2001.

Moore, Robin C. and Susan M. Goltsman, Daniel Iacofano, eds. *Play for All*. Berkeley: MIG, 1992.

O'Boyle, J.G. "Mindsetter: A Cultural Analysis of Disney's Main Street U.S.A." *Persistence of Vision*. 10, 1998.

Oneal, David. *Anaheim Vacationland*. Anaheim: Extinct Attractions, 2009.

Ponzol, Dan. *A Century of Lionel Timeless Toy Trains*. Metrobooks, New York, 2000.

Price, Harrison "Buzz". *Walt's Revolution! By the Numbers*. Orlando: Ripley, 2003.

Snyder, Chuck. *Windows on Main Street*. New York: Disney, 2009.

Sorkin, Michael, ed. *Variations on a Theme Park*. New York: Hill and Wang, 1992.

Stewart, James B. *DisneyWar*. New York: Simon & Schuster, 2005.

Strodder, Chris. *The Disneyland Encyclopedia*. Santa Monica CA: Santa Monica, 2008.

Thomas, Bob. *Walt Disney: An American Original*. New York: Simon & Schuster, 1976.

Thomas, Bob. *Building a Company: Roy O. Disney*. New York: Hyperion, 1998.

Walt Disney Productions. "The EPCOT Film." Script by Marty Sklar. The Walt Disney Company, 1966. Available in *Walt Disney Treasures—Tomorrowland* (DVD), 2004.

Venturi, Robert and Denise Scott Brown, Steven Izenour. *Learning from Las Vegas*. Cambridge: MIT, 1977.

Whyte, William H. City: *Rediscovering the Center*. New York: Doubleday, 1988.

Acknowledgments

Let me begin by thanking you. When this project began, my goal was to write something I wanted to read. There is so much great stuff out there from all of the writers, thinkers, and historians who have come before. The fact that you bought the ticket and went on the ride is just the coolest thing ever.

A readable book would not be possible without a second pair of eyes. I was lucky to have Marsha Rood, Werner Weiss, and David Zanolla contribute to the process. Their influence cannot be overstated. However, I have to pay special tribute to Susan Foster de Quintana. What you have in your hand would not be without her help.

When I got started writing about the Disney theme parks, I discovered a wonderful group of people who have encouraged and inspired me. They include Len Testa, Aaron Johnston, the Burgess family, Chad Emerson, Mike Scopa, Mike Newell, Matt Hochberg, Deb Wills, David Price, Tim Halibur, John Kaliski, Laura Dahl, Jeff Kober, Lee Cockerell, Mark Brodeur, Todd Gish, Kevin Yee, Jim Korkis, Steve DeGaetano, Michael Broggie, Bob Gurr, Jack Lindquist, Richard Harris, David Koenig, Christopher Alexander, Bill Fulton, Andres Duany, Mark Broduer, Vaughn Davies, Tim O'Day, Al Lutz, James Rojas, Dan Burden, Dena Belzer, Lou Mongello, Beth Dunlop, Michael Crawford, Nate Cherry, Kurt Nagle, Todd Regan, Paula Sigman Lowery, Roberto Quintana de Foster, Elaine Carbrey, Harrison "Buzz" Price, Ann Price, John Zinner, David Malmuth, Doug Marsh, Robert Chattel, Norm Gidney, Barbara Gurskey, Mark Taft, Matthew Parrent, AJ Wolfe, Ryan Wilson, David Picasso, George Taylor, Bob McLain, and everybody else that I forgot to mention.

Finally, there is my mom, Jeanette. When asked where I got this bug for Disneyland, I point to her. She unknowingly unleashed my curiosity about what could be. Answering those questions became a lifetime quest and the foundation for this book.

About the Author

Sam Gennawey is a prolific author and Disney historian, a contributor to *Planning Los Angeles* and other books, as well as a columnist for the popular MiceChat website.

His unique point of view built on his passion for history, his professional training as an urban planner, and his obsession with theme parks has brought speaking invitations from Walt Disney Imagineering, the Walt Disney Family Museum, Disney Creative, the American Planning Association, the California Preservation Foundation, the California League of Cities, and many Disneyana clubs, libraries and podcasts.

He is currently a senior associate at the planning firm of KPA.

Other Books by Sam Gennawey

Universal vs. Disney: The Unofficial Guide to American Theme Parks' Greatest Rivalry (2014)

The Disneyland Story: The Unofficial Guide to the Evolution of Walt Disney's Dream (2013)

About the Publisher

Theme Park Press is the largest independent publisher of Disney and Disney-related pop culture books in the world.

Established in November 2012 by Bob McLain, Theme Park Press has released best-selling print and digital books about such topics as Disney films and animation, the Disney theme parks, Disney historical and cultural studies, park touring guides, autobiographies, fiction, and more.

For more information, and a list of forthcoming titles, please visit:

ThemeParkPress.com

More Books from Theme Park Press

The Vault of Walt: Volume 3

Even More Unofficial Disney Stories Never Told

Best-selling author Jim Korkis brings forth from his famous Vault of Walt two dozen new stories about Disney films and theme parks, Disney stars and attractions, and of course, Walt himself. Disney fans and historians alike will relish these little-known tales.

ThemeParkPress.com/ books/vault-walt-3.htm

The Unofficial Story of Walt Disney's Haunted Mansion

Welcome, Foolish Readers!

Haunted Mansion expert Jeff Baham recounts the colorful, chilling history of the Mansion and pulls back the shroud on its darkest secrets in this definitive book about Disney's most ghoulish attraction.

Foreword by Rolly Crump.

ThemeParkPress.com/books/ haunted-mansion.htm

More Books from Theme Park Press

The Book of Mouse

When a mouse as famous as Mickey turns 85 years old, he has lots of stories to tell.

In this comprehensive "biography" of Mickey Mouse, Jim Korkis tells all of those stories, and more, including plenty of "Mouse-ka-Tales" and an annotated filmography of Mickey's cinematic career.

ThemeParkPress.com/ books/book-mouse.htm

Disney's Grand Tour

Join Walt Disney on a whirlwind tour through Europe at the dawn of Disney's Golden Age of Animation.

Didier Ghez follows in Walt's footsteps on a "vacation" that set the stage for Disney's classic films and influenced everything from Disney animation to its theme parks.

Foreword by Diane Disney Miller.

ThemeParkPress.com/books/ disneys-grand-tour.htm

More Books from Theme Park Press

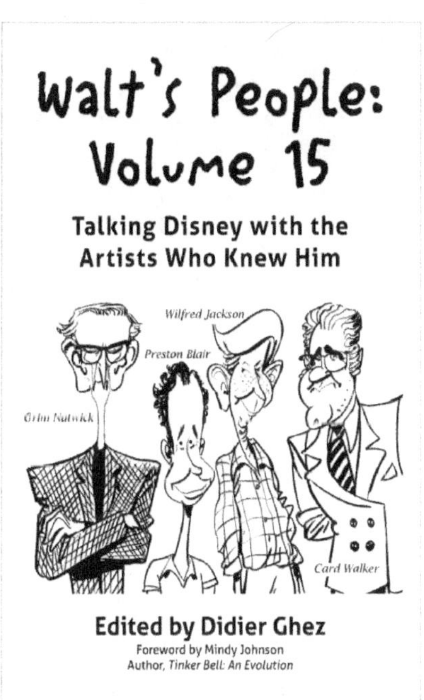

Walt's People: Volume 15

Kimball, Evans,
Zorro and More!

Disney's most prestigious series returns for its 15th volume. Among the Walt's people sharing stories this time: Ward Kimball, Grim Natwick, Card Walker, Wilfred Jackson, and twenty others.

ThemeParkPress.com/books/
walts-people-15.htm

Service with Character

Disney Goes to War!

As Hitler's tanks rolled across Europe, the U.S. government informally drafted Walt Disney. David Lesjak chronicles those dark years, when the Army took over the Disney Studios and even Donald Duck went to work for Uncle Sam.

ThemeParkPress.com/books/
service-character.htm

Discover our many other popular titles at:

www.ThemeParkPress.com

www.ingramcontent.com/pod-product-compliance
Lightning Source LLC
Chambersburg PA
CBHW051513150726
47997CB00001B/230